David Dutton is Senior Lecturer in Modern History at the University of Liverpool. He is the author of several studies in twentieth-century British and diplomatic history, including *Austin Chamberlain: Gentleman in Politics* and *British Politics since 1945: The Rise and Fall of Consensus.*

The International Library of Historical Studies
Series ISBN 1 86064 079 6

The International Library of Historical Studies (ILHS) brings together the work of leading historians from universities in the English-speaking world and beyond. It constitutes a forum for original scholarship from the United Kingdom, continental Europe, the USA, the Commonwealth and the Developing World. The books are the fruit of original research and thinking and they contribute to the most advanced historiographical debate and are exhaustively assessed by the authors' academic peers. The Library consists of a numbered series, covers a wide subject range and is truly international in its geographical scope. It provides a unique and authoritative resource for libraries and scholars and for student reference.

The Politics of Diplomacy

Britain and France in the Balkans in the First World War

DAVID DUTTON

I.B. Tauris Publishers
LONDON · NEW YORK

For Christine – and a very special Anglo-French
relationship

Published in 1998 by I.B.Tauris & Co Ltd,
Victoria House, Bloomsbury Square, London WC1B 4DZ
175 Fifth Avenue, New York NY 10010

In the United States of America and in Canada distributed by
St Martin's Press, 175 Fifth Avenue, New York NY 10010

Copyright © David J. Dutton, 1998

A full CIP record for this book is available from the British Library
A full CIP record for this book is available from the Library of
Congress

ISBN 1 86064 112 1

Library of Congress catalog card number: available

Set in Monotype Dante by Ewan Smith, London
Printed and bound in Great Britain by WBC Ltd, Bridgend

Contents

Preface

Over the many years since I began research on Anglo-French policy in the Balkans during the First World War, I have incurred a large number of debts and obligations. The more a scholar pursues his own inquiries, the more conscious he becomes of what he owes to colleagues in the same profession. Some indication of this indebtedness is given in the Notes and Bibliography of this work. In addition, many fellow historians have offered me the benefit of their own scholarship in conversations and letters. My studies would have been far more onerous without the help and co-operation of the archivists and librarians of the various institutions in Britain and France in which I have worked. I am grateful to them all, but some key individuals must be elevated from this otherwise anonymous vote of thanks – though none, of course, bears any responsibility for the errors of omission and commission which no doubt remain in the finished work.

It was Professor Douglas Johnson who first proposed the Salonika campaign to me as a suitable topic for scholarly inquiry and who guided my initial researches. Once again, my good friends Philip Bell and Ralph White have given freely and willingly of their time to read the text with sympathetic but perceptive and gently critical eyes, and to offer valuable suggestions for its improvement. Lester Crook of I.B.Tauris has seen the project through from inception to publication with commendable professionalism. Alison Bagnall typed the entire manuscript, remaining cheerful in the face of all adversity. And my wife Christine not only rekindled my interest in the First World War after several years in which it had been diverted into other research channels, but also provided a more expert approach to the translation of French documentation than I could hope to attain. Though her role in anything I have achieved cannot possibly be expressed in a brief acknowledgement, this book is dedicated to her.

Acknowledgements

The author acknowledges the gracious permission of Her Majesty The Queen to use material which has been previously published and is subject to copyright.

Transcripts of Crown-copyright material in the Public Record Office and elsewhere appear by permission of the controller of HM Stationery Office.

For permission to quote from unpublished material in their possession or of which they own the copyright, the author willingly thanks the following: Mr Leo Amery; the Chef du Service Historique de l'Armée de Terre; Colonel J. A. Aylmer; the Clerk of the Records of the House of Lords, acting on behalf of the Beaverbrook Foundation Trust; Miss J. M. Bonham Carter; the Trustees of the Bridgeman Papers Trust; the Master, Fellows and Scholars of Churchill College in the University of Cambridge; the Rt Hon. Alan Clark, MP; the Rt Hon. the Earl of Derby; the Rt Hon. Earl Haig; Sir Charles Hobhouse; the Trustees of the Imperial War Museum; the Trustees of the Liddell Hart Centre for Military Archives; Mr A. J. Maxse; the Rt Hon. Lord Milne; the Archivist of the Ministère des Affaires Etrangères, Paris; the Warden and Fellows of Nuffield College, Oxford; the Lord Robertson; Mrs Joan Simon; the University of Birmingham. Every effort has been made to trace the owners of copyright material cited in this book and the author offers his apologies if any copyright has been inadvertently infringed.

For permission to print extracts from published material the author offers his thanks to the following: Addison Wesley Longman Limited; *Canadian Journal of History*; Frank Cass and Co. Ltd; *The Historical Journal*.

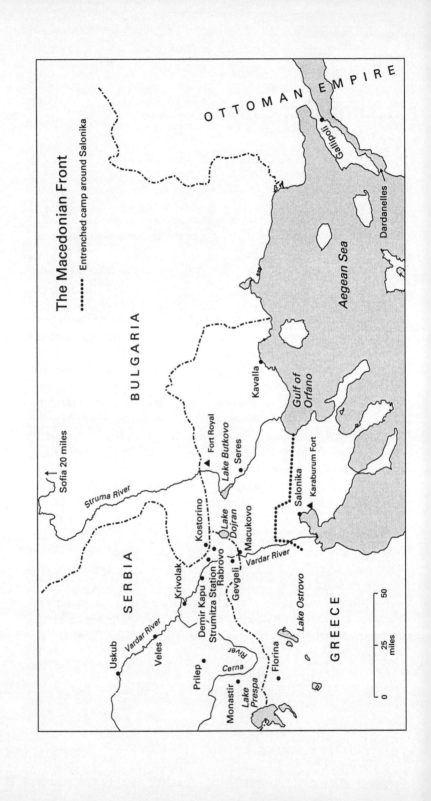

The Macedonian Front
.... Entrenched camp around Salonika

OTTOMAN EMPIRE

Aegean Sea

Gallipoli

Dardanelles

BULGARIA

Sofia 20 miles

Struma River

Fort Royal
Lake Butkovo
Seres

Kavalla

Gulf of
Orfano

Salonika
Karaburum Fort

Kostorino
Lake Dojran
Macukovo
Vardar River

SERBIA

Krivolak
Demir Kapu
Strumitza Station
Rabrovo
Gevgeli

Uskub
Vardar River
Veles

Prilep
Cerna River

Florina

Lake Ostrovo

GREECE

Monastir
Lake Prespa

0   25   50
      miles

. . . .

CHAPTER I

The Uncertain Alliance

I n the context of the long and often troubled relationship between
Britain and France in the course of the twentieth century, the
wartime alliance of the two countries between 1914 and 1918 stands
out as something of a beacon. In marked contrast to the catastrophic
schism of 1940, the Anglo-French partnership survived unbroken for
the duration of hostilities. Yet the two countries entered the First
World War with no real tradition of alliance or even friendship.
Though the celebrated entente cordiale had been concluded by
Foreign Ministers Lansdowne and Delcassé a decade earlier, the fact
that Britain and France had been enemies in war no fewer than eight
times between 1689 and 1815 was probably a more important element
in the popular psyche of the two nations. More recently Britain and
France had clearly been rivals rather than friends in the colonial
scrambles of the 1880s and 1890s, a situation which produced a lively
jousting in the press of the two countries and, at the time of the
Fashoda incident in 1898, serious talk in both capitals of the possibility
of actual armed conflict.[1] The time at which France – and indeed
another future ally, Russia – emerged as threats to Britain's imperial
interests in Africa and Asia was, of course, also that at which the
generation who would dominate British public life during the First
World War reached maturity and formed their lasting attitudes. This
future elite came to see France and Russia as the main enemies in the
international arena some time before any German menace became
apparent.[2] The emergence of Wilhelmine Germany supplemented
and ultimately dominated Britain's list of potential military opponents, but it never fully eliminated from British calculations the
dangers which an untrammelled France might pose to the country's
international position.

The entente of 1904, moreover, neither removed the potential for Anglo-French antagonism nor determined Britain's future partici-pation in a European war at France's side. Even after 1904 Britain continued to have disagreements with France over, *inter alia*, Egypt, the French arms trade and Morocco. It was some commentary on the differing historical perceptions of the two countries that in 1913 the British were beginning to consider how to commemorate the forthcoming centenary of the Battle of Waterloo, a celebration from which the French Embassy in London had decided to absent itself.[3] Indeed, as late as 1 July 1914 Maurice Hankey, the influential secretary to the Committee of Imperial Defence, composed a memorandum which envisaged the possibility of a French attack on Britain.[4]

It is true that, by 1906, Germany had become the national enemy in the calculations of the British Foreign Office. Moreover, the solidification of the entente cordiale, which began life as little more than the mutual recognition by Britain and France of one another's predominant influence in Egypt and Morocco, was largely the result of German reactions to it. But this process of solidification never succeeded, before the outbreak of war, in converting the Entente into an alliance. Periodically, Foreign Office officials such as Eyre Crowe, who saw the German threat as a fundamental challenge to British security, sought this transformation. Many French politicians and diplomats shared the same objective. But all went without success. So while the original entente of 1904 evolved, it was never quite clear precisely what it had evolved into. Under Sir Edward Grey, British foreign secretary from December 1905, the agreement developed, in the words of one historian, into 'a habit of diplomatic cooperation, supported by military and later by naval conversations'.[5] Tentative contacts, begun while Lansdowne was still foreign secretary, developed into more detailed plans for military co-operation should Germany attack France. Increasingly, many British policy-makers came to view Germany as the country's only possible enemy, in which situation France would be the essential ally. In an important exchange of letters in November 1912, it was agreed that the two governments would consult as to the action they might take in the event of extreme tension between the European powers. Still the British stopped short of an alliance. It was never established that Britain was committed to taking the French side in a Franco-German war irrespective of the circumstances in which that war came about. In some situations, in fact, Britain would probably not intervene.[6] On balance, Britain judged that the dangers of offering France the certainty of a formal alliance, in terms of its possible encouragement to provoke Germany into a conflict which the British preferred to avoid, outweighed any perceived advantages.

Thus, in the absence of a formal commitment, Britain's line of action in any given situation remained uncertain. As has been noted: 'It was never in doubt that British troops would defend India. But it remained in doubt until 4 August 1914 whether they would defend France.'[7] So while in unofficial calculations French strategists placed some hope in British support, Plan XVII, the formal battle plan with which France met the German attack in 1914, never assigned the British Expeditionary Force (BEF) any definite role. Yet by eschewing an attack through Belgium – which might have been the best strategic option – Plan XVII left open the possibility of British intervention. An invasion of Belgian territory by French forces would almost certainly have forfeited all hope of British support.[8] Even so, just four months before the start of hostilities Sir Arthur Nicolson, permanent under-secretary at the Foreign Office, judged that 'should war break out on the continent, the likelihood of our despatching any expeditionary force is extremely remote'.[9] This was an exaggeration. Political constraints left the British government less freedom to manoeuvre than Nicolson imagined. But the uncertainty continued into the war crisis itself. As the European Powers moved towards conflict, Asquith's Liberal government repeatedly restated the absence of a formal British commitment to France. As late as 1 August, Grey was still telling the French ambassador in London that France would have to make up its own mind about involvement in a Russo-German war, without any assurance of British assistance.[10]

The important point is that Britain's ultimate decision to intervene was based, above all else, neither upon a 'moral' commitment to France after a decade of ever-closer relations, nor upon a commitment of 'honour' to Belgium, of whose neutrality it was a guarantor, but upon a calculated assessment of its own national self-interest.[11] Indeed, in one sense Britain became involved in order to control France as well as to assist it. For if France and Russia were to prevail in a war against Germany without British support, this might create a situation of confrontation between Britain and the victor powers in which its rivals of the late nineteenth century would now be unrestrained by a German counter-balance to their power.[12] Yet at the same time a mutual dependence existed between Britain and France from the very beginning of the war. As John Keiger has argued, it was an overriding aim of French decision-makers as they tried to manage the July crisis to ensure that their country would enter the conflict with British support.[13] The consensus which emerged inside Asquith's cabinet on 4 August that it was in Britain's own interests to resist the challenge of imperial Germany ensured that this was the case. But it was also the *sine qua non* of British involvement in a European land war that it would fight that war in conjunction with France. Quite simply, Britain lacked the resources to think in any other terms. Looking back in 1917, the South African General Smuts, by that time a member of Lloyd George's War Cabinet, recalled that 'we entered the War in a very small way with a small military force and not as a principal combatant but rather as an auxiliary to France'.[14] It was, after all, Britain's long-standing tradition to fight a land war in Europe by proxy, making the best possible use of continental allies. Britain's intention in 1914 was to stick to this pattern, using its navy to control the seas, subjecting the enemy to a blockade, and using its wealth to help its allies to finance their own war effort. Britain's army would play only a subordinate role in securing victory.[15] The general assumption was that France and Russia would bear the main burden of the land war. Granted that France's manpower resources were considerable and Russia's almost unlimited, such a strategy made good sense, at least in British terms. The British Expeditionary Force of just six infantry divisions and one cavalry division represented little more than a token contribution to the land war.[16]

These factors ensured a certain shape to the wartime coalition which emerged from the old triple entente of Britain, France and Russia. The alliance existed at four main levels: political, military, economic and naval. 'Only in the naval sphere', writes David French, 'was Britain the undisputed leader of the alliance from the start to the finish of the war.'[17] Indeed, granted that it had by far the smallest army and given that naval power was essentially a long-term weapon, there were good grounds for seeing Britain as the weakest partner in the coalition. But all three countries were recognized as independent great powers, with long-standing traditions, aims and ambitions. In a coalition of more patently unequal partners, such as existed between the central powers, the question of who should dominate the alliance was easy to answer.[18] In the case of Britain, France and Russia, such a question could scarcely be asked. Certainly, Britain had few claims to aspire to such a position in the first half of the conflict. This situation did change. By the end of 1914 it was coming to be seen that the war, whose outcome almost everyone had assumed would be decided by a single pitched battle following the supposed pattern of the Franco-Prussian conflict of forty years before, was in fact developing into a war of attrition, to which Britain, contrary to its original intentions, would have to make a sizeable contribution in terms of manpower.

In February 1915 Lloyd George called upon Britain to adopt a very different attitude towards the war from that which had existed hitherto. He wanted the three allies to hold a joint military conference to co-ordinate their plans and argued that the time had come for Britain and its empire to throw their full weight into the alliance. The maxim of 'business as usual' would have to be abandoned if victory was to be secured. In its place Britain needed to build a war economy in which only a basic minimum of resources would be left to meet civilian needs.[19] By 1916 Britain had achieved a rough military parity with its French and Russian allies. Drained by the blood-letting at Verdun, France became increasingly dependent on British support. That dependency extended to the economic sphere as Finance Minister Alexandre Ribot found it ever more difficult to raise loans independently, without British support, in the American market. By the following year, however, Britain itself was beginning to look distinctly war-weary, its potential to dominate the alliance now threatened by the entry of the United States into the conflict that April. Thus, at no point in the war did Britain really enjoy the sort of preponderance which would have enabled it to dominate the coalition and ride roughshod over the interests, opinions and wishes of its co-belligerents. Increasingly, historians have come to recognize that the needs and the constraints imposed by membership of an allied co-alition were one of the most important determinants of Britain's strategic planning throughout the conflict.[20] The possible defection of France – as indeed the defection of Russia – remained an ever-present concern to British policy-makers from first to last. As it soon became clear that the Germans hoped to break up the allied coalition, its preservation became a central allied war aim.[21] And, in the early stages of the conflict, it was clearly Britain which had most to lose if this objective were not secured.

The outbreak of war inevitably changed much in the Anglo-French relationship. Above all, it created a formal alliance where none had existed hitherto. Under pressure from Russia, and at a time when the fall of Paris looked a distinct possibility, Britain, France and Russia signed the Pact of Paris on 5 September 1914. Thereby they promised not to conclude a separate peace with the enemy, or to define peace terms without prior agreement. This was an important step, especially in symbolic terms, affirming a new unity of purpose, though the pact did not create a framework for military or even economic co-operation between the parties to it. In other respects the coming of war marked a less dramatic break with the past. Long-standing animosities, suspicions and prejudices might have been obscured, but they did not disappear overnight. British politicians and military commanders still had sufficiently long memories to look back beyond the last ten years of comparative cordiality to a period when France had been seen as Britain's principal global rival. Georges Clemenceau would later remember a revealing conversation with David Lloyd George. 'I have to tell you', said the French prime minister, 'that from the very day after the Armistice I found you an enemy to France.' 'Well,' retorted Lloyd George, 'was it not always our traditional policy?'[22] Similarly, French perceptions of Britain as 'Perfidious Albion' went back centuries and were ready to be reawakened if the wartime alliance should in any way falter.[23] Germany was certainly the enemy for the time being, but no one knew how long such a situation would endure, or whether it would eventually be replaced by the re-emergence of a more traditional pattern of international antagonisms. Each party to the coalition hoped that the war would enable it to profit not only in relation to its current enemy but also vis-à-vis its current allies. When the British War Council discussed war aims in March 1915 it thought in terms of a territorial settlement which would not arouse lasting German enmity and an overall world picture in which the British empire would be safe from French and Russian incursions.[24]

David French and others have argued persuasively that the British war minister, Lord Kitchener, in particular, never lost sight of this strategic goal. His purpose in raising a continental-scale army during

1915 and in husbanding its strength was to enable Britain to assume a major role on the Western Front at the very moment when the French would approach a point of exhaustion. In this way Britain would be in a position to dictate the terms of peace to foe and 'friend' alike.[25] Lord Derby later recalled a conversation he had had with Kitchener in 1915. 'What I am anxious for', insisted the British war minister, 'is that when it comes to peace we shall have the biggest army in the field. It would never do for the French to have more than us.'[26] Britain's purpose in entering the conflict in 1914 was, after all, to preserve a continental balance of power and that state of affairs ruled out an overwhelming French preponderance in Europe. Indeed, a strong, but not over-mighty, Germany was a key component in Britain's desired European balance.[27] The French may well have suspected that Britain did not wish to see their unqualified victory in the war. Throughout the conflict, resentment was felt at what was seen as Britain's inadequate contribution to the common purpose. The length of line held by the armies of the two countries on the Western Front remained an on-going bone of contention for the duration of the war. Tension was at its greatest in the crisis days of May and June 1918, following an important German breakthrough on 27 May. As one French official complained, 'I am horrified by the disproportion between France's effort and her share in the diplomatic game ... the English make use of us. There is no equality of sacrifice.'[28] Neither country felt it could afford to let the other enhance its prospective postwar position without a compensating gain for itself. Confronted with the possibility of a unilateral British expedition to Syria, the French minister of war insisted that 'the English should not land there by themselves. We must therefore ... be in a position to intervene rapidly ... if not at the same time as the English, then immediately in their wake.'[29]

Some elements of closer co-operation were forced upon the Allies by the course of events. For example, the war greatly increased France's economic dependence on Britain. In January 1915 the firm of J. P. Morgan and Co. was appointed sole purchasing agent for the allied powers in North America. This meant the establishment of a single channel for the negotiation of contracts in the New World and underlined Britain's growing economic pre-eminence within the coalition.[30] But in other areas institutional deficiency impeded progress.

Unfortunately, at the outbreak of hostilities the alliance lacked any formal machinery for formulating diplomatic policy or military strategy. Such a situation was bound to hinder the amicable settlement of inter-allied disputes and differences. It was by a slow and sometimes painful process of trial and error that the two governments moved hesitantly towards a greater understanding of how to conduct coalition warfare. As this study will illustrate, the problem was compounded by the fact that neither country, anticipating a very different type of war from the one it now confronted, had really sorted out its own domestic command structure or the working relationship between its political and military leaderships. There thus existed a four-fold division of authority between the French and British governments and high commands.[31] In the absence of an allied co-ordinating machinery, personal contacts became extremely important. The process began sporadically with individual ministers crossing the Channel to consult with their opposite numbers, though there was no guarantee that agreement at this level would be endorsed by the full cabinets in London and Paris. Gradually, official diplomatic channels were supplemented by a plethora of liaison officers and official and unofficial representatives. But the information provided by such individuals was often idiosyncratic, inaccurate or just plain wrong, doing little to foster harmony and understanding between the two countries.[32]

It was not until July 1915 that the prime ministers of the two countries met for the first time. That month also saw the first formal Anglo-French conference of the war held at Calais. But, as experience showed, these conferences, usually called to resolve existing disagreements rather than to prevent new ones, were but a poor substitute for the sort of permanent decision-making machinery which the requirements of total war demanded. As Arthur Balfour noted, early in 1917, soon after becoming foreign secretary:

> What impresses me most painfully is the futility ... of our various international conferences. They have not been few in number, but in many cases the resolutions – long discussed and embodied in formal minutes duly signed by the governments concerned – have been departed from as soon as the Conference separated.[33]

Sir William Robertson, whose appointment as chief of the Imperial General Staff (CIGS) coincided with the most sustained incidence of these inter-allied gatherings, was of like mind:

The conferences were assembled on no kind of system either as to time, place, or purpose, while all the attempts to regularize them failed because so many people were concerned that it was impossible to make arrangements to suit the convenience of everybody. When arranged, they had more than once to be deferred, adjourned or abandoned altogether, because some unforeseen event, such as the sudden irruption of political troubles at home, made it undesirable for the Ministers of one country or another to be absent from their posts ... The number of people present rendered the preservation of secrecy and the prompt dispatch of business impossible. It was seldom that less than a score would attend, and when all countries were represented the number might amount to as many as a hundred, made up of Prime Ministers, Ministers for Foreign Affairs, Army, Navy, Munitions and Finance, Ambassadors, Commanders-in-Chief, and other technical delegates, secretaries, assistant secretaries and interpreters.[34]

In practice, Britain and France tended to treat their conferences less as an opportunity to reach a genuine consensus between them than as the occasion to launch their particular points of view. As prime minister, David Lloyd George became so exasperated by long and often inconclusive meetings that he began to come to inter-allied conferences with resolutions already drafted.[35]

While the politicians and commanders of the two countries sought to co-ordinate their strategy at a succession of inter-allied conferences, the armies on the ground had the practical task of trying to fight the war together. The question of a unified command was obviously critical. But whatever chances existed of this coming about were probably dashed by early experiences on the Western Front. Though the French were relieved by the news of Britain's decision for war, British mobilization was nevertheless three days behind that of France. What was seen as British indecisiveness left a legacy of misunderstanding and suspicion which scarcely augured well for the future.[36] Recent research has revealed much more Anglo-French friction in the first stages of the conflict than was once believed. The alliance in fact got off to a bad start.[37] The instructions sent to Sir John French, commander of the BEF, made his position abundantly clear: 'your Command is an entirely independent one and ... you will in no case come in any sense under the orders of any Allied General.'[38] During 1915, with the failure of the Anglo-French offensive in Artois in May and against the background of the continuing retreat of the Russian army, French War Minister Alexandre Millerand constantly urged the principle of a unified command – naturally enough under the French commander General Joffre – upon his British opposite number, Lord Kitchener. But, notwithstanding Joffre's acclaimed success at the Battle of the Marne in September 1914, this was never a likely development. A man of few words and no great intellect, Joffre succeeded in convincing some observers that his silence concealed unfathomed depths. His 'sparingness of phrase ... formed a protective screen which baffled their subtler wits and tongues'.[39] Most British observers, however, reached the conclusion that Joffre was too slow-witted to risk entrusting the British army to his direction. In any case Kitchener was determined to husband Britain's armed strength as far as possible for later use and wanted gradually to take the entire allied war effort under British control. Kitchener's instructions to Haig allowed for closer co-operation with France than had those sent to Sir John French and the two countries did develop general plans for combined military operations before the start of the 1916 and 1917 campaigning seasons. But the British always stopped short of a unified command.

According to the liaison officer, Edward Spears, who was well placed to judge, Anglo-French relations on the Western Front actually deteriorated after Joffre's fall from power in December 1916:

> The French began to feel that their early efforts, when they had borne the brunt of the war, were being forgotten, and that as the claims and pretensions of their allies grew in proportion to their own diminishing strength, they would find themselves helpless and deprived of all influence when the time came for the final great settling of accounts between the nations.[40]

Spears also points to an important determinant of the day-to-day relations of the two countries – a certain similarity in French eyes between the British and the Germans: 'to many Frenchmen the sight of part of their country in enemy hands, and of allies, however well-intentioned, exercising some measure of authority over another part, was exasperating.'[41]

Under Joffre's successor, Robert Nivelle, military unity was established on the Western Front, albeit briefly. But this owed more to the mounting animosity between Prime Minister Lloyd George and the British commander in France, Douglas Haig, than to any thoroughgoing reappraisal of the mechanics of allied warfare. Not until

November 1917 was the Supreme War Council – a permanent instrument of inter-allied command – set up at Versailles. Even this failed to surmount a host of practical obstacles hindering the full integration of the two countries' war efforts. The council did not supersede the existing allied commanders, and the national general staffs retained responsibility for the conduct of operations by their own armies and were answerable to their own governments. But it was a senior body, consisting of the prime minister and one other representative of each member nation and, through monthly meetings, was expected to 'watch over the general conduct of the war'.[42] Finally, with the German spring offensive of 1918 threatening to split the British and French armies apart and then defeat them individually, the Allies agreed to the appointment of General Ferdinand Foch as commander-in-chief on the Western Front. Even then, a caveat must be inserted. Despite Foch's title, the British, French and American armies placed under his control remained in the last resort answerable to their own governments and provision was made for individual commanders to appeal against Foch's orders if they believed that these threatened the safety of their armies. Only in the last year of the conflict, therefore, and even then imperfectly, did Britain and France really possess the institutions and habits of a genuine alliance.

Of course, it was always possible that the exigencies of war, bringing representatives of both countries into close contact, would ultimately lead to a better appreciation of each other's qualities. In given situations this no doubt happened. Lloyd George developed a good working relationship with Aristide Briand, based perhaps on a common Gallic temperament and a shared liking for the oratorical flourish. A bond of respect and friendship also evolved between Lloyd George and his French opposite number as minister of munitions, Albert Thomas. Such experiences were no doubt replicated in many situations where representatives of Britain and France came into contact. If this had been the norm, the Anglo-French war effort would certainly have progressed more smoothly than it did. In general, however, the evidence points the other way. Such evidence is often necessarily anecdotal, but too common to be ignored. Day-to-day association between French and British politicians and soldiers served largely to confirm the sort of unfavourable racial stereotyping which had existed before the outbreak of hostilities. Three years into the war Lord Robert Cecil, junior minister at the Foreign Office, clearly thought he had got to the heart of the matter:

> There is undoubtedly a difference between the British and the continental point of view in international matters. I will not attempt to describe the difference, but I know that you will agree in thinking that, where it exists, we are right and the continental nations are, speaking generally, wrong.[43]

'It is rather absurd,' judged even the relatively cosmopolitan Lord Esher, 'but you cannot bring an Englishman and a Frenchman, if they are pure bred of their race, together. The Anglo-Saxon ... has so little in common with the Gaul in temperament, education, habits or feeling.'[44] William Robertson agreed. The French commanders and their staff were, he judged, 'a peculiar lot'. But 'the great thing to remember in dealing with them is that they are Frenchmen and not Englishmen, and do not and never will look at things in the way we look at them.'[45]

Fighting together demanded trust, but many Englishmen could not bring themselves to place their trust in their neighbours across the Channel. 'Truly,' remarked Sir John French, commander of the BEF, 'I don't want to be allies with the French more than once in a life time. You can't trust them.'[46] His successor, Douglas Haig, who reasonably enough assumed that the French were very much the same as they had been in Napoleon's day, concluded that 'few realize the difference between right and wrong, between honest, straight-forward dealing and low cunning'.[47] Such sentiments were fully reciprocated. As one French general explained, British deviousness meant that it was Britain 'who will reap the main benefits of this war. Once again, she will have persuaded the continental nations of Europe to cut each other's throats for her greater advantage.'[48]

It was perhaps important, particularly in the military context, that British observers tended to attribute 'feminine' characteristics to their nearest neighbours. Frenchmen were seen as inherently emotional and unstable, their lack of steadfastness a clear sign of female weakness and frivolity. Thus, writes Philip Bell, 'the stereotype of France became a capricious woman – the flighty Marianne as against the solid John Bull'.[49] Even General Henry Wilson, one of the few senior British soldiers of the Great War who might claim the title of francophile, judged the French 'half men, half children and half women'. It was, moreover, 'this last half that always beats us'.[50] Such sentiments, their arithmetical imprecision notwithstanding, ultimately translated into a nagging feeling of regret that the great-power alignments had worked out in the way they had, pitting Britain against the more 'manly' Germans. 'If only we and the Boche were allies,' Robertson is said to have remarked at one inter-allied gathering, 'how easily we could beat all this crowd!'[51] Haig at least reserved such sentiments until after the armistice. 'The French!' he then declared. 'They're the fellows we shall be fighting next.'[52]

So, while the three allied armies were confronting a common enemy, they were always likely to develop different strategic plans to achieve their objectives. But such an argument should not be taken too far. An American observer overstated his case. Writing in 1922, and no doubt by then reflecting the sense of disillusionment with which his country viewed its own involvement in the war, Tasker Bliss, who had been the United States military representative on the Supreme War Council, argued that the entente powers 'were allied little more than in the sense that each found itself fighting, at the same time with the others, its own war against one enemy, and too largely for separate ends'.[53] Conflict is no doubt more interesting than harmony, but there are two sides to the same coin for, as Winston Churchill once pointed out, there is only one thing worse than fighting with allies, and that is fighting without them.[54] Britain and France did achieve considerable feats of co-operation to survive more than four years of warfare with their partnership intact. Coalition warfare imposed enormous stresses and strains, but in the last resort it did bring the conflict to a successful conclusion. 'Whilst the alliance creaked and groaned,' writes Douglas Johnson, 'it remained firm until the armistice.'[55] In a very real sense there was no alternative for either Britain or France – short of a humiliating peace with Germany – to co-operation with one another. The alliance had to be made to work. As Kitchener once famously remarked, 'unfortunately we have to make war as we must and not as we should like to'.[56]

In practice, the Allies were obliged to balance their own interests against those of the coalition itself. By 1915 it was becoming increasingly clear that success in the war could be achieved only as a consequence of close co-operation between Britain and France (and Russia) in the military, diplomatic and economic spheres. Lord Esher put his finger on the problem as early as December 1914:

With regard to France, it would be comparatively simple to establish ties of intimacy. This is an essential condition to carrying on a war with a highly organised and concentrated military power such as Germany. We cannot afford to procrastinate and muddle along, owing to the economic strain upon France.[57]

Both sides, and particularly the British, came to see the alliance in itself as critical to eventual victory. Its maintenance became an overriding objective of Britain's wartime diplomacy. As a result, though France's behaviour was often exasperating from a British point of view, Britain was reluctant to push criticism too far. British observers never really got to grips with the political structure of the French Third Republic – 'I do not understand French politics,' conceded General Callwell. 'Nobody does.'[58] But they were always wary about doing anything which might endanger the survival of the French government, lest such a move might also endanger the alliance itself. It is above all against this background that the present study charts the history of the Salonika campaign, launched by Britain and France in October 1915.

The Salonika campaign seems to defy rational comprehension. It began as an attempt to save the Serbian army from defeat and destruction in the terrible winter of 1915–16. This task proved impossible. Once its failure was apparent, there were frequent appeals for the campaign to be abandoned. Yet it remained in being for the rest of the war. What was it doing? In much of the general historiography of the conflict it has merited only cursory treatment, its soldiers constituting – as many of them felt at the time – a forgotten army. In reality Britain and France could scarcely ignore the existence of an allied force which at times exceeded half a million men. Size, however, did not translate into military effectiveness. For most of its lifetime the expedition seemed to lack military purpose and its continuation was a source of mystery and confusion to many who looked on. This sense of puzzlement was all the greater because the main impulse and support for the expedition came from France, where every eye should surely have been focused on the Western Front. With enemy troops firmly entrenched on French soil, at least one leading French politician saw the paradox. 'Is it so difficult to understand', asked Georges Clemenceau, 'that with the French front in the position that it is, the conquest of France is the vital concern of the war, which can end only with a German victory in France, or a French victory in Germany?'[59] The surprise was that not all his fellow citizens seemed to share Clemenceau's logic. The allied forces based on Salonika were effectively locked up in what the Germans referred to as 'the biggest internment camp in Europe'. The real war in the Balkans, suggests one critic, 'was waged against the malarial mosquito'.[60] Overall, something like ten times as many British soldiers entered hospital with malaria as did those with wounds inflicted by the enemy. Only in the autumn of 1918 did the Salonika army seem to play a part in the securing of victory – and even the importance of this contribution is open to dispute.

Some comparison with the best known 'side-show' of the First World War is inevitable. The Dardanelles campaign has attracted an altogether larger literature, with many writers becoming almost lyrical about its possibilities. There is something rather grandiose and splendid about the whole of that operation, including even the miraculously successful final evacuation, which fires the imagination. 'It was', writes one enthusiast, 'the most imaginative conception of the war and its potentialities were almost beyond reckoning.'[61] The future prime minister, Clement Attlee, who served at Gallipoli, saw the Dardanelles campaign as 'an immortal gamble that did not come off ... Sir Winston [Churchill] ... had the one strategic idea in the war'.[62] By contrast few, if any, British writers have been equally enthusiastic about the Salonika expedition. Two factors are probably important here. The Dardanelles was a relatively short-lived campaign, which had less time to become enveloped in political intrigue. And Salonika was as much a French enterprise as the Dardanelles was British. At the latter, France played the role of 'docile supernumerary';[63] in the Balkans it tended to dictate the course of events. Not for many decades, moreover, had a British government embarked upon a military venture with greater reluctance than it did in October 1915. As Paul Cambon, the experienced French ambassador in London, noted, just as the French had been rushed into the Dardanelles operation without adequate study and investigation, so Britain was led by France to Salonika without having time to consider the full implications of what it was doing.[64]

Not surprisingly, therefore, such voices as have been raised in defence of the Salonika expedition have been predominantly French. 'A magnificent dream. Its realization was not impossible. It would have meant the war being shortened by more than a year and our financial restoration greatly eased.'[65] For the diplomatic historian Albert Pingaud, Salonika and not the Dardanelles was the great 'might have been' of the First World War. With adequate commitment, the campaign, he suggests, could have led to the defeat of Austria from the south and the shortening of the war by up to three years.[66] Though the present work is not intended as a military history of the campaign,[67] the fact remains that the Salonika armies were for the most part locked in the sort of military deadlock which also characterized the Western Front. The terrain of the Balkans favoured defensive action by the central powers rather than offensive action on the part of the Western Allies. The further the allied army had succeeded in marching into the Balkan interior, the more extended would its lines of communication have become and the more likely the risk of being cut off from its base. Be that as it may, Anglo-French differences served only to exclude any chance of military success. The Allies left the Salonika force large enough to weaken their armies on the main front, but insufficiently strong to make its presence genuinely effective in the Balkans.

'Of all the problems which brought soldiers and statesmen into conference during the years 1915–17,' judged one well-placed observer, 'the Salonika expedition was at once the most persistent, exasperating and unfruitful.'[68] As the campaign proved largely irrelevant to the outcome of the war, it could be argued that the contemporary attention lavished upon it by politicians and military leaders in Britain and France exaggerates its intrinsic significance. But the very fact that it did become so great a preoccupation imposes upon the diplomatic and political historian, if not perhaps his military colleague, the need to examine and analyse it. No campaign of the whole conflict better illustrates the problems of coalition warfare. 'My own opinion', wrote the war correspondent G. Ward Price in 1917, 'is that until all the documents now held secret in different countries ... are revealed there will be very few men indeed who know the inside story of the Allies' doings in the Balkans these two years past.'[69] It is in that spirit that this book is written.

. . . .

CHAPTER 2

The Origins of the Campaign

The allied campaign in the Balkans began with indecent haste. On 21 September 1915 General Maurice Sarrail told French War Minister Alexandre Millerand that, according to Prime Minister René Viviani, Salonika could not be envisaged as a base of action for the newly constituted Armée d'Orient.[1] Yet within forty-eight hours, in the face of Bulgarian mobilization and after urgent pleas for help from Prime Minister Venizelos in Greece, the French government had agreed, without consulting their British allies, to the despatch of forces to Salonika to help Greece fulfil its treaty obligations to the threatened Serbia.[2] Less than a fortnight later Sarrail himself set sail for Salonika to assume command of the newly arriving French troops. The actual concept of an expedition based on the Greek port of Salonika had, however, a more respectable pedigree. Its origins lay in two related but separate developments. The first was the quest for additional allies to join the entente, a quest which began almost as soon as war broke out. To many, particularly in Britain, the countries of the Balkans seemed to offer a promising focus of attention where skilful diplomacy might induce a number of important additions to the allied cause. The second was a reappraisal of the military situation following the realization that original thoughts about the war's nature and duration had been altogether too optimistic. By the end of 1914 it was becoming clear that the conflict, which most had assumed would be decided early on by a massive pitched battle, was now developing into a war of attrition in which frontal offensives, though still widely seen as the only ultimate route to victory, would be hideously costly in terms of casualties. In such a situation, politicians on both sides of the Channel began to explore the possibility of alternative – or at least complementary – strategies which might help bring the war to a speedier conclusion.

As early as August 1914 Greek Prime Minister Eleutherios Venizelos proposed an alliance between Britain and Greece. At the time he was anticipating a declaration of war by Turkey upon Britain, or an attack by Bulgaria on Greece or Serbia. The prospect of a Balkan base offered obvious attractions and while the British government felt obliged to reject Greece's formal offer lest it should actually provoke Bulgaria or Turkey into joining the enemy, the cabinet agreed upon a 'cordial acknowledgement' and took up with enthusiasm the general idea of a Balkan confederation, embracing Serbia, Greece, Romania and Bulgaria.[3] But such an association was far easier to envisage than to secure. 'Desperate efforts are being made to find some territorial formula which will bring Bulgaria and Roumania into the fighting line alongside of Servia and Greece,' noted Prime Minister Herbert Asquith at the end of November 1914. 'It is not an easy job.'[4] The Balkans were 'a tangle of conflicting aims and deep-seated enmities' and 'getting the caldron to brew the right mixture' was no easy task.[5] Twice in 1912 and 1913 these rivalries had spilled over into armed conflict. In 1912–13 Serbia, Bulgaria and Greece had secured a brilliant and largely unexpected victory over Turkey. In 1913, however, Bulgaria, backed by Austria-Hungary, had turned on its recent allies, only to meet with defeat and the loss of most of the gains secured in the earlier conflict. Bulgaria felt particularly aggrieved at the loss of Macedonia, ceded to Greece and Serbia under the terms of the Treaty of Bucharest. The wounds of the Balkan Wars had far from healed and many of the states nurtured territorial ambitions which could only be satisfied at the expense of one another. Those events which began with the assassination of the Austrian Archduke Franz-Ferdinand in the Bosnian town of Sarajevo in June 1914 were, for the states of the area, first and foremost a third Balkan war. As European war unfolded from this latest Balkan conflict, the workings of the alliance system rapidly turned Serbia into the ally of Britain and France. In the first months of the Great War Serbia successfully resisted an Austrian offensive but, isolated from its allies, clearly it remained vulnerable to a renewed assault.

Those who believed that a Balkan confederation might become a reality clearly faced considerable problems in terms of persuading the states in question that it was worth their while to join the conflict, especially after Turkey's entry into the war on the side of the central powers in November 1914. Bulgaria was widely seen as the key to the problem. But while it would have been relatively easy to bribe Bulgaria with promises of territory at Turkey's expense, Bulgaria's other ambitions immediately came up against the interests either of countries which Britain also hoped to win over or, in the case of Serbia, those of a state which was already engaged in the war on the allied side.[5] In short, Bulgaria's ambitions were beyond the capacity of the Allies to satisfy. At times it appeared that such inconvenient realities might be overridden. In December 1914 the cabinet had 'a long discussion on Bulgaria. Ll.G., W.S.C[hurchill] and Masterman wanted us to offer the whole of Macedonia to Bulgaria as a bribe to maintain neutrality'.[6] But Bulgaria bided its time, keeping the prospect of its allegiance at a tantalising arm's length, but in practice awaiting a higher bidder.[7]

Some British ministers recognized from the beginning that the complexities of the Balkan situation made it an unpromising field for allied diplomacy. 'The settlement after the second Balkan War', recalled Foreign Secretary Edward Grey, 'was not one of justice but one of force. It stored up inevitable trouble for the time to come.'[8] Since concessions made to any one Balkan state might only result in driving others into the arms of the enemy, Grey preferred to develop the whole area into a neutral zone. Others, however, most prominently David Lloyd George, the chancellor of the exchequer, were more sanguine. His ideas relied heavily on information provided by the two brothers and radical Liberal MPs, Noel and Charles Buxton, who embarked upon a semi-official mission to the Balkans in August 1914. For more than a year the Buxtons encouraged Lloyd George and others in the belief that the Balkan states could be organized into a confederation mobilized against Turkey and Austria-Hungary.[9] Arguing that the death of King Carol of Romania had removed the greatest single obstacle to a pro-alliance coalition, the Buxtons developed a seductively simple programme of territorial rearrangements designed to bring the whole peninsula into the allied camp. As Asquith explained:

> They ... are quite sure that if we offered (1) Bulgaria, the slice of Macedonia Irredenta which (Monastir etc.) the Serbs stole from her 2 years ago (2) Servia, Bosnia and a good bit of the coast of Dalmatia (3)

Roumania, Transylvania and one or two oddments and (4) Greece, Southern Albania, Rhodes and the other islands, and perhaps Smyrna and a
strip of the shore of Asia Minor in that region – we could bring the
whole lot in to fight on our side. They all hate one another and are as
jealous as cats – particularly the Serbians and Bulgarians; but in the case
of the 2 latter we cd. save them from the repulsive necessity of fighting
side by side, by putting them back to back – the Serbs going for Austria
and the Bulgars for Turkey.

'On the whole,' concluded the prime minister, '(tho' the difficulties
are prodigious) I am attracted by the plan.'[10]

Such schemes continued to be considered almost until the moment
that Bulgaria threw in its lot with the central powers. At one point
Lloyd George even put himself forward in the role of ambassador
extraordinary to visit the Balkan states and try to bring them into the
conflict. Not surprisingly, Grey was 'dead opposed to anything of the
kind' and the idea was dropped.[11] But increasingly the realization
dawned that it would be the course of the war itself and, in particular,
the physical presence of an allied army in the Balkans which would
have the most dramatic impact. As Lloyd George put it at the end of
January 1915, 'I am fairly confident you will not get these Balkan
States to decide until they see khaki!'[12]

By this time, however, the second strand in the origins of the
Balkan campaign had come into play. Debates about the possible
creation of alternative theatres of war were an inevitable consequence
of the rapid emergence of a military stalemate on the Western Front.
By the end of 1914 it was clear that recent developments in the
techniques of defensive warfare had invalidated the careful plans of
the army high commands on both sides for a rapid war of movement.
The existence of a continuous line of trenches from the Channel
coast to the Swiss frontier ruled out even the possibility of a flanking
attack. In Britain the quest for strategic alternatives was no doubt
encouraged by the country's reluctance to be involved in a European
land war and by its desire to pursue the sort of campaign for which
historically and materially it was better fitted. David French has
argued persuasively that 'the real division between British policy-
makers did not lie between "Easterners" and "Westerners"', and that
this 'sharply defined division into two separate schools of thought
was a caricature of the debate about war policy conducted within
the British government', the creation of the later memoirs and bio-

graphies of the participants.[13] But, in emphasizing that there were other key debates and divisions about the way in which the war should be fought and that very few, if any, policy-makers seriously believed that an eastern strategy offered a simple alternative to engagement on the Western Front in terms of a cheap and easy road to victory, Professor French may have overstated his case.[14]

No one can study the debate over the Salonika expedition without appreciating that an 'easterner' point of view did exist and that it involved a considerable shift of emphasis from concentration on the battlefields of France and Flanders. Both the vocabulary and the reality of an easterner/westerner debate existed at the time, long before they were enshrined in the polemics of autobiographical self-justification. As another scholar has put it, easterners

> believed that with the current balance of forces between the protagonists a decisive victory could not be won on the western front, and that until Russia had developed her overwhelming military strength on the eastern front the Central Powers could not be defeated. Therefore, while recognising that the western front was the main front for the Anglo-French armies, they argued that it was only necessary to hold this front in sufficient strength to prevent a German victory ... They hoped to use military resources surplus to these requirements to diplomatic and military advantage elsewhere.[15]

Only indeed as a result of increased pressure on the central powers on other fronts would the enemy be obliged to reduce its strength in the west, thereby enabling the Allies to drive Germany's soldiers from occupied France and Belgium.[16] Thus the young Conservative MP, Leopold Amery, who understood the Balkans better than most British observers, argued that the function of an allied force in Macedonia 'should be that of Wellington's Army in the Peninsula, to create a constant drain on the enemy's resources, and only to attempt the advance on Belgrade when the enemy's resistance has begun to crumble everywhere else'.[17]

There is some uncertainty as to who was the first public figure in France to come up with the idea of a campaign in the Balkans. It seems safe to assume that several individuals must have envisaged it at much the same time as a reaction to the evident lack of progress on the Western Front. In November 1914 Aristide Briand, minister of justice in Viviani's government, produced a plan to send an allied force of 400,000 troops to Salonika so as to protect Serbia, influence other Balkan states and bring about an offensive against the southern flank of Austria-Hungary.[18] In addition to the strategic motivation Briand seems also to have been responding to a section of French public opinion which, notwithstanding the military emergency in France, believed that the wide diffusion of French money, language, thought and influence in the Eastern Mediterranean would indissolubly tie its inhabitants to France. This pressure, which had spawned a number of organizations interested in the affairs of the area, had been joined at the outbreak of war by a section of the press in urging the government to take prompt action to safeguard French interests.[19]

At this early stage of the conflict the final arbiter of French strategy was the army commander-in-chief, General Joseph Joffre. And Joffre, whose power in the direction of the French war effort had been supreme ever since the government's evacuation to Bordeaux in September 1914 had signalled a virtual abandonment of its authority, was quick to quash Briand's scheme, arguing that the war could not be won outside France. At very much the same time as Briand evolved his plan, General Franchet d'Espérey, commander of the French Fifth Army, drafted a long memorandum in which he too proposed the despatch to Salonika of five army corps, which would then be transported along the Vardar and Morava valleys to Belgrade so as to mount an offensive aimed at Budapest in the spring of 1915.[20] This document was handed to the president of the republic, Raymond Poincaré, at the beginning of December 1914. Others have attributed the paternity of the idea, as early as October 1914, to General Galliéni, military governor of Paris, though the general himself claimed no responsibility for the concept in his published diaries.[21] Be that as it may, by February 1915 Galliéni had become an enthusiastic convert to the idea of an expedition to Salonika, to use it not for an advance into the Balkans but as a base for a march upon Constantinople with an army large enough to encourage the Greeks and Bulgarians to join the entente.[22] Even Poincaré later attempted to claim some credit for himself for originating the conception of a Balkan campaign.[23] At all events the question was raised again on the first day of the new year.

At a reception at the Elysée Palace Briand told his ministerial colleagues that he no longer believed in the possibility of a breakthrough on the Western Front and that it was now necessary to

search for a decision elsewhere. He proposed the formation of an
Anglo-French expeditionary force to be sent through Serbia into
Austria-Hungary.[24] This plan seems to have won the support of
Viviani and it was decided that the whole question should be placed
before General Joffre, without whose assent no action would be
possible.[25] A few days later Joffre was summoned to the Elysée but
resolutely refused to countenance any diversions in southern Europe,
arguing that his own plans involved an attack in the spring against
the enemy's defensive line in Artois and Champagne for which he
would require every available soldier. The government could only
give way in the face of the general's opposition. Joffre was delighted
at his success in winning the government round to his point of view
and the idea of a Salonika expedition was, for the time being, allowed
to drop.[26] But concurrent developments on the other side of the
Channel meant that the plan would not be buried as definitively as
Joffre might have wished.

As has been well documented, by the end of December Colonel
Maurice Hankey, secretary to the newly constituted War Council,
David Lloyd George and Winston Churchill, the First Lord of the
Admiralty, each acting independently, were coming to similar conclusions about the war situation. All were alarmed at the prospect of
an interminable war of attrition on the Western Front and each was
anxious to bring in new allies in the Balkans, to increase the pressure
on Turkey and Austria-Hungary and to relieve that on Russia. Their
concern was given added emphasis with the arrival on 2 January of
an urgent appeal from the Russian commander-in-chief, the Grand
Duke Nicolas, for some diversionary action to relieve the pressure on
his own front. There was no consensus among the three men as to
precisely what should be done, but broad agreement that the war
could be won on the Western Front only at an intolerable cost. As a
result it would be worthwhile to explore the opportunities for military
action in the Eastern Mediterranean, especially as Britain would soon
be in possession of far greater military resources than at the beginning
of the war as Kitchener's New Armies began to come into existence.
This rethinking came at the right psychological moment. Asquith
summed up the mood: 'When our new armies are ready, as they will
soon begin to be, it seems folly to send them to Flanders where they
are not wanted, and where (in W[inston]'s phrase) they will "chew
barbed wire", or be wasted in futile frontal attacks.'[27]

Even Kitchener, who at heart knew that the war would be won or lost in the west, was sympathetic to a strategic initiative which might relieve pressure on the Russian front. As he explained to a sceptical Sir John French, Britain's commander in France, 'the feeling here is gaining that although it is essential to defend the line we hold, troops over and above what is necessary for that service could be better employed elsewhere'.[28]

Lloyd George's thoughts, which he put together in a long memorandum for the cabinet entitled 'Suggestions as to the Military Position', are the most relevant in the present context. There was a real danger, the chancellor argued, that the people of Britain and France would sooner or later get tired of long casualty lists justified on spurious or inadequate grounds. What he had seen of the military situation in France, together with his own study of the subject, convinced him that any attempts to force the German line would only end in failure and an appalling loss of life. Lloyd George was clearly looking for a military success somewhere – precisely where seemed altogether less important.

> A clear definite victory which has visibly materialised in guns and prisoners captured, in unmistakable retreats of the enemy's armies, and in large sections of enemy territory occupied, will alone satisfy the public that tangible results are being achieved by the great sacrifices they are making, and decide neutrals that it is at last safe for them to throw in their lot with us.

But he did put forward two concrete proposals. One was for a landing in Syria should the Turks despatch any substantial force in the direction of the Suez Canal; and the other was for an attack upon Austria either through a landing on the Dalmatian coast or by a force operating out of Salonika. Such a step, Lloyd George hoped, would finally bring a Balkan confederation into being. The British forces would join up with 300,000 Serbs and, all being well, up to half a million Romanians and 200,000 Greeks and Montenegrins. Austria would then face an attack on its most vulnerable frontier which would oblige Germany to send troops to its assistance or abandon it completely. His proposal would thus have the ultimate purpose of 'bringing Germany down by the process of knocking the props under her'.[29]

It was the Balkan option which really attracted Lloyd George and at meetings of the War Council throughout January 1915 he sought to convert his colleagues to his point of view. On 13 January the War Council decided in favour of a naval attack at the Dardanelles, as advocated by Churchill, but as this seemed to have no implications in terms of land forces it did not appear to prejudice the Balkan option. Indeed, as Lloyd George himself recorded, the War Council

> decided that if it becomes apparent in February and March that a stalemate is established on the Western frontier, it is desirable that British troops should be employed in another field of operations. That preparation be made so as to put us in a position to engage in such operations if it be found desirable to undertake them. That a Sub-Committee be appointed to consider such preparations, to consist of the Secretary of State for War, the First Lord of the Admiralty, Mr. Balfour and myself.[30]

With Serbia looking increasingly vulnerable, the argument was clearly going Lloyd George's way. By 22 January it had been decided to send an army corps to the Balkans which would 'in all probability bring in both Roumania and Greece; in which case a really effective blow will be struck at the heart of the situation'.[31] As Asquith explained:

> The main point is to do something really effective for Servia, which is threatened by an overwhelming inrush from the Austrians reinforced by some 80,000 Germans. I have urged Grey to put the strongest possible pressure upon Roumania and Greece to come in without delay, and to promise that if they will form a real Balkan bloc we will send troops of our own to join them and save the situation. I am sure that this is right, and that all our 'side shows' – Zeebrugge, Alexandretta, even Gallipoli – ought to be postponed to this.[32]

One factor, however, was being left out of the equation. As Balfour reminded his colleagues, 'we had to keep on friendly relations with the French'.[33] The opportunity for the two countries to exchange views on the possibility of a Balkan campaign came when War Minister Millerand arrived in London for talks on 21 January. To British dismay the French minister, acting very much as a spokesman for Joffre, demanded that all available British troops be sent to France rather than the Balkans. Asquith described what happened, while also commentating on the rudimentary machinery which so far existed to conduct Anglo-French diplomacy:

> Of course I put to him strongly the Balkan situation, and the irreparable

disaster wh. wd. be involved in the crushing of Servia. He professed to be quite alive to this, but not 'dans ce moment' etc. Ll George (with the aid of an interpreter) and E. Grey after dinner pressed our point. I don't know what the actual upshot will be, but I am sure that it is all to the good that we shd. often have these personal interchanges. They obviate friction, and grease the sometimes rather creaking wheels of the Entente.[34]

A 'rather stormy' interview between Lloyd George and Millerand failed to shift the French war minister and even Kitchener had to give way. Millerand declared that the question should be studied but insisted that immediate action was impossible. Kitchener was not prepared to do anything which might endanger the alliance and promised Millerand that the Balkans scheme would be put on the back-burner.[35]

The matter was raised again at the War Council on 28 January. It was acknowledged that serious differences had arisen between the two allied governments and the hope was expressed that there would be closer co-ordination in the future. Despite Kitchener's assurances to Millerand, Lloyd George once again stressed the need to send an army to the Balkans 'in order to bring all the Balkan states into the war on our side and settle Austria'. His hand was strengthened by the fact that Venizelos had now offered to bring Greece into the conflict providing Romania did the same, Bulgaria remained neutral and Britain and France landed two army corps. The Greek minister in London was reported to have suggested that the appearance of even 5000 allied troops in the Balkans would suffice to influence Bulgarian opinion. Kitchener argued that such a tiny force would be the object of ridicule, but the main difficulty was seen to lie with the French, for Asquith admitted that Millerand had not taken at all favourably to the idea of assisting Serbia.[36] At this stage of the war, however, Lloyd George was not prepared to see British strategy dictated by the French, 'as if we were her vassal'. Strategy in France itself, he conceded, must necessarily be France's to declare. But 'outside we are free after taking counsel with her to take our own course'. It would, he concluded, 'be criminal folly if we allowed [French dilatoriness, timidity and selfishness] to compel us to look on impotently whilst a catastrophe was being prepared for the Allies in the Balkans'.[37]

This then was the situation when Lloyd George visited Paris at the beginning of February, ostensibly to discuss economic problems. In conversation with Finance Minister Alexandre Ribot, he discovered that Millerand had never mentioned to his colleagues that the suggestion of an expeditionary force to Salonika had been made to him when he was in London. After discussions with Viviani, Delcassé and Briand, Lloyd George realized that they too had been kept in the dark and he found them astonished and annoyed that Millerand had not fully reported the matter to them. The chancellor found them much more friendly to the idea than Millerand had been, while Briand told him that, with the possible exception of Delcassé, the rest of the French cabinet were opposed to Millerand and unanimously in favour of the principle of an expeditionary force of two divisions being sent to Salonika at the earliest practicable moment. Briand also indicated that, if Greece and Romania agreed to enter the war, Joffre would be obliged to provide the necessary forces. 'It was incredible that if 80,000 men from the W[est] could bring in 800,000 in the E[ast], any general would refuse his consent to such a proposal.'[38]

Lloyd George's diplomatic initiative certainly seemed to have the desired effect. At a special meeting of the French cabinet on 4 February it was agreed in principle to send an allied expeditionary force to Salonika, subject to Kitchener sending to France four divisions which he had already promised, and to Joffre being ready to provide the necessary troops.[39] With some show of reluctance Millerand secured Joffre's consent to this proposal. So Lloyd George returned from France on 6 February, bringing with him Delcassé, who bore his government's promise to send a division to Salonika if the British would do the same. Majority opinion now clearly believed that this was a cheap price to pay if it induced Greece, and possibly other Balkan states, to join the Allies.

Lloyd George even seemed to have won the support of the figure who would later become his staunchest opponent in the matter of the Salonika expedition. A meeting on 6 February with General William Robertson, the future CIGS, left him greatly enthused. Robertson was a 'shrewd, clear-headed and strong man' who regarded the Salonika idea as 'good strategy', maintaining this attitude throughout their discussion.[40] At a meeting of the War Council on 9 February, Asquith again stressed the advantages of the proposed expedition. But the situation had now become urgent since Bulgaria had contracted a loan with Germany, making its adhesion to the central powers appear imminent. The War Council decided that if Greece promised to enter the war, two allied divisions would be sent to protect its flank from any possible Bulgarian attack. As an earnest of Britain's commitment Kitchener agreed, despite the presence of Sir John French at the War Council, that Britain's last remaining uncommitted regular division, the 29th, should be sent to Salonika.[41] In the meantime Delcassé, still in London, pressed the French War Ministry to provide the necessary rifles to induce the Grand Duke Nicolas to participate in the proposed allied venture.[42] But the Greek king absolutely refused to entertain the idea of Greek participation in the war without the collaboration of Romania, which was becoming increasingly unlikely following the Germano-Bulgarian loan agreement. On 15 February Greece categorically refused to join the entente and when the War Council met on the following day it was agreed that the 29th Division should be sent to the Eastern Mediterranean 'at the earliest possible date ... to be available in case of necessity to support the naval attack on the Dardanelles'.[43] 'Our Serbian démarche is off for the moment', recorded Asquith, 'as the Greeks shy at it ... . So one's eyes are now fixed on the Dardanelles.'[44]

Though attention shifted from Salonika to the Dardanelles, the objective of a Balkan confederation remained a constant. As the War Council heard on 26 February, the immediate aim of the Dardanelles operation was to open up the sea route to the Black Sea,

> but the ultimate object was to bring in the Balkan States. Nearly every member of the War Council mentioned that as our ultimate aim. Some members went further and suggested that we might find scope in the Near East for the employment of the new armies. As Mr. Lloyd George has pointed out, the employment of British military forces in the Balkans is probably indispensable if we are to secure the adherence of the Balkan states to the cause of the Allies. Probably, therefore, the War Council will accept the view that the ultimate object of the operation now commenced is to open the way for military operations against Austria in which a British army will, it is hoped, co-operate with the armies of Roumania, Servia, and perhaps Greece.[45]

Such a prospect once more flickered into life when, on 1 March, Venizelos, encouraged by recent naval successes at the Dardanelles, suddenly offered to land three Greek divisions on the Gallipoli peninsula. It was, according to Asquith, 'far the most interesting moment of the war'.[46] But the Russian government, fearful that Venizelos's offer masked a long-term ambition to include Constantinople inside a postwar greater Greece, quickly made it clear that it would not consent to Greek participation in the campaign. On 3 March and again two days later, the Crown Council in Athens, recognizing Russia's hostility, set its face against Greek involvement. In the circumstances Venizelos had little alternative but to resign on 6 March, making way for a prime minister committed to a policy of strict neutrality. The chimera of a Balkan bloc was, to all intents and purposes, dead.

At the beginning of 1915, therefore, a campaign based on Salonika had been conceived as a means of uniting the Balkan states in coalition against the central powers, thereby effecting a considerable change in the balance of a war which appeared to be stalemated on the Western Front. True, many problems had been ignored or at least only partially thought through. The enormous obstacles in the way of a Balkan confederation had never been successfully addressed. There was in any case a tendency to overrate the military effectiveness of the states in question. Too much faith was placed in simple arithmetical calculations showing the combined manpower resources of the Balkan states, and insufficient attention was paid to their lack of the sort of industrial infrastructure necessary to sustain their effective participation in a twentieth-century total war. The armchair strategy of men such as Lloyd George sounded fair enough in theory, but there was a misleading simplicity in the notion of a march across the Danube to take the central powers in the rear. As Trevor Wilson has pointed out, Lloyd George's notion that Germany might be defeated by 'knocking the props under her' involved allowing an optimistic 'piece of kite flying, expressed in compelling but sometimes dangerously misleading language', to get in the way of a rational discussion of military practicalities. To talk of props whose removal would entail Germany's collapse 'constituted little more than a sleight of hand with a wall map – upon which [Austria-Hungary and Turkey] appear "below" Germany'.[47]

This was understandable enough. At this stage of the war Kitchener retained such a tight and personal control over military policy that other members of the cabinet and War Council had great difficulty in even getting access to professional military opinion and information. 'Were it not for Winston and L.G. asking Kitchener questions,' commented one government minister, 'we shd. have precious little enlightenment on military questions.'[48] As regards the Balkans, Kitchener himself may have had no strategic plans. As he explained to Lord Esher: 'owing to the rapid changes that take place on the political horizon in the Balkans and that part of the world, it seems difficult to see how any very fixed plan of action can be determined upon when we are dealing with such unstable factors.'[49]

But at least at this stage of the war the idea of a Balkan campaign was being discussed in terms of its possible military advantage to the Allies in their struggle against Germany. Early in 1915, the idea of an expedition based on Salonika, designed to unite the forces of the Balkan states against the central powers, was an initiative which demanded careful consideration. By the beginning of March few in either Britain or France still regarded such a campaign as a practical proposition. The Allies were then fully committed to operations at the Dardanelles, now seen very much as a combined naval and military venture, and one side-show was probably enough. Furthermore, as 1915 progressed, the failure of this venture served increasingly to dampen the enthusiasm of many of those who had believed that operations in the Eastern Mediterranean offered an alternative, or at least an indispensable complement, to concentration on the Western Front. By the time that the Salonika expedition finally materialized in October, it was as a last-minute expedient dictated in the first instance by considerations of French internal politics and undertaken with almost no technical evaluation of its strategic possibilities.[50]

To understand how this came about attention must now turn to the evolution of France's war directorate. As is well known, on the afternoon of 4 August 1914, Prime Minister René Viviani addressed the Chamber of Deputies on the new situation created by the out-break of hostilities with Germany. He read out a message from the president of the republic. This ended with a passionate plea for an internal political truce to bring to an end the domestic political strife which had been so characteristic of the Third Republic, and which, in a wartime context, threatened to paralyse the nation's efforts to defeat the enemy. Thus the so-called Sacred Union was born. Political partisans had, however, little reason to regard this as a long-term sacrifice since almost all observers were confident that this war, like its predecessor of 1870, would be over in a matter of months. When later that day the National Assembly adjourned for six months, it did so reasonably confident that when it met again the military emergency would be over. It was appreciated that the parliamentary process was fundamentally incompatible with the sort of strong government required for the waging of war and that its continuation might well produce political and military paralysis. For a few months, therefore, or perhaps only weeks, the legislators were prepared – as a matter of trust – to abdicate their power and defer to the executive authority which would supervise the activities of the High Command.[51]

This was the theory. The practice, of course, turned out to be rather different. The growing realization that this would be a long, drawn-out war of attrition rather than a speedy clash of arms inevitably placed the Sacred Union on altogether less firm foundations. But the expected length of the war was not the only miscalculation upon which the political truce was constructed. In addition, the anticipated war executive failed to materialize. Viviani soon stated that the government had no intention of interfering in the command of the troops nor in the direct conduct of operations.[52] Under stronger political leadership this might not have happened, but apart from his oratorical powers Viviani had few of the qualities of war leadership. Poincaré described him in the early stages of the war as 'absorbed, absent-minded, silent, directing nothing, reaching no conclusions', in short as 'flaccid as a rag'.[53] As a result, power passed almost unnoticed into the hands of the military commander, General Joffre. When, in 1910, a new supreme commander for wartime had had to be nominated to replace General Fémau, the existing functions of General Pau had seemed to mark him out as the strongest contender. The cabinet, however, had refused to consider him 'because he went to Mass'.[54] Joffre therefore took over the post very much by default, but his combination of offices in the years before 1914, when he was both vice-president of the Conseil Supérieur de la Défense Nationale and chief of the Army General Staff, gave him extensive, indeed almost absolute, powers in military matters.[55] With the outbreak of hostilities, the Chamber's two miscalculations coalesced, for the underlying basis of Joffre's almost total control of French war policy and plans lay in the fact that during the years of peace the coming war had never been envisaged as anything other than a short, sharp clash of arms leading to a speedy victory. So it was almost inevitable that the

French government would effectively abdicate its directing authority and leave Joffre unfettered to achieve the desired military results. The government believed that its role was simply to retire from the stage to observe what would be no more than a duel between armies. At the outbreak of war no institution even existed to act as a link between the civilian and military leaderships.

Joffre's power in the early days of the conflict was considerably increased by the decision to transfer the government from Paris to Bordeaux. There, it was almost impossible for ministers to know what was going on at the front, let alone to determine the course of military events. Whether or not the government should remain at Bordeaux largely depended upon Joffre himself. 'Delcassé swears', recorded Lord Bertie on 27 October 1914, 'that the return to Paris has not been discussed in the Cabinet and that the decision when discussed will depend on General Joffre: if he says "Go" the Government will go, and if he says "Stay" the Government will stay at Bordeaux.'[56] Not surprisingly, Joffre soon became conscious of the extent of his authority. When General Galliéni was sent to check on the situation at the besieged town of Liège on 14 August, the commander-in-chief seemed sorely offended. As Joffre later recalled:

> I sensed that Galliéni was trying to broach the question of operations and that M. Messimy [war minister until 26 August] must have charged him with presenting to me the manner in which he thought they ought to be conducted. One can easily imagine how disagreeable this suggestion was to me, if one considers the responsibility I was bearing. Accordingly, I broke off the conversation sharply enough.[57]

In some ways Joffre seemed singularly ill-equipped for the elevated position he now occupied. He had reached his late fifties with almost no experience of the command of troops and no higher study of warfare. 'His equipment was the experience of a single little colonial expedition in early life and a technical knowledge of fortification and railway construction.'[58] But after the 'miracle of the Marne', a victory for which he perhaps received an undue share of the credit, Joffre was endowed with a popular reputation as a military commander which he would take with him to the grave. As the months passed, however, the promised breakthrough on the Western Front failed to materialize. In political circles whispers of discontent at the lack of achievement became ever more insistent as 1915 progressed. Indeed, the stalemate on the battlefield was a key factor in re-creating parliament as a significant element in the politico-military structure of wartime France. In particular, the Foreign Affairs and Army Commissions of the Chamber and Senate emerged as important instruments in the reassertion of parliamentary control after the military dictatorship of 1914. These committees of the French parliament provided the opportunity for the sort of detailed interrogation of ministers which was not possible in open debates of the Chamber and Senate. In so doing they created a powerbase for the government's most influential critics. A struggle now developed between parliamentarians seeking to exercise what they regarded as their legitimate rights and Joffre, supported by War Minister Alexandre Millerand, determined to preserve the autonomy of the Grand Quartier Général (GQG).[59] The government was caught somewhere in the middle.

In this climate the feeling grew that Joffre, notwithstanding his victory at the Marne, was not the general most likely to win the war for France. Criticism ranged from dissatisfaction at his military strategy to a concern that he might be trying to set up a dictatorship at his headquarters at Chantilly. But removing Joffre was not an option for the government while his prestige among ordinary Frenchmen remained high.[60] Moreover, Joffre had become so pampered through the zeal of Millerand in shielding him from criticism that he had grown to regard the War Ministry as little more than a buffer between himself and the government. Those who wanted a change in the high command came to understand that they would not get it from Millerand. So to reach the general it became necessary to attack the minister. The solidarity between the two men was such that a crisis in the command would almost certainly entail a ministerial upheaval.[61] As Joffre later recalled with gratitude, as parliamentary opinion became more anxious and insistent, all the more firmly and consistently did Millerand defend his liberty of action.[62]

Inevitably, Millerand's position became even more uncomfortable than that of Joffre. He was severely attacked in the Chamber as early as March 1915, but managed to extricate himself.[63] Poincaré found it necessary to criticize Millerand's attitude, his apparent inertia and his obstinate unwillingness to give precise information to the parliamentary commissions.[64] The president of the republic was himself becoming restless at the constitutional restraints which limited his own freedom of initiative. Millerand, 'one of my oldest friends, aspires to leave me less power than a senator or a deputy'.[65] But Poincaré was not alone. Millerand's uncritical defence of Joffre set him at odds with his ministerial colleagues and by early July each meeting of the French cabinet seemed to produce a 'Millerand incident'.[66] The unremitting efforts of the commissioners to inspect men and material at the front and the reluctance of the War Ministry to admit them posed a dilemma which only Millerand's removal or a drastic reduction in the powers of the parliamentary commissions could resolve. The war minister displayed an uncritical faith in Joffre and seldom questioned his decisions and proposals. He regarded it as his duty to defend the commander, even when the attacks directed against Joffre seemed only too justified.

Unfortunately for both Joffre and Millerand, the early months of the war saw the emergence of a new popular hero in the person of General Maurice Sarrail, a soldier whose views and associates made him an embarrassment, indeed a threat, to Joffre. For Sarrail appeared to have imagination and flair, whereas Joffre seemed dull and devoid of new ideas. His political views, moreover, immediately set him at odds with his superior officer, while making him a focal point for those politicians who wanted to criticize the high command. Sarrail was one of the few figures in the senior ranks of the French army whose allegiance to the republican ideal was thought to be beyond question. He had emerged before 1914 as the darling of the political Left and in particular of the Radical Socialist party. This was the party which had grown out of Gambetta's Republican Union and had become associated with an unswerving defence of the institution of the republic.[67] Sarrail had been one of the few high-ranking officers in the 1890s who did not join in the witch-hunt against Captain Dreyfus and he had subsequently found the way open to rapid advancement under the anti-clerical war minister, General André. Then, with the coming of war, his stature had risen dramatically as a result of his part in the Battle of the Marne, in which he had commanded the French Third Army.[68] But it was Sarrail's political backing which now made him such an important figure, particularly at a time when the semblance of parliamentary government was returning to France after the virtual military dictatorship of the early months of the war.

In the general election of May 1914 the Radical Socialists had captured 136 seats in the Chamber which left them well short of an

overall majority, but stronger than any other single party. The unofficial but acknowledged leader of the Radical Socialist group was
the former prime minister, Joseph Caillaux, a politician whose
questionable activities during the war would eventually bring him
before the High Court. A figure who aroused much suspicion and
distrust, Caillaux was widely believed to retain a lurking sympathy for
the German cause. As one historian has put it, 'everywhere that there
was intrigue and rebellion, everywhere that people shirked their duty,
his name appeared as a standard, a rallying post'.[69] Even so, Caillaux
might have been able to push his own claims to the premiership but
for the fact that, on 16 March, Mme Caillaux had shot and killed the
editor of *Le Figaro* as revenge for publishing letters between herself
and her husband, dating from before their marriage. As it was, Louis
Malvy, minister of the interior in Viviani's cabinet, emerged as the
key link between Caillaux's parliamentary following and the influence
exercised by the Radical Socialists in the direction of the government.
That parliamentary following was one which no French government
nor the high command could afford to ignore.

The rise of Sarrail served to reopen one of the central debates of
the French Third Republic. The army and the republic had never
been fully reconciled and, if the Sacred Union were to be fractured,
this would be one of the first issues to resurface into the political
conflict. There existed in left-wing circles in wartime France an on-
going, if no doubt exaggerated, fear that military victory might prove
the occasion for a right-wing, possibly clerical, *coup d'état* by the
victorious generals which would effectively sound the deathknell of
the republic. In some minds it remained as easy to associate the
army with the persecution of Dreyfus and the threat of Boulanger as
with the defence of the *patrie*. The intensity of feeling on this issue
is best expressed in the words of a contemporary. Early in the war
Joffre became acquainted with the fears nurtured by Sarrail. 'Yes,'
Sarrail told one deputy,

> we are headed straight for a dictatorship. When the Germans give in
> General Joffre will be promoted Marshal and will hand over the reins to
> General Foch. That means the return of imperialism and the end of the
> Republic. You are going to Paris for the opening of parliament. You must
> remain there, do not come back. It is essential for the Chamber to remain
> in session and to see that no *coup d'état* takes place.[70]

By contrast, figures on the centre and right of the political spectrum viewed with unease the 'revolutionary' tendencies of the Left and their few associates in the higher echelons of the army. The influential French ambassador in London, Paul Cambon, believed that the Radical Socialists'

> single preoccupation ... is to be in power on the day of the election and to impose themselves on the country by fair means or foul. They would be capable like the Convention in its last days of reserving themselves two-thirds of the seats in the next Chamber. I think they are capable of anything, even an 18 Fructidor with Sarrail as the executioner-in-chief.[71]

The fact that there was little if any substance in either of these fears is of less significance than the contemporary reality that they were genuinely felt.

Sarrail was therefore an obvious embarrassment to Joffre while he remained among the French military elite, and the relationship between the two men was further strained by the fact that whenever the possibility of Joffre's replacement was mentioned, the name of Sarrail was never far distant. As early as February 1915 two memoranda were circulated from the headquarters of the Third Army – whether or not with Sarrail's connivance is unclear – which concluded that if Joffre found himself indisposed for even a fortnight and command passed to Sarrail, the enemy would without question be chased out of France because of the new strategical ideas which Sarrail would bring to the higher direction of the war.[72] Joffre, it was said, did not want capable republican generals to have commands which could attract attention to themselves and so demonstrate his own incapacity.[73] The animosity between the two men inevitably grew stronger and by the end of March Sarrail was complaining bitterly to President Poincaré about Joffre and the barrage of orders and counterorders which he received from the GQG.[74] In June Alfred Margaine, deputy for the Marne, urged upon the president the need to replace Joffre with Sarrail at the head of the French army.[75] In such circumstances the commander-in-chief was understandably on the look-out for the means to ruin his rival.

Joffre's opportunity came at the beginning of July as a result of a military setback suffered by Sarrail. A German attack on 30 June inflicted heavy casualties on Sarrail's Third Army and the general's counter-offensive, based on two divisions of reinforcements dispatched by Joffre, was delayed too long. In addition, it was reported that on some occasions Sarrail had not been wholly truthful in his reports to Joffre: he had lost trenches and had failed to announce the fact in the hope of winning them back before the deception had been discovered.[76] Joffre wrote immediately to General Dubail, commander of the Group of Armies of the East, instructing him to carry out an investigation of the operations in the Argonne and of Sarrail's role in them. Joffre showed uncharacteristic subtlety in his choice of Dubail, since the latter was a staunch republican and a favourite of the political Left in very much the same way that Sarrail was. In the event that his report proved unfavourable to Sarrail, Joffre calculated that it would be difficult for Sarrail's friends to claim that he had been the victim of a political witch-hunt.[77] Joffre later wrote that it was in order to show that action was being taken for purely military reasons that he entrusted the inquiry to a commander whose uprightness and independent judgement had never been brought into question.[78] Others, however, regarded it as nothing but 'a manifestation of spite' and believed that the tone of Joffre's letter to Dubail dictated the required response.[79] Joffre wrote: 'I wonder … if the answer is not to be found higher up and if the moral atmosphere in the Third Army is such as to permit the free development of that energy, initiative and devotion which are essential in war.'[80] Certainly, it was noted at the GQG that what was held against Sarrail was not so much his military failures as the fact that his command of his army and his relationships with his subordinates were determined by his own political leanings. Sarrail seemed to assess a man's value less on the basis of his military prowess than on the radicalism of his politics.[81]

Dubail presented his findings to Joffre on 20 July in the form of two long reports. The first, on the subject of the recent military operations, was both critical and complimentary about Sarrail's conduct. The most significant criticism made against the general was that he had failed to constitute any reserves.[82] The second report on the atmosphere at Sarrail's headquarters and inside his army was more damaging. Dubail found in Sarrail's dealings with his junior officers, 'conduct which hamstrings the lower command and harms its prestige'.[83] Sarrail had not acted the part of an army commander to the full. He had, for example, shown a reluctance to visit his troops and interest himself in their welfare. The overall tone of Dubail's two reports was therefore not favourable to Sarrail, but neither was it as damaging as has sometimes been suggested.[84] Sensing what was afoot Margaine now wrote a long letter to Viviani protesting that the 'republican general' was being molested by the GQG.[85] Joffre, however, wasted no time. Just a day after receiving Dubail's reports he sent his liaison officer with a letter announcing Sarrail's replacement at the head of the Third Army. Joffre expressed a willingness to give Sarrail command of an army corps unless the government had another mission for him – a phrase which perhaps hinted at Joffre's desire to see his rival removed from French soil.[86] Be that as it may, on 22 July the Council of Ministers was presented with the *fait accompli* of Sarrail's dismissal.

At the cabinet meeting Finance Minister Ribot, himself no friend of Joffre,[87] voiced the feeling of many of his colleagues that it was unfair to punish Sarrail for his recent setback in the Argonne, while no one had been disciplined for comparable failures around Arras. But for most of those present an unwillingness to do anything which might arouse Joffre's anger and perhaps prompt his resignation was a limiting factor on the discussion. The suggestion that Sarrail should be entrusted with the command of the Army of Lorraine was shouted down by Briand, who argued that Sarrail's continued presence in France would only provide an excuse for renewed political agitation. Many ministers had the impression that Joffre would like to see Sarrail sent out to the Dardanelles and it was decided to sound out the commander-in-chief on this idea.[88] The existing French commander in that theatre, General Gouraud, had recently suffered a serious injury and a replacement was required, although when Millerand had discussed the matter with Poincaré earlier in the month there had been no question of Sarrail being offered the post.[89] But political and military considerations were becoming inextricably intertwined. According to Abel Ferry, the under-secretary for foreign affairs, of those present at the cabinet meeting only Poincaré had managed to rise above the level of party political intrigue.[90] Kitchener heard that Briand had supported Sarrail simply because he hoped to strengthen his standing with the Radical Socialists in order to fulfil his ambition of replacing Viviani at the head of the government.[91]

Sarrail learnt of the blow which had befallen him on 22 July and was instructed to report to the War Ministry on the following day. Before doing so, however, he was informed by Interior Minister Louis Malvy that the government was thinking in terms of making him commander of the Dardanelles expeditionary force.[92] Once the news of Sarrail's dismissal became known, his supporters tried to stir up a wave of protest. An article was prepared for the newspaper *Le Radical* in which it was argued that the general was the victim of the intrigues of a cabal, but the censor stepped in before this could appear.[93] Joffre's liaison officer at the Ministry of War quickly gained a picture of the parliamentary agitation which had been aroused: 'Sarrail is a symbol ... he shouldn't have been touched. To deprive him of his command is to slap parliament in the face by striking out at the only republican general.'[94] The head of the British mission at French army head-quarters reported that Sarrail was 'a dangerous man' and that it was more than probable that he would organize a political campaign against Millerand and Joffre.[95] Millerand certainly came in for severe criticism. 'The Left of the Chamber are "going for" Millerand,' noted Bertie. 'There is even a talk amongst the Rue de Valois lot of deputing a Commissary to watch the Army: a return to the days of the Convention.'[96] The minister had been obliged to take on three under-secretaries, one for munitions, one for supplies and one for sanitary and hospital questions, thereby severely restricting his authority, but now the Chamber wanted his head. Partly because of Joffre's astute choice of Dubail, however, the Left found it difficult to use *l'affaire Sarrail* as the linchpin of their attack on Millerand.[97]

Sarrail now had to decide whether he would accept the command at the Dardanelles should a formal offer be made to him. No doubt aware of the motivation which lay behind the projected offer, he declared to Millerand and Viviani on 23 July that, having been relieved of his command in France, he could not accept what was evidently an inferior appointment. His career, he insisted, was at an end and he would go into retirement. Somewhat to Poincaré's irritation Viviani now suggested trying to obtain Joffre's consent to giving Sarrail the command of the Lorraine army. Perhaps this would lessen the parliamentary agitation. In the game of politics, Viviani reminded the president of the republic, one had to learn to live with the Chamber.[98] On 24 July the Council of Ministers heard that Joffre, although he had already designated General Gérard for the Army of Lorraine, was not opposed to giving Sarrail command at the Dardanelles.[99] Convinced that the political unrest had to be quelled, the government decided to send the minister of public instruction, Albert Sarraut, one of Sarrail's political sympathizers, to try to persuade the general to reconsider his decision concerning the Dardanelles command.[100] Sarrail was also visited by Briand and his resistance began to weaken, although he remained adamant that he would accept only if the expeditionary force were strengthened.[101] On 25 July, Viviani was therefore able to tell Poincaré that Sarrail might after all go back on his earlier refusal, while on the following day the radical-socialist deputy, Henry Franklin-Bouillon, confidently announced to the Chamber Foreign Affairs Commission that Sarrail would shortly be leaving to head the Dardanelles expedition.[102]

An examination of the issue of reinforcements was requested from General Gouraud, who insisted that three or four new divisions would be needed. The Council of Ministers, meeting on 27 July, came to the same conclusion and Viviani and Millerand were entrusted with the task of extracting Joffre's consent. But the latter proved reluctant to allow Sarrail to take command of a reinforced expeditionary force. His change of heart appears to have been dictated by little more than his personal antipathy towards Sarrail, for he now expressed the hope that the command would be offered to General Franchet d'Espérey.[103] 'The exercise of power and the ruin of a rival appear to have become more important to Joffre than the immediate task of finding a way to defeat the enemy.'[104] Joffre was summoned to appear before the cabinet on the last day of July, when his excuse that he was unable to spare four divisions from the Western Front was summarily rejected. Meeting again later in the day, but this time without Joffre, the ministers decided to nominate Sarrail as commander of the Dardanelles expedition and to get him to prepare a plan of operations straight away.[105] But on 3 August Sarrail, conscious of his own strength, placed three conditions before Millerand which, he said, would have to be fulfilled if he were to accept the command. He insisted that an 'Armée d'Orient' should be constituted, that he should not be placed under the British commander, Sir Ian Hamilton, and that he would not depart without the agreed reinforcements.[106] Millerand was in no position to resist. His own situation was weakening as the chambers clamoured for the appointment of travelling commissions which would effectively transfer much of the government's authority over the army to the Senate Army Commission. Sarrail's close associate, the deputy Paul Doumer, was deeply involved in this intrigue, in which, it was said, the general himself was rather more than a passive observer.[107]

Bertie was able to keep the British government sketchily informed of the development of events. He understood that General Bailloud, the acting French commander at the Dardanelles, would prefer to return home rather than serve under Sarrail. Franklin-Bouillon had informed the British ambassador that the Radical Socialists hoped that Sarrail would receive the command as compensation for his earlier dismissal by Joffre, but Bertie could get no confirmation of this from Foreign Minister Théophile Delcassé. After leaving the Quai d'Orsay, however, Bertie read of Sarrail's appointment in *Le Temps*. He concluded that Delcassé 'must be deaf or an awful liar'.[108] Sarrail's political supporters were now certainly very active on his behalf and, on 4 August, an article by Gustave Hervé intended for the *Guerre Sociale* was seized by the authorities. In it Hervé predicted the end of the Sacred Union if Sarrail did not receive entire satisfaction.[109] When the cabinet met again on 5 August several ministers voiced their reluctance to do anything which appeared to humiliate a republican general. In the circumstances the cabinet readily accepted the conditions that had been laid down by Sarrail and later that day the general was informed that he had been selected to command the Armée d'Orient.[110] For perhaps the first time in the war, Joffre's wishes in a significant military matter had not been respected.[111] *L'affaire Sarrail* had served as an unwelcome reminder of the precariousness of the Sacred Union. It was clear that deep political divisions still lay just beneath the surface veneer of unity in wartime France. These divisions would have enormous implications not only for the future expedition to Salonika, but also for the development of Anglo-French relations.

When Joffre had been confronted with the news that the French government intended to reinforce the Dardanelles, his reaction had been to stress the impossibility of withdrawing any troops from the Western Front until September, when the results of an offensive which he proposed to carry out in Champagne and Artois would be known. He called for a rational plan of operations and suggested that an officer of his General Staff should be sent out to the Dardanelles to collect the necessary information.[112] Asked by Poincaré on 31 July whether it would be possible to keep a certain number of divisions ready to be transported to the Dardanelles, Joffre replied that the present circumstances were far too uncertain to allow any such movement of troops. Joffre stressed his pressing responsibility for the defence of France and argued that he must be left free to act in the main theatre offensively or defensively as he saw fit – and with the full complement of his armies.[113] Obviously, while Joffre maintained this sort of attitude, it was going to prove very difficult for the government to keep its promise to Sarrail to provide him with reinforcements. In the circumstances Sarrail's continued lukewarmness towards his new command was entirely explicable. Moreover, haggling with Sarrail made Millerand impatient and provoked him into a slip. 'The desire to see me removed from the French front and from France', Sarrail later recalled, 'emerged in a phrase which escaped the minister's lips: "if you think that I am going to let you remain in Paris until 15 September!"'[114] Nevertheless, on 11 August Sarrail produced a written appreciation of what a French force might be expected to achieve in the eastern theatre. He suggested a number of schemes but seemed himself to favour the idea of a Serbian expedition through Salonika.[115] Joffre quickly dismissed Sarrail's study as too flimsy, and when questioned by Poincaré a few days later became vehement in his opposition to any extension of existing operations at the Dardanelles. The president of the republic had to remind Joffre that Generals Gouraud and Bailloud had also both recommended extending the scope of operations for purely military reasons. Grudgingly, Joffre promised two army corps for September. But it seemed evident that, if pressed any further, he might resign.[116]

On 17 August the cabinet decided to ask Sarrail to study more closely the strategy of an operation to force the Straits, leaving aside all the other possibilities which he had considered. Just over a week later Joffre was informed that the government now felt it indispensable that reinforcements should be sent quickly to the Dardanelles. But Joffre insisted that he would have to hold on to the four divisions requested until 20 or 22 September when he would know whether or not his Champagne offensive had been a success.[117] Sarrail's report, dated 24 August, was limited to discussing, without final conclusions, the possibilities of a landing at a number of points on the European and Asiatic coasts. There was no detailed analysis of the number of troops required nor of the prospects of success.[118] Joffre therefore had the whole question examined by his own secretariat in the Section d'études de la Défense Nationale. The conclusions of this body, which must have delighted Joffre, were emphatically opposed to the resumption of offensive operations at the Dardanelles on the basis of the forces currently envisaged.[119] Joffre now requested that, if the plan should still proceed, the divisions previously promised for the end of September should be held back until the first days of October. In addition, Sarrail should be required to go out to the eastern theatre to assess the situation and its requirements at first hand.[120]

Arguing that the operations carried out so far at the Dardanelles under the command of Sir Ian Hamilton had been a failure, Millerand called on 28 August for a new approach to the problem.[121] Three days later the French cabinet concluded that the four divisions already earmarked should be ready to start out on 20 September.[122] The British government was informed of this French decision and was requested to use its own units to replace the two divisions under Bailloud at Cape Helles so that France would have the whole of its forces at its disposition.[123] Joffre, appearing before senior ministers, repeated his wish that Sarrail should leave as soon as possible to study the possibilities at the Straits and again stressed that he could not accept responsibility for the detachment of a single division from the Western Front before October. He would sooner resign. Even in October, the four divisions would probably be quite insufficient to force the Straits. Viviani, Millerand, Delcassé and Poincaré bowed before Joffre's obstinacy and on 3 September the full cabinet agreed to ask Sarrail to set out to study the possibilities of a reinforced expedition.[124] But Sarrail still appeared reluctant to leave France. At the same time Joffre's desire to see him depart was growing apace. The commander-in-chief thought that Sarrail was stalling in the hope of acquiring another command in France, and felt that the government was too frightened to order him to leave. But Joffre's enthusiasm to see Sarrail depart made him no more willing to provide reinforcements and, in answer to Millerand's request of 7 September that he should have four divisions ready to embark at Marseilles in the first week of October, Joffre now replied that he would not be able to spare these troops by that date and urged the government to reconsider his earlier objections before deciding on a course of action.[125]

An inter-allied conference held in Calais on 11 September turned out, in practice, to be a triumph for Joffre. The hope was expressed that the troops would be ready to leave on 10 October and that operations could begin around the middle of November. But no definite arrangements were made and, if Joffre's offensive in the west proved successful, it was agreed that the Dardanelles enterprise would be cancelled to allow him every opportunity to push home the victory in France.[126] In fact, the constant postponement of operations at the Straits into the winter months was making their ultimate realization increasingly unlikely.[127] Joffre followed up this tactical success by presenting the government with a further note from the Section d'études de la Défense Nationale. This argued that the coming offensive in the west was of such critical importance that Joffre must be allowed to employ all available troops until its outcome was known.[128] As this seemed to postpone the possibility of serious action at the Dardanelles into an indefinite future, Millerand reminded Joffre that the Calais agreement had been based on the assumption that the general would prepare four divisions to be ready on 10 October.[129] Joffre replied that he could not promise that the divisions designated for the Near East would be ready on time, and voiced further objections to the whole concept of the proposed operation which, he suggested, might deal a fatal blow at the French war effort.[130] Prime Minister Viviani was beginning to despair that the operation would ever get under way. 'The Dardanelles operation will not take place. The GQG doesn't want it to, because it is General Sarrail who will command it.'[131] If the government's troubles with Joffre were not bad enough, Sarrail was also stepping up his demands. A force of 100,000 troops was now being mentioned, while Sarrail insisted on command of all the existing allied contingents as well as a guarantee of Italian assistance.[132] At the same time there was growing parliamentary agitation for some action in the eastern theatre. As Caillaux argued on 22 September, a great operation was imperative to provide a success somewhere in the area. The right-wing deputy Denys Cochin argued that this success should be sought not at the Dardanelles but elsewhere.[133]

It was in this still fluid situation that the rapid development of diplomatic events in the Balkans intervened to overtake the internal political wrangling in France. Sofia decreed general mobilization on 22 September. Bulgaria, still anxious for revenge against Serbia after the second Balkan War, was now prepared to throw in its lot with the central powers in the belief that Austria too was ready to move against Serbia. The mobilization of the Bulgarian army rendered any further discussion of renewing operations at the Dardanelles irrelevant and revived the prospect of a Balkan campaign, such as had been discussed at the beginning of the year. Military factors were still present. The desire to save Serbia, an ally since the outbreak of hostilities, was genuine. The possibility of a Balkan coalition once again captured some imaginations. But the speed with which the French government now gave up its existing plans and seized upon the idea of an expedition to Salonika is a clear indication that the dominant consideration was not so much military strategy as the desire to be rid of Sarrail. As one observer put it, 'it's necessary to remove Sarrail – even at the price of an army'.[134]

The Serbian government, under the very real threat of being overrun, appealed immediately to London and Paris for aid, while from Greece Venizelos called for allied assistance to enable his country to honour its treaty obligations to Serbia. The French minister in Athens, Jean Guillemin, had already discussed with Venizelos the possibility of an allied expedition based on Salonika. He understood that the Greek king would feel obliged to make a formal protest against the violation of his country's neutrality, but that the Greek government would in practice 'allow its hand to be forced'.[135] So when the news of Bulgarian mobilization came through, Guillemin forwarded Venizelos's urgent request to the Quai d'Orsay that the Allies should provide 150,000 men, adding that Venizelos hoped that a reply would be made within twenty-four hours and, significantly, that the replies from London and Paris would be made without consultation between the two capitals. Guillemin urged acceptance of Venizelos's proposal, arguing that if the Allies did not respond the armed assistance of Greece would be lost for the duration of the war.[136]

Despite some hesitation on the part of Foreign Minister Delcassé, the French cabinet agreed on 23 September to inform Venizelos that France was ready to supply the troops which the Greek leader had requested.[137] The decision was taken in some haste – and it was one which belonged to the politicians. Joffre merely acquiesced, with the result that the campaign got under way with a total lack of strategic planning and forethought. Just as importantly, no attempt was made to co-ordinate a response with Britain. Indeed, Paul Cambon, the French ambassador in London, argued that the French decision was somewhat premature in view of the fact that no prior agreement had been reached with Lord Kitchener.[138] France's decision had been arrived at, as Venizelos had urged, without reference to London. Only when the French commitment had been made was Cambon instructed to express the hope that the British government would make Venizelos a similar offer.[139]

Venizelos's appeal found British opinion divided. Hankey, for example, was clear that 'the idea of committing the allies to yet another campaign in this part of the world ... is most objectionable from a military point of view'.[140] But Grey argued that, while it was not possible for Britain to send a force to Greece immediately, this might not be ruled out later on.[141] Some ministers felt inhibited about taking a decision because of Kitchener's temporary absence from London. Lloyd George, on the other hand, felt no such constraints. Reviving his old enthusiasm for a Balkan campaign, he produced wildly optimistic calculations to suggest that an intervention by 150,000 allied troops would result in the adhesion of 500 or 600,000 Romanians and possibly 200,000 troops from Serbia and 150,000 from Greece. These figures added up to not far short of one million men, whom the Austro-Germans would have to attack, which in winter would be a very difficult operation. Surely, argued Lloyd George, it was worth sending 150,000 men in order to reap so rich a reward.[142]

By 24 September, however, the British government had effectively been presented with a *fait accompli* by their French allies. Ministers and officials went through the motions of evaluating the advantages and disadvantages of the proposed new venture, but in practice their options were now extremely limited. The Dardanelles Committee unanimously agreed that the British government should associate itself with the reply of France, guaranteeing the forces requested to enable Greece to fulfil its pledge to Serbia. Asquith summed up what had happened in a subsequent letter to the king. 'The French at once agreed to comply and ... it was impossible for us in the circumstances to hold back.'[143] In the course of the meeting, however, Kitchener read out an appreciation drawn up by the General Staff. Its wording merits attention since it defined the limits within which British military authorities were prepared to accept a second eastern front – limits which, if adhered to, would soon have put a stop to the essentially futile confinement of large numbers of British troops in this unproductive theatre for the remainder of the war. The document read:

It must be clearly understood that the role of the 150,000 allied troops for which Greece has asked and which will, if necessary, be sent to Salonika will ... be restricted to enabling and assisting the Greek army to protect the Serbian flank and the line of communication with Salonika.[144]

It was not long before the relevance of the British reservations became apparent. Just before the first allied troops actually landed at Salonika, Venizelos, finding his position in relation to the Greek monarch untenable, resigned. So the Anglo-French force, which was arriving in Greece in order to enable that country to fulfil its treaty obligations to Serbia, was likely to confront a Greek army, in the process of mobilization, which would at best be neutral and which might – granted Constantine's personal and family sympathies for the German cause – even prove hostile.[145] Paul Cambon reflected on the unpromising position: 'We are now landing at Salonika to bring help to the Serbs who are in danger of being squashed between the Austro-Germans and the Bulgarians. Here we are with a new war front.' But he remained unconvinced of the soundness of the Allies' new strategy: 'It is in Champagne and Artois that matters will be decided and where the impact of events will determine the fate of the Balkans.'[146]

Meanwhile, in Paris, one central personality – General Sarrail – had been kept curiously ill-informed of the development of events. On 25 September he heard from the Sorbonne historian Alfonse Aulard that the Council of Ministers had decided to send one of the Dardanelles divisions to Salonika, while three days later he learnt that the destination of the newly designated Armée d'Orient would be Salonika and not the coast of Asia Minor.[147] Millerand now asked him to draw up a note on the subject of French intervention in the Balkans. Sarrail complied and concluded that 'if the total of French troops directed to the Balkans is to consist only of the three brigades presently earmarked ... this can have no real military impact'. As it was, the expedition could not be regarded as anything more than 'a gesture'.[148] The French government responded none the less by issuing official orders designating Sarrail as commander-in-chief of the French army operating in Serbia. His mission in the first instance was to cover the communications between Salonika and Serbia against all threats from the Bulgarian troops and eventually to co-operate with the Serbian army in active operations against the enemy forces.[149] In an attempt to clarify these somewhat vague instructions Sarrail called on Delcassé on 5 October, but neither from him nor from the president of the republic did Sarrail receive clarification.[150] The general seems to have concluded that he could achieve little further by waiting around in Paris and on 7 October he departed for Salonika from Marseilles. Perhaps this new campaign would yet offer the opportunity to refurbish his military reputation. The prospects probably appeared more inviting than enforced inactivity in France. By the time he arrived, however, the situation had been transformed by Venizelos's resignation. As Sarrail later recalled: 'I arrived in Greece on 12 October 1915, without information and without official instructions; knowing nothing of the country, the people or what had happened [in Greece] since the beginning of the war.'[151] It was not a hopeful start.

Be that as it may, out of a combination of unconnected themes a Balkan campaign had now emerged. Consideration of the possible advantages to Britain and France of opening up a new theatre of war had been overtaken by a crisis in French domestic politics as Joffre and Sarrail paraded their respective merits as military commanders. The mobilization of the Bulgarian army and Venizelos's response to this event brought these two developments together and made the Salonika expedition a reality. It was, by any standards, a bizarre basis upon which to embark upon a major new initiative in the war. Only time would tell whether the campaign could recover from this unpromising beginning.

CHAPTER 3

The Pattern Set

During the remaining three months of 1915 the essential pattern of Anglo-French relations over the Balkan campaign was fixed for the duration of the war. It was a pattern which revealed just how restricted Britain's potential for diplomatic and military initiative was as a result of its alliance with France. With Venizelos's resignation, the whole supposed justification for British intervention in the Balkans – to assist the Greeks to fulfil a specific treaty obligation – was undermined, especially when the new Greek premier, Zaimis, offered his opinion that the *casus foederis* in relation to the Graeco-Serbian treaty had not arisen in the present situation.[1] The logic of the position was that Britain should now either withdraw completely or conform to the rather more extensive plan of operations apparently envisaged by France. A statement of these French plans was sent by Joffre to Kitchener on 9 October. Here it was argued that the mission of the allied troops should be to cover and hold the railway line between Salonika and Uskub in order to secure communication with the Serbian army and the supplies of that army, while preventing any enemy attack on central Serbia.[2]

The divergence which was beginning to emerge between the conceptions of the two governments was further revealed when Viviani, the French prime minister, arrived in London for talks with Asquith and the British government. Viviani argued that the unopposed entry of the Bulgarian and German armies into Serbia would have dire consequences for allied prestige in the Near East and the entire Islamic world. He denied that the offer of military assistance had been made solely in relation to Greece's treaty obligations to Serbia. Indeed, the resignation of Venizelos ought to lead not to the abandonment of the operation but to the recognition that the force of 150,000 men,

originally envisaged, would no longer be sufficient. Somewhat ominously, Viviani made it plain that France's imperative need to defend
its own soil meant that it could make only a small contribution to
any additional reinforcements which the Allies might judge necessary.[3]
Further difficulties emerged when Viviani sought British approval for
a statement of explanation which he intended to make to the Chamber of Deputies on 12 October. The British did not like any mention
of 'assistance to Serbia' which left out the original Greek invitation,
since they believed that without Greek co-operation Serbia could be
saved only by a really large allied force, which would be most unlikely
to arrive in time. The declaration, as Viviani proposed to make it,
seemed like an open-ended commitment by Britain and France, rather
than the clearly defined involvement which the British government
was prepared to accept.[4]

The British General Staff was in no doubt as to what should now
be done. In a joint memorandum General Murray, the CIGS, and
Admiral Jackson, the First Sea Lord, stated their position with commendable clarity. They had

> not lost sight of the desirability, for material as well as sentimental
> reasons, of assisting Serbia. They have not lost sight of the connection
> between this Balkan problem and the security of our Eastern Empire ...
> But the prospects of favourably affecting the situation, in any of these
> respects, by such operations as have been considered above, seems so
> poor, while the chances of unfavourably affecting the situation everywhere
> by want of success ... are so evident, that the Combined Staffs have no
> hesitation in placing on record their opinion that the weight of argument
> is against these operations being undertaken.[5]

The British cabinet, by contrast, was deeply divided. Few ministers
favoured complete withdrawal from the Eastern Mediterranean, but
opinion differed as to the relative merits of Gallipoli and Salonika.

At the Dardanelles Committee on 11 October the decision had
almost been taken in favour of Gallipoli when Lloyd George 'broke
in and opposed it most vigorously. He said he thought it was madness
to send a force of men to support a hopeless cause when Serbia was
so terribly in need of help.'[6] Asquith sought to postpone a decision
and the committee accepted a formula whereby 150,000 men would
be sent from France to Egypt, leaving open the question whether
they would ultimately be employed at Gallipoli or Salonika. A

specially chosen general would go out to advise on the best course of action.[7] It was, reported Lloyd George to his mistress, 'pitiable to see the relief of the PM when it was decided not to commit the Cabinet to anything definite'.[8] Asquith's procrastination was too much for Sir Edward Carson, the attorney-general, who resigned from the cabinet, giving as his reason the government's refusal to recommend an expedition to support the Serbs. Meanwhile Lloyd George and Churchill, on the evening of 12 October, pressed the prime minister into sending a telegram to Romania and Greece offering these countries military support if they came into the war on the side of the Entente.[9] Hankey was horrified:

> Imagine my astonishment at finding a telegram in the morning offering Greece and Roumania that we would send 200,000 men on condition that they entered the war – this in the face of the warning in the recent General Staff appreciation on Serbia regarding the difficulty of operations there! Presumably Churchill and Lloyd George had bounced everyone into this. They are a danger in the Cabinet and I deeply regret and dread the consequences of a campaign in the Balkans.[10]

The government, it seemed, was in some difficulties. Grey's statement to the Commons on 14 October was singularly uninformative. 'No more than any one of us could have said,' noted one MP. 'I think he is played out.'[11] In the event, however, it was – as so often over the next two years – political events in France rather than in Britain which really shaped the course of British policy.

In France the enthusiasm of Briand, Viviani and others for the Salonika expedition had run up against the passive opposition of Foreign Minister Théophile Delcassé. The latter's return to ministerial service in August 1914 had done much to enhance the prestige of Viviani's administration. His standing on the international stage still reflected his diplomatic triumphs in the early years of the century. But, as he later disclosed to a secret session of the Chamber of Deputies, Delcassé could not conceal the misgivings he felt at sending French soldiers overseas while the enemy remained on French soil.[12] He hoped to abandon the proposed eastern expedition and concentrate all resources on the Western Front.[13] At the height of the Balkan crisis the French minister in Athens, who had the task of smoothing the path for the arrival at Salonika of the Anglo-French expeditionary force, found himself without instructions from the Quai d'Orsay, which had not replied to any of his telegrams since 26 September. Delcassé's apparent paralysis obliged the political director, Pierre de Margerie, to send instructions on his own initiative.[14] Finance Minister Alexandre Ribot concluded that Delcassé was frightened to associate himself with the responsibilities which the government was assuming,[15] and it was no real surprise when Delcassé offered his resignation to Viviani on around 10 October.[16] This, however, was no time for the Viviani government to be confronted with internal convulsions, especially as the prime minister's efforts to induce Britain to provide extra troops for the expedition, which led to his hurried trip to London on 7 October, were proving unsuccessful. Ribot and War Minister Millerand were designated to try to persuade Delcassé to withdraw his resignation.

The Sacred Union was again under threat since Viviani could lessen domestic criticism only by assuring Sarrail's supporters that the expedition had the full support of the government and that the general would be given all the forces he needed. Delcassé seemed initially to yield to the entreaties of his two colleagues, but by 12 October he had changed his mind again, sending the prime minister a categorical letter of resignation. This provoked a sharp response from Viviani – a reaction for which there was some justification since Delcassé appears not to have voiced his objections to the expedition during earlier meetings of the French cabinet.[17] The foreign minister, who had previously sought to retire on grounds of ill-health, now insisted that he could not agree to the policy of his colleagues.[18] He could not associate himself with the Salonika expedition, especially as it now seemed doubtful whether British or Greek collaboration would be forthcoming.[19] Poincaré could only express his amazement that Delcassé should be speaking of disagreements of which he had shown no sign during meetings of the cabinet.[20]

The resignation of so distinguished a figure as Théophile Delcassé inevitably shook the Viviani government to its foundations and caused widespread misgivings throughout France. As one sympathetic correspondent inquired, 'what can we be heading for that you should quit the ship?'[21] It was a sign of Viviani's desperation that he informed the Chamber on 12 October that there was complete agreement between the French and British governments as to the need to assist Serbia and on the number of troops required for the expedition – a remark for which there was no justification.[22] Indeed, it was a prophetic comment on this ill-fated venture in Anglo-French co-operation that the first victim of the Salonika campaign should have been the man who, over a decade earlier, had done so much to construct the entente cordiale itself.

The debate in the Chamber on 13 October was the most acrimonious parliamentary session since Poincaré's appeal for a Sacred Union. In an attempt to secure unrestricted debate Pierre Renaudel, leader of the Socialist Party, called unsuccessfully for the Chamber to meet in secret session. On a vote of confidence only nine deputies voted against Viviani, but more than a hundred left-wingers abstained.[23] Broadly speaking, the most vociferous voices in the Chamber were in favour of the Salonika expedition, while those in the Senate opposed it. It fell to Viviani to chart an awkward course within this increasingly polarized situation. Taking over the foreign affairs portfolio himself, the prime minister attempted to explain the position to anxious senators in the Foreign Affairs Commission on 15 October, but six days later Clemenceau, Pichon and d'Estournelles were still pressing for additional information on Delcassé's resignation and for clarification of the current situation at the Quai d'Orsay.[24] On 19 October Viviani, while still refusing to disclose Delcassé's letter of resignation, admitted that the foreign minister had not been an active supporter of the Salonika expedition. But he assured the Chamber Commission that Delcassé had told Ribot, Millerand and himself that there was no rift in the cabinet and that he had resigned because of his health. The chairman of the commission, Georges Leygues, ended what had obviously been a most uncomfortable meeting for the prime minister by warning that there would be political repercussions unless Viviani succeeded in persuading both Britain and the Grand Quartier Général to support the Salonika enterprise.[25]

Not prepared to concede that his own position was hopeless, Viviani sent Millerand to London to attempt to persuade the British government to send extra divisions to the Balkans. Arriving on 15 October Millerand voiced the French government's concern that, according to reports received from General Sarrail, British troops were showing every intention of remaining at Salonika during the winter months instead of pressing north in support of the Serbs.[26] The military situation was deteriorating daily as the plight of Serbia became ever more desperate. As the Serbian legation in London confirmed, the Serbian army on its own was not strong enough to

withstand the enormous pressure exerted by the combined forces of
Germany, Austria and Bulgaria.²⁷ But Millerand's most telling argument was of an entirely different order. The war minister bluntly
declared that if the British did not continue to send troops to Salonika
the French government would have to resign and the alliance itself
would be endangered. Meeting Lloyd George on 19 October,
Millerand learnt that he could count on the support of the minister
of munitions, even though Lloyd George feared that action in the
Balkans had probably come too late and that the campaign might
prove a forlorn gesture.²⁸ Viviani readily prolonged Millerand's stay
in London in the hope of reaching agreement and the war minister's
persistence was rewarded to the extent that a joint declaration committed the two governments to continue to send the 150,000 men
already agreed upon, while each reserved the right to re-examine the
situation if circumstances so demanded.²⁹

British military leaders looked on askance. Major-General Charles
Callwell, the director of military operations, felt that the French must
be in abject terror of Sarrail and of their public opinion, which fondly
imagined that saving the Serbs was a perfectly simple operation. In
fact, according to Callwell, the expedition's task was an impossible
one. The French plans did not appear to have been properly thought
out by their General Staff and he could not understand how they
proposed to manage for transport.³⁰ Callwell assured General
Robertson, who was anxiously watching the situation from army
headquarters in France, that the British General Staff was totally
opposed to operations in the Balkans which were 'objectionable from
every point of view'.³¹ Robertson took heart from this statement and
urged that Britain should be wary of having its hands forced by
Millerand or any other French politician. He did not take the implied
threat to the alliance all that seriously. 'After all,' he wrote to Callwell,
'the French have a certain interest in this war.' In any case, Robertson
considered that strained relations with the French would be preferable
to losing two or three divisions in the Balkans and perhaps even
losing the war.³²

Millerand's dire warnings of possible political chaos in France were
confirmed by reports from the British Embassy in Paris. London
interpreted the abstentions on Viviani's vote of confidence as evidence
of a worrying increase in war weariness. In the background lay the
spectre of a return to power by the former prime minister, Joseph

Caillaux, on the platform of a compromise peace with Germany.[33] Lord Bertie noted that French public opinion might well become exasperated if the British showed any signs of backing out of the Salonika expedition. Joffre had expressed the view that it was necessary, both from military and political points of view, to continue operations based on Salonika and indeed to send additional troops.[34] Inside the British Foreign Office the permanent under-secretary, Sir Arthur Nicolson, seemed inclined to accept this line of argument. 'Our relations with France', he concluded, 'will be seriously impaired if we do not meet their wishes by sending immediately the division to Salonika.'[35]

The effect which French pressure was having upon the British government became apparent when the Dardanelles Committee met on 25 October to consider the Balkan situation. This meeting was crucial in exposing the reality of the British position. The nature of the decisions reached, and more particularly the arguments used to support them, go far to explain that British readiness to acquiesce in French policy decisions which would characterize the country's conduct of the campaign as a whole. At the meeting Kitchener announced that he had received a strongly worded note from the French military attaché requesting that British troops should be sent immediately to Salonika, since any delay would mean the destruction of the Serbian army. In the war minister's opinion the terms in which the French note was couched suggested that there was a political motive behind it and that it was not entirely based on the requirements of strategy. The question which arose in his mind, therefore, was whether a refusal on Britain's part to comply with French demands would place the French government in any political difficulty. Grey wondered whether Joffre really thought the expedition strategically sound, or whether he was obliged to back it for different reasons, possibly the fear that otherwise Millerand would fall and the barrier protecting Joffre from criticism in the French Chamber would be removed. To this Kitchener added that if Millerand resigned, Joffre would not be able to maintain his own position, a development which would entail considerable changes in the policy of France. His advice, therefore, was that the British government should tell the French that they intended to take the correct course, but that if this involved any danger of upsetting the French government, they would send the troops which had been requested to Salonika.

Sir John French, hastily summoned from his headquarters in France, then expounded upon the state of French internal politics in a way that revealed that the British were fully acquainted with the intricacies of *l'affaire Sarrail*.[36] The picture drawn was of a most delicate edifice, which any false move by France's ally might serve to upset. This description prompted a pertinent question from Austen Chamberlain, secretary of state for India. If the Salonika expedition was completely futile from a military point of view, he asked, was it worth going on with it in order to save Millerand, Joffre and the French government? But political and military issues could not be separated so easily. Kitchener, whose priorities as secretary of state for war were necessarily military, answered with ponderous authority that more was at stake than Chamberlain seemed to realize – it was to save the alliance itself. If France were to break with Britain, the war would be over and Britain defeated.

In the end the Dardanelles Committee resolved not to take any firm decision until Generals Murray and Callwell had visited Chantilly to put the British point of view to Joffre.[37] Nevertheless, the drift of the discussion had been unmistakable. The implications of this meeting were considerable for, though it would not have been appreciated at the time, Britain was abdicating its right to have any more than a nominal voice in the direction of allied strategy in the Balkans. The principle was well on the way to being established that the maintenance of the existing regime in France should have priority over all other considerations, military and diplomatic, in this theatre of the war. This meant that France would be able to justify all future development of and modifications to its policy in this area, and secure the adherence of the British to them, on arguments relating to the stability of its own domestic politics. In adopting this stance, Britain risked enveloping its freedom of manoeuvre in the Balkans in a paralysing cocoon of submission to the will of its ally. Arguably this is precisely what happened, at least until the spring of 1917. All attempts to reassert a degree of independence and sovereign authority in British policy towards the Salonika venture were doomed to failure in the face of fear over their disruptive political effect on the other side of the Channel.

Joffre made it clear that Murray and Callwell lacked the necessary authority to conclude a definitive agreement. He regarded British hesitations in the present situation as tantamount to 'desertion in full battle'.[38] With the French commander in this frame of mind, it was no surprise that the military conference held on 27 October failed to resolve the impasse. At the suggestion of the president of the republic, therefore, Joffre decided on a personal trip to London. Grey expressed delight at the news of Joffre's visit, especially when he heard that the French commander would be discussing the question from a purely military point of view.[39] Such expectations were, however, to be rudely disappointed. The views which Joffre put forward at 10 Downing Street came as a surprise to British ministers, who had suspected that his enthusiasm for the Salonika expedition was at the most lukewarm. Yet he now insisted on the importance of doing everything possible to save the Serbian army and argued that, if the enemy were checked, Greece could still be brought in on the side of the Allies. More importantly, Joffre hinted after the formal meeting that his own retention of the post of commander-in-chief of the French army and even the permanence of the alliance itself might well depend on the reply of the British government.[40] Kitchener's account of this episode was that Joffre 'pointed a pistol at the Cabinet and said: "If you back out of Salonika it is the end of the Entente", and he thumped the table and the Cabinet gave way'.[41] It is true that Joffre's instincts were not sympathetic to the Salonika expedition. He had recently told Millerand that any transfer of troops from the Western Front must be kept to a bare minimum. Neither the fact that the enemy was installed on French soil only eighty kilometres from Paris, nor the state of French resources in men and munitions, permitted France to constitute a large expeditionary force for the Balkans.[42] But Joffre was well aware that Sarrail's political supporters were vehemently championing the campaign and gaining fresh backing all the time, and he evidently felt that his own position would be compromised unless he gave the expedition his public support and secured a substantial British participation in it.[43]

Yet, ironically, Joffre's *démarche* had come too late to save Viviani. The president of the republic had already turned to Aristide Briand, minister of justice in Viviani's cabinet, and during the evening of 29 October Briand succeeded in forming a new ministry from which Millerand was excluded. The latter was to be the sacrificial victim whose dismissal might quieten parliamentary discontent. Viviani himself kept a place in the new administration, going to the Ministry of Justice which Briand now vacated. To inspire public confidence

General Galliéni, officially designated as Joffre's successor in the early days of the war and seen by some as the real victor of the Marne, replaced Millerand at the Ministry of War, while protesting that he had neither the political finesse nor the health to stand the strain.[44] The parliamentary situation, however, remained extremely difficult and Briand was soon being subjected to the same sort of pressure which had driven his predecessor from power. The Foreign Ministry, which Briand now chose to keep within his own hands, already had evidence from its London embassy of attempts by French and British opponents of the Salonika campaign to join forces in a combination which would have the destruction of the French government as one of its objectives. The Comte d'Aunay, a close associate of Georges Clemenceau, was said to be conducting secret negotiations in London.[45] Briand's response to this potentially dangerous situation was to enlarge his government by the inclusion of several prestigious elder statesmen as ministers without portfolio. Their presence would, he hoped, serve to buttress his ministry against the attacks of disaffected sections of the Chamber and Senate. It made for the broadest-based French government during the entire war. Even the venerable former premier, Charles de Freycinet, was recalled to office despite being almost ninety years of age, while Clemenceau was left to surmise that, in his mid-seventies, he was as yet too young for ministerial service.[46] Not everyone, however, was impressed with Briand's tactics. One cynical observer noted that the affairs of France were now to be conducted by the union of a man of great talent but no character (Briand) with a general of character but no talent (Joffre), under the aegis of an irresponsible and intellectually limited chief executive (Poincaré).[47]

The fact that the Anglo-French wartime alliance comfortably survived the fall of the Viviani government in no way lessened the argument that the maintenance of French political stability required British acquiescence in the continuation of the Salonika campaign. Two points should be noted. In the first place Briand came into office as a declared champion of the Balkan expedition, which he had first proposed at the beginning of the year. Though he was sceptical of the military prowess of General Sarrail, this guaranteed Briand, at least for the time being, the support in the Chamber of the numerically important Radical Socialist group, from which Sarrail drew his political strength. This group, led by the former prime minister, Joseph

Caillaux, was itself strengthened by the inclusion of such party icons as Léon Bourgeois and Emile Combes among Briand's ministers. At the end of 1915 Ambassador Bertie reported that Caillaux could rely on the votes of 150 deputies – a figure which, granted the party political fragmentation of the Third Republic, no French ministry could afford to ignore.[48] Second, Briand appeared to offer the prospect of greater political stability than his predecessor. The new cabinet represented a widening of the Sacred Union. In addition to the elderly ministers without portfolio, Denys Cochin, from the Catholic Right, now joined a government which already contained the socialists Guesde, Sembat and Thomas. Cochin was the first representative of the Catholic Right to serve in government since the early 1880s.

For Britain, Briand's ability to keep the lid on France's domestic political divisions was his greatest virtue. To do this required many of the skills of wheeling and dealing in the parliamentary corridors which the British usually regarded with contempt. As Lloyd George once heard, Briand could be ruthless. Though he would not murder his own mother, he 'would murder someone else's mother'.[49] In the years before the outbreak of war Briand had already become skilled at manoeuvring his way through the 'Republic of Pals'. The important thing in the wartime context was that these skills still seemed to work. Over the next year and a half Briand surmounted a series of political crises, particularly in secret sessions of the Chamber, which would have destroyed a less skilled political operator. After one such occasion a British observer reported:

> The sitting was opened by a long speech from Briand which produced an excellent impression. The soporific qualities of his oratory were at their best and I believe that most of the deputies wondered why they had asked to have a secret sitting, after they had listened to the President of the Council.[50]

It was significant that Briand's most ardent admirer inside the British cabinet was the minister of munitions, David Lloyd George. Lloyd George had singled Briand out as early as February 1915 as 'much the ablest man in the Ministry' and once explained that the Frenchman, who spoke no English, had such 'a beautiful voice and talked so distinctly that he was able to follow what he said'.[51] The Breton son of an innkeeper who had studied law before going into politics had much in common with the romantic Welshman brought up in unpretentious surroundings, who became a practising solicitor in Porthmadog. Both were outsiders in the political world they inhabited; both developed reputations for ambition and unscrupulousness; neither was ever quite seen as a gentleman. The two men even bore a certain physical resemblance. Arthur Balfour once remarked that, except for the fact that they spoke a different language, he 'never could tell the difference between them. They were exactly alike.'[52]

Throughout his tenure of office Briand remained an asset in British eyes. British policy-makers were concerned that his fall might precipitate the sort of political crisis in France which would endanger that country's continued participation in the war. Speeches such as that which the French premier made to the Chamber in late September 1916, in which he 'praised Britain's efforts and nailed his colours to the mast for war *jusqu'au bout*', securing a positive vote of 421 against 26, proved particularly comforting for the British.[53] But Briand's parliamentary survival could never be taken for granted. Those most often spoken of as potential successors were Caillaux, who was believed to favour the sort of compromise peace with Germany which would take no account of British interests, and Georges Clemenceau. Though Clemenceau might be expected to wage the war with renewed vigour, his relations with the president of the republic were so bad that British observers found it difficult to see how the two men could forge a working partnership. As late as January 1917 Bertie judged that, as an alternative prime minister, Clemenceau had 'made himself impossible'.[54] In short, the majority of British political opinion judged that the maintenance of the Salonika campaign was a price worth paying for Briand's political survival.

Given the considerations which were now shaping British policy it was no surprise that a memorandum by Joffre on the role of the allied armies at Salonika was soon accepted by the Asquith government. Joffre's document conceded that the original mission of the Salonika force could no longer be achieved, but argued that the possibility still existed of re-establishing communications with the Serbian army.[55] The Dardanelles Committee decided to recommend support for the French army in its task of securing communication with the Serbs.[56] Kitchener's reply to Joffre, dated 30 October, did appear to safeguard the British position:

In view of the French Staff statement dated 29 October 1915, including definite calculations of the capacity of the port of Salonika and of the carrying power of the railways into Serbia ... and in view of the strictly limited role that the French General Staff and General Joffre desire British troops to fulfil, viz, to ensure the position of Salonika to Krivolak inclusive, in order to support the French army ... and with the full understanding that if communication with the Serbian army cannot be opened and maintained, the whole Allied force will be withdrawn to be used as circumstances may require, the British Government are prepared to cooperate energetically in the manner proposed by the French government.[57]

Few British ministers, however, were prepared to risk a quarrel with a French government which was clearly deeply committed to the Salonika expedition. In practice the British had now conceded that any decision to withdraw from Salonika would have to be a French one. British diplomacy was in some disarray. Bertie heard that the confusion at the Foreign Office was 'indescribable'. Grey, in particular, was very tired and disgusted at the failure of his Balkan policy.[58]

Acquiescence in what was essentially a French policy inevitably brought the British government up against the advice of its own military authorities. At the Dardanelles Committee on 30 October the CIGS was emphatic that the opinion of the General Staff and of the principal officers of the British Expeditionary Force in France was unanimously opposed to the Serbian enterprise.[59] The diversion of troops from the western theatre of war could not be justified from a strategical point of view and could only endanger allied prospects of victory in the war as a whole.[60] Added force was given to this argument when the British commander at Salonika, General Sir Brian Mahon, reported that no action which the Allies could now take would be in time to save Serbia.[61] On 22 October the Bulgarians had advanced across the railway south of Uskub, severing the communications of the Serbian army with Salonika. Meanwhile, Grey tried to put the best possible gloss on the situation. Joffre's visit to London had, he said, resulted in complete agreement between the two countries. The foreign secretary merely hoped that in future there would be closer co-operation between the military authorities of France and Britain and that neither power would find itself committed to operations involving the forces of the other without prior consultations between the respective military chiefs.[62] Yet the difficulties of meaningful allied co-operation were well illustrated when Kitchener, on his way to the Near East to survey the scene at first hand, stopped in Paris for talks with the new French government. The French chargé d'affaires in London warned that Kitchener might be hoping to find the new war minister, General Galliéni, less favourable to the Salonika expedition than his predecessor.[63] If this was indeed the case, Kitchener was to be disappointed. Galliéni admitted that the relief force would arrive too late to save Serbia, but was unwilling to face the consequences of disengagement from the Balkans. After talks with Briand and Galliéni, Kitchener reported back to Asquith in London:

> As regards Salonika it is very difficult to get in a word; they were both full of the necessity of pushing in troops and would not think of coming out. They simply sweep all military difficulties and dangers aside and go on political lines, such as saving a remnant of Serbs, bringing Greece in and inducing Roumania to join. I could get no idea from them as to when the troops would come out, they only said they must watch events.[64]

The French cabinet, taking advantage of Kitchener's presence in Paris, decided on 6 November to seek a firm assurance that Britain would supply 90,000 out of the total of 150,000 men without further delay.[65] On the same day Kitchener met Joffre at Chantilly and, somewhat surprisingly, seems to have given such an undertaking, without, however, telling the French commander that he would soon be going to Salonika to assess the situation for himself.[66]

This left open the question of the precise role which Sarrail's army could now be expected to fulfil. Within the broad scope of the instructions which he had already received, Sarrail was in practice left considerable room for manoeuvre.[67] His mission was simply to save and reconstitute what he could of the Serbian army, in such a way that, joined with the allied contingents, it would once again form a realistic fighting force.[68] But in view of the retreat of the Serbian army towards Montenegro and the development of events in Macedonia, it became increasingly probable that the Anglo-French forces would have to retire to Salonika. In such an eventuality the French government felt that the Allies should take full control of the port, suspending Greek management of it for the time being.[69] On 13 November the French cabinet decided that Sarrail should be left free to decide whether or not to retreat to Salonika, depending on his assessment of the military situation.[70] On the previous day, however, the newly constituted British War Committee had again voiced its concern at the uncertainty surrounding the whole operation. It was decided to inform the French that it was essential that the military advisers of the two countries should come to an understanding as to the proper military policy to be adopted by the allied forces in the Balkans.[71]

Meanwhile Kitchener had arrived in the Near East on his fact-finding tour of inspection and had begun to voice his apprehensions concerning the Salonika expedition. If the operation was going to be pursued, he now felt that as many as 400,000 men would be needed. He made no secret of his resentment that the French government had gone into the campaign without consulting its allies, who had been obliged to follow suit largely to preserve the entente.[72] It was a sign of the gravity with which he viewed the situation that Kitchener now told Asquith that the decision to be made on the future of the campaign would have such a momentous effect that it could prove to be the turning point leading to the loss of the war by the Allies. He regarded the chances of saving Serbia as non-existent. Even more seriously, he feared that, with attention shifting to the eastern theatre, the offensive arranged for early 1916 in the west would be very greatly weakened. Then, if the war were to drag on through the winter of 1916–17, he warned that some of the Allies would be unable to take the strain.[73] Kitchener was even able to cite Sarrail's opinions in favour of his argument. The French general believed that it would require at least 300,000 men to hold Salonika and generally confirmed the war minister's assessment of the seriousness of the military position.[74]

In view of the confusion surrounding the Salonika expedition and with that at the Dardanelles remaining uncertain, the French government requested a conference to review and co-ordinate policy in the Near East. Any hope that the British might use this occasion to impose their wishes proved to be short-lived. When the delegates assembled in Paris on 17 November the French found that Lloyd George was still an ardent supporter of the Balkan campaign. His enthusiasm served to counteract the hesitation of his colleagues, and the British government once again ended up by promising that its full commitment of 90,000 men would be sent out as soon as possible, but this time with the addition of two extra divisions.[75] The biggest concession that the British representatives could extract from Briand was the promise that, if junction with the Serbs became manifestly impossible while the forces of Greece posed a threat to the rear of the allied troops, then the French government would be prepared to examine the question of total evacuation.[76] In practice, however, domestic political considerations meant that evacuation would never be expedient for the French premier, whatever the military and diplomatic situation might dictate.

Sarrail now considered that a retirement to Salonika was essential but that it would be difficult to execute unless begun immediately.[77] The Dardanelles Committee also saw this as the best available option, deciding on 19 November to inform the French military attaché in London that Britain would be sending fresh forces to Salonika, as had been agreed two days earlier, but only for the purpose of giving support to the retiring troops.[78] Although the initiative lay with Sarrail himself, French opinion was also hardening in favour of a retreat and on 22 November Denys Cochin, minister without portfolio in Briand's government, who had been sent to Greece to view the situation at close quarters, reported Sarrail's belief that Serbia was now doomed and that he should retire to Salonika where nothing could be done without a force of 300,000 men.[79] In the British camp General Mahon seemed close to despair. The expedition had not prevented the Bulgarians from fighting, nor had it encouraged Greece to attack Bulgaria, and it was no longer realistic to think in terms of saving Serbia. In fact the whole enterprise had degenerated into a 'useless errand'.[80] The existing uncertainty as to whether it was intended to go forward, to remain still or to retire adversely affected all arrangements and made it difficult to reach decisions on even minor matters. Sarrail and his chief of staff had twice been approached with a view to formulating definite proposals about the conduct of a possible, if not probable, retreat and to consider the various problems involved. But their attitude had been to dismiss the whole subject with the 'enunciation of a few broad tactical principles and a wave of the hand'.[81] Sarrail did at least clarify the situation to some extent with his decision, notified to the French government on 27 November, to bring back to Salonika all the divisions which had advanced into Serbia. The problem now, as Sarrail fully recognized, was to determine what role could be given to the allied forces, which had evidently failed in their original mission. The general himself concluded that, unless a diplomatic or political motive existed for retaining Salonika itself, it would be preferable to re-embark the troops as soon as they returned to the port.[82]

The retreat to Salonika inevitably raised the hopes of all those who wished to see an end to the campaign. These ranged from the king of Greece to the British General Staff. Within the British military hierarchy, General Henry Wilson was one of those pressing for complete evacuation. But, as Andrew Bonar Law, the Unionist leader in Asquith's coalition, warned him, the French would not permit this. Their government would feel that if the troops were withdrawn from Salonika after what would amount to a complete defeat, the position of the ministry in France would be untenable.[83] Nevertheless, a paper drawn up by the CIGS, even before Sarrail's definite decision to retreat, reached the conclusion that the weight of military argument against holding Salonika was overwhelming. It was recommended that all further transport of troops should be stopped at once and that the evacuation of Salonika should proceed as fast as possible.[84] Reluctant perhaps to adopt these conclusions in their entirety, Grey argued that, as the prospective danger to the whole Anglo-French force was considered to be very serious, the French government should take the matter into immediate consideration.[85] At the same time General Callwell was despatched to Paris to try to elicit a positive statement of intention from the French. Callwell informed Galliéni that complete evacuation was 'virtually' British policy, though that policy awaited the final confirmation of the government. But he also warned the War Office in London that his mission would become pointless unless a definite decision could be communicated to the French on the following day, 26 November.[86] In fact there was little chance of the French government agreeing to a policy of evacuation. As Briand told Guillemin on 28 November, the French intention was to make Salonika a fortified base for future offensive or defensive operations.[87] Not surprisingly, Callwell's mission proved a complete failure. As Sir Archibald Murray told the War Committee on 29 November, Callwell had found it impossible to get a definite expression of opinion from the French General Staff on the strategy to be adopted in Greece and Serbia. Asquith dejectedly concluded that the government was absolutely in the dark as to French plans. Grey was authorized to represent to the French government Britain's concern at receiving no definite opinion from the French General Staff as to the future of the Anglo-French forces in the Balkans, as to whether they were to retire on Salonika and whether it was safe for them to remain at Salonika or not. He was also to press for a conference of Anglo-French ministers and military authorities to take place in London or elsewhere without delay.[88]

For the last time for some months to come the British government was bracing itself for a showdown with the French. As one Foreign Office official put it: 'the first thing necessary is a decision by France and ourselves as to remaining at or evacuating Salonika.'[89] In fact the inter-allied conference was to be precipitated at very short notice by a startling development within the British government itself.

On the evening of 29 November Kitchener left for London from Paris, where he had spent the day on his way home from his mission to Gallipoli and Greece. Kitchener had been deeply impressed by what he had seen for himself in the Near East and was now ready to add the weight of his authority to the call for the evacuation of Salonika. At the War Committee on 1 December he insisted on the need to reach a clear decision in advance of any meeting with the French. If British delegates attended an inter-allied gathering without having made up their own minds, 'the French would press for the retention of Salonika'. Lloyd George's attempts to procrastinate were impatiently brushed aside. Kitchener argued that the want of decision which had so far characterized British action might lead to the loss of the war itself. 'This had been going on for some time, and our changes in policy were having a deplorable effect on neutrals and in depressing our own troops.' The War Committee now decided to implement the letter of the agreement reached with Joffre at the end of October.[90] The French government was to be told that, as the Armée d'Orient's attempts to open communications with the Serbian army had failed, the earlier agreement that the whole of the allied force should be withdrawn to Salonika, for use as circumstances might require, had come into effect. If the French government dissented there should be a conference as soon as possible to settle the matter.[91] If further arguments in favour of the new British line were needed, General Mahon in Salonika was ready to provide them. The military situation, he insisted, was becoming increasingly worrying with news of the concentration of Bulgarian forces. He urged that a decision about evacuation should be arrived at immediately. Further delay might prove ruinous to both possible options, that of remaining at Salonika and that of leaving.[92]

General Joffre had already warned his war minister that French occupation of Salonika could not be sustained in the face of Britain's formal opposition. So although Joffre had prepared a list of objections to put before the British General Staff if they arrived in France demanding evacuation, it was unlikely that he would maintain this attitude if the British proved resolute.[93] The political situation remained uncertain, however, with Paul Cambon reporting that while Edward Grey favoured total evacuation, he was not sure whether the British government as a whole shared this view. Cambon sensed a total lack of agreement not only between the allied governments and their General Staffs but within these bodies themselves.[94]

After a fresh examination of the problem, the French cabinet confirmed its intention to remain at Salonika and even decided to ask for additional British troops to bring the total strength of the expeditionary force to 300,000 men. Salonika should be held as a base for future operations in the Balkans with a view to keeping Greece neutral and persuading Romania to enter the war.[95] Cambon was instructed to inform Grey of this new resolve, but Briand's despatch had scarcely left the Quai d'Orsay when news arrived from the London embassy that, having heard Kitchener's first-hand reports, the War Committee had decided in favour of evacuation.[96] Once Bertie had confirmed the British position it was clear that a crisis in Anglo-French relations was imminent. The ambassador's statement had caused great consternation to Briand and his secretary-general at the Quai d'Orsay, Jules Cambon. Bertie added that the situation between the British and French governments would become very difficult if Britain insisted on withdrawal, which the French would regard as pandering to the Germanophile sympathies of the Greek king and his government. The French view was that if Salonika were abandoned it would be occupied by an enemy force either in collusion with the Greeks or in spite of them, and that withdrawal would have far-reaching and disastrous consequences throughout the Balkans and everywhere in the East.[97] Briand urged that no steps should be taken committing the British government to withdrawal before Paul Cambon had had the chance to make representations. He warned that if the British attitude became known to French public opinion the consequences would be most serious.[98]

Briand's influential *chef de cabinet*, Philippe Berthelot, now set about preparing a long and cogent list of the diplomatic, military and political disadvantages which would result from the evacuation of Salonika. He objected to the fact that Britain was proposing to retire even before it had fulfilled its long-standing commitment to send 90,000 troops.[99] But the French were left in no doubt as to the strength of British feeling. Cambon now reported that the War Committee had definitely decided upon the need for evacuation and that instructions had been sent to General Mahon to co-operate with the French commander in preparations to this end.[100] From the British War Office the French liaison officer, Captain Doumayrou, told Galliéni that for the first time for many months the British government was completely united in its determination and that the vote in the War Committee had been unanimous.[101] Kitchener wanted Galliéni to know that he had never seen such agreement among British ministers. If French representatives came over to Britain, they should not expect to change any opinions.[102]

The French cabinet none the less agreed to back Briand in resisting the British determination to quit Salonika. The French prime minister was to leave for London as soon as possible to try to win round the British government to the French point of view.[103] Joffre confidently informed Sarrail that the French intention was to remain at Salonika and that negotiations were in progress to secure British agreement on this point and on the future line of conduct in the Balkans. Sarrail was even instructed to begin immediate defence works at Salonika.[104] But Grey, while admitting that there might be objections to evacuation from a political point of view, was emphatic that the question was one to be settled by military opinion – and in Britain this was unanimous. Evacuation, he stressed, was preferable to the loss of the whole force, which the British military authorities believed must ensue if Germano-Bulgarian forces advanced on Salonika. Kitchener and his advisers believed that, unless the decision to re-embark all the troops was taken without delay, the whole Anglo-French force would probably be lost.[105] As long as there was a prospect of a military disaster, it was not worthwhile discussing anything but military considerations.[106] In the face of such pronouncements the French military attaché warned Galliéni of the serious situation which might arise, so determined was the British government to pursue its own policy to a conclusion.[107]

This, then, was the situation when the full British cabinet assembled on 3 December and was faced with a bombshell from its secretary of state for war. Kitchener bluntly informed his colleagues that he took so grave a view of the position and prospects in the eastern theatre that he could take no further responsibility for the conduct of the war unless British troops were at once withdrawn from Salonika so that the earliest and most certain of the catastrophes which he envisaged in the east could be averted.[108] As he reminded Douglas Haig later in the day, the British had gone to Salonika only to satisfy the French and to give employment to General Sarrail.[109] Kitchener's power within the British government was now on the wane. Indeed, plans were already being hatched to remove him from the day-to-day control of the war by increasing, to an unprecedented level, the authority of the chief of the Imperial General Staff. Of an earlier stage in the war, Churchill would later write, with only slight exaggeration:

> When Kitchener gave a decision it was invariably accepted as final. He was never, to my belief, over-ruled by the War Council or the Cabinet in any military matter, great or small. No single unit was ever sent or withheld contrary, not merely to his agreement, but to his advice.[110]

Such a description no longer fitted the situation. Kitchener's dismissive attitude towards politicians, his refusal to confide in them and his unwillingness to make full use of the General Staff because of the confidence he retained in his own opinions and abilities all meant that many government ministers would have preferred to see him relieved of his responsibilities.[111] But, with the British government yet to grasp the nettle of conscription, Kitchener still had value as a recruiting symbol which no figure in the country could seek to rival let alone replace. The war minister's popular prestige remained undimmed and it was still unthinkable that his services could be dispensed with altogether. It is in this light that Kitchener's threat to resign should be viewed. Its impact upon the government may easily be imagined.

Not surprisingly, the cabinet accepted the war minister's conclusion and it was decided that the French government should be informed at once of the crisis which had arisen as a result of Kitchener's statement and to point out that the gravity of the situation was such as to make it desirable to hold an inter-governmental conference the following day, either in London or Calais.[112] On leaving the cabinet meeting, Grey told Cambon that Kitchener's resignation would bring about a general crisis and that it was absolutely necessary for the two governments to reach an agreement before the military conference which had been arranged for 5 December.[113] Soon after 5 p.m. Bertie received Grey's despatch, informing him of the cabinet crisis which had developed earlier in the day. He went at once to the Quai d'Orsay, but neither Briand nor Jules Cambon was available and he was unable to see the French premier before 6.30 p.m. The latter was very perturbed by Grey's message and announced that he, Galliéni and Admiral Lacaze, the well-respected navy minister, would go to Calais the following morning so as to meet with British ministers as quickly as possible.[114] Significantly, the British delegation to this conference did not include Lloyd George. As his secretary and mistress recorded:

> On [4 December] D[avid] discovered that the French had sent an urgent telegram requesting members of the British Government to meet them at Calais that day. The P.M., Balfour and Kitchener had already started. D[avid] had not been asked, either because he was not available, or (which is more likely) because he held different views from the others on the question of Salonika.[115]

Prior to the conference Berthelot prepared a briefing note for Briand in which he forcefully argued that Britain's insistence on evacuation should be met with intransigent opposition from France. The political effects of giving way would be catastrophic. The confidence of French public opinion in the outcome of the war would be shaken, the Briand ministry would fall, General Joffre's position would be weakened and even the president of the republic might not be safe. A long series of military and diplomatic arguments should therefore be placed before the British to convince them of their lack of wisdom. As a trump card, Berthelot suggested that Briand might dangle the offer of placing the campaign under the command of a general acceptable to both powers – General Lyautey, the royalist resident-general of Morocco.[116] Whether the replacement of Sarrail would have been a practical proposition, granted his strong political following in Paris, was, however, another matter. In practice the question was never raised at Calais.

At the conference itself a clash of wills was inevitable as both sides followed predictable set-pieces. Briand put forward the views of the French government as to why evacuation was undesirable and then, with some emotion, Kitchener announced that if it were decided to remain at Salonika he would have to resign as he could not accept responsibility for a decision which he believed would lead to military disaster.[117] After a brief adjournment Asquith read out a statement declaring that to keep 150,000 men at Salonika was likely to prove catastrophic and insisting in the name of his government that preparations should be made for evacuation without further delay. This left the French with little scope for manoeuvre or even further discussion. As a result, Asquith's declaration was accepted by Briand for the French government, which in consequence abandoned its own declared wish to remain at Salonika, although it was insisted that the responsibility for the decision lay with Britain.[118] Briand said that if the British government declared that it could do nothing at Salonika then the question was settled. If Britain refused to stay, 'France can only give way'. He considered it a huge mistake to leave Salonika, but the responsibility for that would establish itself at a later date.[119]

Delegates returning to London and Paris on the evening of 4 December could thus easily be forgiven for assuming that the Salonika expedition had now in effect been wound up. So when, on the same day, Sir Francis Elliot, the British minister in Athens, pressed to know whether the final decision was to remain at Salonika or to depart, only one possible answer could be given him.[120] Philippe Berthelot certainly seems to have believed that the campaign had been abandoned for, just before midnight, he submitted an impassioned note to Briand 'under the impression that we had accepted the evacuation of Salonika'. This note underlined the folly of capitulating in the face of the imaginary danger posed by the king of Greece in association with the German emperor, and the perils entailed in giving up control of the Mediterranean and thereby leaving Germany with freedom of action in the Near East. As the Calais decision would materially affect the course of the war, France should make it public that no real agreement existed between the Allies on this issue and that it was merely following the British line for the sake of the entente. Britain's policy since the beginning of the campaign had been disloyal and dilatory. The British conception of the war, limited as it was to northern France and Egypt, was infantile and selfish. They were heading for defeat and were dragging the French along with them. Wildly, Berthelot suggested that France should look to its own interests and seize Crete and Corfu immediately.[121]

Clearly, the impression given by Briand's foremost biographer that the Calais Conference had come to no definite conclusion over Salonika is far from accurate.[122] As Asquith recalled a decade later:

> I soon came to the conclusion [at Calais] that if we stuck to our guns we should not only hold our own, but the French would on the whole feel relieved. So I turned on Kitchener again, who played his part of the sullen, morose, rather suspicious, but wholly determined man with good effect ... [The French] acquiesced with some show of reluctance and regret and we parted ostensibly, and I think really, on excellent terms.[123]

Back in Paris, however, Briand faced a cabinet crisis of the first magnitude. Ironically, Minister of State Denys Cochin, newly returned from Greece, had just told his colleagues that he had become convinced that no useful purpose could be served by remaining at Salonika.[124] But Briand met uncompromising opposition to the idea of evacuation from the socialists in his government, led by Marcel Sembat and Albert Thomas. By contrast, the veteran de Freycinet thought it impossible to remain at Salonika without British support, as did War Minister Galliéni. In the face of this impasse Briand, knowing that the Sacred Union could not survive if the Socialists left his cabinet, readily clutched at the compromise offered by Léon Bourgeois, that nothing should be done until Russia and Italy had been consulted.[125]

As Paul Cambon appreciated, this manoeuvre had no other motive than to gain time.[126] He was convinced that Briand had agreed to evacuation at Calais but that, in the face of the objections of important cabinet ministers, the premier had gratefully sought refuge in Bourgeois' suggestion. Cambon found his government's inability to reach a firm decision lamentable.[127] He had met the British Admiralty chief of staff, Admiral Oliver, who had been present at Calais and who had informed him that the Allies had agreed on evacuation,[128] but he now received a despatch from Briand to the effect that the Calais Conference had merely been between governmental representatives, whereas a final decision could be made only after consultation between the two governments themselves.[129] It was a flimsy argument, but Briand was determined to use any means available to reverse the Calais decision. The senior Foreign Office official, George Clark, was understandably annoyed: 'I made careful notes of M. Briand's language at Calais ... and it certainly justifies an assumption that the French Ministers present accepted our decision, reluctantly certainly, but without reserve and on behalf of the French government so far as regards the main point – withdrawal from Salonika.'[130]

The French government now embarked upon a two-pronged strategy. While hoping that the military conference at Chantilly would see Britain forced to give way over Salonika in the face of the united will of France, Russia and Italy, it also sent Albert Thomas to London to work on the British cabinet and, in particular, Lloyd George. Thomas and George having ties as radicals and ministers of munitions, Briand hoped that it might be possible to use the Welshman to win over his cabinet colleagues.[131] The familiar process was now about to be repeated, whereby Britain's apparent determination to pursue its own policy in relation to the Salonika campaign would be undermined by the priority it felt obliged to give to the dictates of French domestic politics. By the time that the War Committee met on 6 December it was evident that all was not well, and Asquith anxiously asked Kitchener if he had any information as to the French government having gone back on the agreement reached at Calais. Kitchener replied that the French military attaché, Colonel Panouse, had informed him that the French government had decided it could not accept the Calais decision until the Italians and Russians had been consulted and had given their agreement. Asquith noted that there had evidently been trouble inside the French cabinet after the conference, while, according to Admiral Oliver, Briand would have to resign if the forward Salonika policy was upset. Lloyd George, who had already met with Albert Thomas, reported that the unanimous feeling in the French cabinet had been one of consternation. The effect of the French agreeing to evacuation would be the ultimate overthrow of the Briand government.[132] In the vistas of potential political chaos in France, Britain's resolve to enforce the Calais decision began to weaken. Could Britain afford to see the end of the Sacred Union with the Socialists renewing their factious criticism in the Chamber? Was domestic political strife in France a price worth paying for the ending of the Balkan venture, when its consequences might deal the overall allied military effort a crippling blow?[133]

Meanwhile Briand had felt obliged to take drastic measures. As Paul Cambon recognized, 'the whole question is dominated in the minds of Briand, Viviani and the President of the Republic by the fear of a ministerial crisis'.[134] The French cabinet, examining the record of the Calais meeting, came to the conclusion that the document did indeed represent a reluctant acceptance on France's part of the decision to evacuate.[135] But such a step remained a political impossibility, even though the conflict of wills between Britain and France had created, in Cambon's opinion, the gravest crisis since the start of the war.[136] Accordingly, Briand, in his own hand, carefully changed the wording of the procès-verbal of the conference, as drawn up by de Margerie, so as to alter the sense of what had been decided upon. It was now made to appear as if the French representatives had merely taken note of the British pronouncements for reference to their own government.[137] Bertie soon heard that the British government's resolve was slackening. He gathered that Lloyd George was now saying that if Britain deserted the French over Salonika he would resign. Asquith might therefore have to choose between Lloyd George and Kitchener, though Bertie suspected that the war minister, when he saw which way the votes were going, would 'after trumpeting, fold up his trunk and accommodate to circumstances'.[138] The ambassador himself did nothing to encourage a strong British line when he reported that a withdrawal from Salonika might cause the fall of Briand's ministry. Britain would be held responsible by French public opinion for leaving France in the lurch.[139] The French premier was now suggesting that if British objections to holding Salonika were of a military nature, then the matter should be settled by the discussions currently taking place at Chantilly between the allied chiefs of staff, where the British representative would have the opportunity to hear Joffre's point of view.[140]

At Chantilly the whole question was discussed once more, 'just as though it had never been up before the Calais meeting at all'. Generals Joffre, Gillinsky and Porro for France, Russia and Italy were all resolutely in favour of remaining in the Balkans.[141] Isolated, the CIGS reiterated his own view that the expedition should be abandoned and that all the forces thus liberated should be concentrated in France. The position at Salonika was already dangerous and would become quite untenable should Greece decide to throw in its lot with the central powers. But, as he reported to the War Committee two days later, Murray could not bring his colleagues to consider the actual military situation.[142] All that the conference was able to do was to conclude that, while the ultimate decision of the war could only be sought in the main theatres, the delegates – with the exception of the British – were unanimous in requesting the maintenance of the occupation of Salonika.[143]

Meanwhile Thomas's diplomatic offensive was clearly bearing fruit. Asquith sensed the difficult situation in which the alliance might be placed. As he informed his latest female confidante:

> The French have stiffened their backs and claim to have the sympathy of both Russia and Italy. 'La Belle Alliance' has its drawbacks. We had here at lunch M. Thomas [who is] a delightful shaggy creature, full of *esprit* and good sayings. After lunch Grey and Ll. George and I had an hour with him. It is clear that the Briand Govt. would not survive an announcement that they had agreed with us ... But *que faire?* Our joint 150,000 are in real peril, which is impossible to make the Frogs realize or appreciate.[144]

The news from Chantilly had a profound effect on British ministers, many of whom had hoped that Joffre would have revealed his own lack of enthusiasm for the campaign. The War Committee, meeting on 8 December, might have been more prepared to dig in its heels, had it known that Sarrail himself had, only the day before, informed his government that, with the forces currently at his disposal, no meaningful result was possible and that, diplomatic and political considerations aside, evacuation seemed the logical conclusion.[145] As it was, Lloyd George now announced that it would be better that Britain should lose all its forces in the Balkans than that any serious misunderstanding should arise with the French. He received support from Arthur Balfour, elder statesman of the Conservative Party and First Lord of the Admiralty in the coalition government. Balfour argued that it would be quite impossible to desert the French and that, since the British were at Salonika at the instigation of their allies, they should throw the responsibility for conducting the matter further on to France, asking that country to take over both the military and diplomatic command. Eschewing this radical proposal, the War Committee decided instead that Kitchener and Grey should go to Paris with *carte blanche* to settle the matter as they should think best.[146] As the military situation deteriorated, Asquith gave vent to his true feelings in a private letter:

> I have had a pretty hellish day. The situation at and near Salonika could hardly be worse. Our poor 10th Division ... has been hammered and battered a lot in sustaining their self-denying role of guarding the French flank ... It is no longer a question of retaining or evacuating Salonika as

a policy; but of preserving the whole Allied force from the imminent menace of destruction. You can guess (and share) my feelings for the Frogs at this moment.[147]

Grey assured Bertie that he and Kitchener were coming not to press for either the retention or the evacuation of Salonika, but because the military situation had become so serious that it was necessary to be in the closest touch and consultation with their French opposite numbers.[148] But the visit to Paris was effectively a tactical victory for France. As the British position had already been made perfectly clear, it could only be modified by Kitchener and Grey in the direction of the French point of view. According to Frances Stevenson, the trip was very much Lloyd George's idea. 'He knew that once K. got over there he would be entirely in the hands of the French, who would make things so hot for him that he would be obliged to give way.'[149] Kitchener himself seems to have been rather unhappy about the mission which had been entrusted to him. Somewhat plaintively, he told General Callwell that the cabinet no longer paid any attention to his views and always asked instead for the opinions of the General Staff. Callwell feared that the war minister's journey to Paris could only make matters worse.[150]

In fact, in the conversations with Briand and Galliéni, the question of whether the Allies should continue to hold Salonika with a force of 150,000 men was only briefly touched upon. All discussions seemed to start from the tacit understanding that the campaign would continue.[151] As Grey reported back to the Foreign Office, he and Kitchener had told their opposite numbers that the sole object of their visit was to arrange with the French government how British troops could best support the French forces and secure the safety of the whole allied army. The subsequent question of remaining at Salonika was left to be decided by the course of events. 'Strained feeling', Grey comfortingly concluded, 'on the part of the French government is, we think, very much diminished by our visit.'[152] But the possibility theoretically envisaged by Grey in this despatch, that the expedition might yet be abandoned, was in fact illusory, since 'the course of events', to use Grey's phrase, which exerted ultimate influence over British policy was the course of political events in France, and this was not likely in the foreseeable future to make the abandonment of the Salonika campaign a feasible proposition.

Some British ministers were readier than Grey to concede the reality of what had happened. Lord Selborne, the president of the Board of Agriculture, voiced his concern that Kitchener had abandoned the position, which at one point the whole British cabinet had endorsed, that he would resign rather than stay at Salonika. Selborne thought it pure self-deception to pretend that the question of evacuation was really open. The French were going to have their way again, the Greeks would be turned into hostile neutrals or even enemies, and the exact situation would be created which the British General Staff had always said would be fatal.[153] The reality of the situation was apparent in Asquith's letter to the king following the cabinet meeting of 14 December. In effect, the prime minister argued, the French had asked, and Britain had agreed, that the Allies should stay on for a while, under arrangements which from a military point of view were equally necessary whatever the final decision might be, leaving 'as far as the French are concerned that final decision in suspense, but our own views as to what it ought to be remaining unchanged'.[154] What Asquith did not comment upon, however, was the difficulty of translating British views into allied action. When Grey returned from Paris he was able to tell the War Committee that his visit had changed the whole aspect of affairs in the French Chamber. Putting to one side the fact that he had had to go back on a unanimous decision of the British cabinet, Grey almost congratulated himself for having given priority to French political considerations over the expert military opinion which he had earlier held to be sacrosanct. His assessment of his mission was that it had taken place at the right psychological moment and that it was 'essential that it should have been made'.[155] Briand's position had certainly been eased, though perhaps not to the extent which Grey imagined. Bertie heard that the subsequent debate in the French Chamber had been much more stormy than the newspaper accounts suggested and that at one time 150 Radical Socialists were thinking of abstaining.[156]

The train of events begun by Kitchener's resignation threat thus came to an end. Ministers such as Grey had managed to present the collapse of British policy as a tactical success. Other observers were less convinced. Maurice Hankey, the influential secretary to the War Committee, believed:

the Government are really dreadfully to blame. They put off decisions, squabble [and] have no plan of action or operation, and allowed themselves to be dragged into this miserable Salonika affair at the tail of French domestic politics. I see only one solution – to suspend the constitution and appoint a dictator.[157]

At all events, Britain's Balkan policy had been undermined and its freedom of action curtailed. A pattern had been set which would characterize the conduct of the Salonika expedition for the next two years at least. As a result, carefully considered evaluations of the military situation in this theatre, such as the General Staff continued to produce, could in the last resort be no more than pious statements of intent, susceptible to the modifying influences of French political pressure. Grey had repeatedly insisted that the Salonika expedition should be judged solely on the criterion of its military value. But this assertion was true only up to a point. In the last resort factors other than military ones would play the dominant role in determining the actions of the British government. The British had come very close to asserting their right to an independent voice. Had they done so, the Balkan expedition would almost certainly have come to an end. As it was, the British government had finally allowed political considerations to override military ones. There was a justification for this. Britain's still subordinate and dependent position within the wartime coalition meant that, even after more than a year of hostilities, it could not afford to risk losing the French alliance. But it was an unedifying position for a great power to find itself in. As Asquith put it, 'the damned alliance is costing us a heavy price'.[158] Certainly, the events of late 1915 had revealed what little progress Britain and France had so far made in co-ordinating their war strategies. The conclusion which General Henry Wilson drew in the light of the Chantilly Conference was that the two countries needed to set up a small executive body to direct the allied war effort.[159] In the absence of such a development, the experience of the Calais and Chantilly Conferences was almost bound to be repeated.

. . . .

CHAPTER 4

Soldiers and Statesmen; Generals and Politicians

The fortunes of the Salonika expedition were determined not merely by the changing relationship between Britain and France, but also by the interaction of the civil and military authorities in both countries and by developments within all four bodies. Achieving a consensus between four sources of authority was no easy matter in relation to any disputed issue in the allied conduct of the war. As regards Salonika, that consensus was almost impossible to secure. Nineteen sixteen saw significant changes in all these areas which in turn reacted upon the campaign in the Balkans. As between Britain and France, the balance was clearly shifting. By early 1916 the rate of French casualties could no longer be met by French replacements. Increasingly, France had to look to Britain to take an ever greater role in the overall military struggle.

In Britain 1916 saw a clear waning of political authority as Asquith's first coalition failed in the eyes of many critics to galvanize the country's war effort. Gradually, David Lloyd George, still the cabinet's most enthusiastic advocate of an eastern campaign, emerged as the champion of those who wished to see a more dynamic system of war management instituted. Meanwhile, the military authorities, and in particular the new CIGS, General Sir William Robertson, achieved unprecedented control over the direction of Britain's strategic policy. 'During 1916', writes Dr Rothwell, 'Robertson virtually dictated British strategic policy to a government which had become supine and he used his influence methodically to bring about the maximum possible concentration of efforts on the Western Front.'[1] He 'knew what he wanted and he nearly always got his way'.[2] Another scholar has confirmed that 'Robertson ... dictated British military policy through-out 1916'.[3]

In France the picture was more complex. For much of the year the Briand government and Joffre's high command were engaged in a mutually supportive embrace, but the most significant change of 1916 was probably the steady advance of the French parliament at the expense of the country's executive. Nineteen fifteen had seen the return of parliamentary democracy to France after what was effect-ively a military dictatorship in the first months of the conflict when parliament had been prorogued between August and December 1914. During 1916 parliament's still growing powers made the positions of both Briand and Joffre more vulnerable than hitherto, especially in the light of mounting casualty figures at Verdun and Joffre's apparent inability to achieve a military breakthrough on the Western Front. By the end of the year the prime minister had concluded that his own survival necessitated the general's removal from power.[4] The question of Salonika remained entwined around all these developments. The campaign both helped to shape and was in turn shaped by the changing forms of war government in the two countries.

William Robertson was appointed to succeed Sir Archibald Murray as CIGS in December 1915, and given unprecedented powers in the post, largely so that he might act as a counterweight to Kitchener, the secretary of state for war, whose management of Britain's milit-ary efforts was causing increasing concern to his cabinet colleagues. It was strong pressure from figures within the government which finally nerved Asquith to take advantage of Kitchener's temporary absence at the Dardanelles to create an alternative source of military authority. Established in his new post, Robertson quickly made the most of his powers, benefiting from the indecision of the prime minister and the apparently waning authority of the foreign secretary, Edward Grey, to become a leading member of the War Committee. He rejected the notion that, as an appointed official, he should simply advise and then leave it to ministers to accept or reject his advice. He believed rather that the politicians should accept his views and that he was in practice himself a maker of policy.

Early in 1915 Robertson had given a succinct statement of his policy for victory in the war as a whole. 'There is only one way of ending this war satisfactorily,' he concluded with commendable clarity, 'and that is by putting our troops where they can kill the most

Germans and by trusting to ourselves and not to other people.'[5] This formula appeared to rule out the then unborn Salonika expedition on two grounds: the enemy involved was primarily non-German and the directing voice was that of Paris rather than London. Theoretical opposition was sustained by practical experience. Robertson had himself visited the Balkans in 1906 to complement his 'close study of the literature regarding this complicated part of the world'. His overall conclusion had been that the mountainous nature of the terrain rendered military operations exceptionally difficult.[6] In practice Robertson did recognize the primary importance of the French alliance, but he also shared the sort of francophobic prejudices which were common among his generation.[7] More than a year into the war he told the king's secretary that the French were 'as good allies as any country could have'. He merely wished to emphasize 'the great difficulty there has been and always will be in operations conducted by allied armies. It is only natural.'[8] But only four months later he concluded that, with very few exceptions, every British general in France shared his assessment of the French commanders, which was 'not very high'. The problem, he explained, was that 'France is apt to be swayed more by emotion and sentiment than by cool judgement and common sense'.[9] Granted the strains which it imposed upon the Anglo-French alliance, the Balkan expedition was to become one of the most intractable and pervasive problems which Robertson had to confront throughout 1916, the year when his authority within the British war directorate was at its greatest.[10]

The General Staff position on the Salonika campaign was well established before Robertson succeeded to the post of CIGS. Murray had expressed it concisely in late November 1915:

> As to holding Salonika the General Staff have no hesitation whatever in urging that it should be vacated, as quickly as possible ... The only argument for holding it that is worth considering is to deprive the enemy of a submarine base. We cannot for a moment consider that as a sufficient justification for locking up an army of 150,000 men ... The weight of military arguments against holding Salonika is overwhelming, and, in addition to these arguments, there are other considerations: we might make Greece actively hostile, and offend the conscience of Americans and other neutrals by attempting to hold it.[11]

In the wake of the Calais and Chantilly conferences, however, the prospects, at least from a British point of view, were far from promising. 'We were committed to the defence of Salonika for an indefinite time ... We had engaged ourselves, probably for the duration, in a venture which at the moment had scarcely a friend among our statesmen, our soldiers or our sailors.'[12] Matters were scarcely helped when Kitchener accepted the principle of unity of command at the Salonika front under a French general. The British war minister originally expressed the hope that a high-ranking French officer might be placed above both Mahon and Sarrail, but withdrew this proviso when it was explained to him that it might be embarrassing for the French government if Sarrail's authority was publicly undermined in this way.[13] 'Thus was instituted, at a moment when the British government had not finally decided whether their troops were to remain at Salonika, the unified command in French hands which was to endure until the end of the war.'[14]

Yet Robertson, on taking over from Kitchener the day-to-day direction of the war, had not given up hope that Salonika might even yet be evacuated. In a note for the War Committee dated 23 December, the very date of his appointment, Robertson reiterated Murray's conclusion that Flanders remained the main theatre of operations and that all other commitments should be reduced to a minimum. In support of an existing General Staff paper – which argued that 'to employ our surplus divisions in the Balkans next spring and summer would not only not promise any adequate results as against the Central Powers, but might possibly ruin our chance of ultimate victory' and that 'it would be most advantageous to be relieved of our present commitments in the Balkan theatre'[15] – Robertson urged that the War Committee should aim 'to persuade the French to withdraw with us from Salonika'.[16] But British ministers, still smarting from their recent experience of French politics and diplomacy, not surprisingly rejected this conclusion at their meeting on 28 December 1915.[17] Indeed, there were still those, most noticeably Lloyd George, who retained their faith in an eastern strategy. At the War Committee on 13 January the minister of munitions argued that it was Britain's 'business to sit tight on the Western frontier and then take the offensive in Egypt, Mesopotamia or Salonika'.[18]

If withdrawal had become a political impossibility, Robertson remained determined that the option of any large-scale operations from Salonika should be excluded. He was pleased to sense an ally in the French commander-in-chief, General Joffre, who agreed with him on the 'limitations which the difficulties of the country, the lack of roads and communications and the shipping situation impose upon the Army of the East'.[19] In conference in Downing Street in January 1916 the representatives of Britain and France managed to agree that for the moment there was no question of other than defensive operations in the Balkans, and that the immediate needs were to reconstitute and make use of the depleted Serbian army and to ask the Italian government to participate in the expedition.[20] By the following month, however, it was clear that the French government was beginning to contemplate offensive operations. Joffre now seemed to be much less of a stumbling-block than hitherto. In conversation with Robertson on 14 February, the French commander argued that, while a great offensive from Salonika was out of the question, he did propose to increase the size of the force by a further 100,000 troops so as to be in a position to make a large-scale 'demonstration'.[21] For a real offensive Joffre considered that as many as six or seven hundred thousand men would be required, but he was prepared to bow before his government's judgement that a 'mock offensive' might be sufficient to bring in Romania on the side of the Allies. The CIGS disagreed. The best way to help Romania, he insisted, would be through an Anglo-French attack on the Western Front.[22]

Robertson had reached the conclusion that 'the French politicians are at the root of the trouble ... From every point of view to attempt anything big in the Balkans would be the height of folly.'[23] Joffre had 'sprung rather a bomb' on him in suggesting a demonstration northwards with 400,000 men to keep the Bulgarians and Germans from attacking Romania. The politicians in France seemed to think that if anything went wrong with Romania their ministry would be turned out. But Joffre was 'really rather tiresome in this matter because he knows that the operations would be foolish and useless yet apparently will not so tell his Government openly'. Even so, Robertson was prepared to oppose the project 'to the utmost of my power' and was working hard to make his government take a stronger line. In general he felt that Britain was not taking nearly enough lead in the conduct of the war, considering the great amount it was now contributing towards it. But the French 'really are rather difficult people to deal with'.[24] As a precaution, Robertson reminded General Mahon, the British commander at Salonika, that no change had taken place in British policy with regard to the employment of his troops and stressed that the question of undertaking offensive operations was not being considered by the British government.[25] Robertson realized that 'Sarrail must be a great trouble' to Mahon, but assured him that he would never be party to any offensive operations in the Balkans. These would be 'both futile and foolish'.[26] At the same time the CIGS confided to Sir Douglas Haig that he intended to 'knock the Salonika thing clean out' at the next inter-allied conference. It was, he flatly stated, 'utter nonsense'.[27]

On 23 February the War Committee expressed its basic concurrence with Robertson's views without feeling the need to take up his suggestion of concluding a separate peace with Turkey, thereby ending the need for allied involvement in the Balkans. It was agreed that the adoption of an offensive in the Balkans on a scale sufficient to ensure the co-operation of Romania and Greece was ruled out at present by the lack of mercantile shipping and the strain it would impose on British resources, while the adoption of a partial offensive would not offer sufficient military advantage. Robertson argued that, from what he had seen of the French generals and their staff, the sooner Britain acquired overall control of operations the better.[28] On 24 February, three days after the launching of the great German offensive at Verdun, Robertson stressed that his long-term objective remained to use some of Mahon's troops 'elsewhere, more usefully than at present'. The attack around Verdun, a desperate attempt to cripple the French army beyond hope of recovery, might at least have the effect of demonstrating the futility of keeping large forces idle when the main decision was being fought out on the Western Front.[29] Robertson was disappointed in Joffre who, despite his misgivings about the campaign, still declined to consider a withdrawal from Salonika. The reason, insisted the CIGS, was that Joffre 'is so much in the hands of the politicians'. If the Allies withdrew from Salonika the futility of having sent troops there in the first place would be apparent to the French public and the French government would 'get into trouble'. The French had become 'even more tiresome than before', but Robertson was determined not to deplete the British force in Egypt for the benefit of the French front while Britain and France had five divisions 'sitting in Salonika doing nothing'.[30] Mahon was therefore warned to avoid giving Sarrail any suggestion that the British government might depart from its existing policy which was restricted to the defence of the base at Salonika.[31]

In fact, the German attack at Verdun brought into focus the changing balance of power in France's war directorate, of whose implications Robertson was only partially aware. As in Britain, the politico-military structure was now subtly different from that which had existed earlier in the conflict. With the formation of Aristide Briand's government in October 1915 and the elevation of General Galliéni to the Ministry of War, the era of Joffre's unchallenged ascendancy was at an end. His absolute authority was incompatible with the growing realization that victory in the war would not be quickly or cheaply secured. The general's military failures inevitably undermined his military dictatorship. As the president of the republic noted, 'if things had gone better for France, it is probable that we could have accustomed ourselves, for the time being, to Joffre's regime'.[32] But Joffre's inability to produce a military victory made some readjustment of the politico-military balance in France's war directorate inevitable.

A further cause of his waning authority derived from the Anglo-French alliance. One of the reasons why the French government had tolerated Joffre's dictatorship was that it enabled France to exercise some control over the whole allied war effort in the west in the early months of the conflict. Although the British forces under Sir John French (and subsequently Sir Douglas Haig) were never formally subjected to his authority, Joffre's prestige was sufficient to elevate him almost to the position of generalissimo. By 1916, however, British misgivings about his military and intellectual capacity had reached the point where no further gestures towards unity of command were likely while Joffre remained at the helm. In this way Joffre's usefulness to his political masters began visibly to diminish. But for the French government to take any action against him, it would be necessary for his popular standing in the country to decline. And this is precisely what happened in the course of 1916, particularly against the back-cloth of the epic struggle for Verdun.

By February 1916 discontent with Joffre in French political circles was coming into the open. Ambassador Bertie heard that his position was 'very shaky'. There were constant rumours that his days were numbered and that General Lyautey would be brought back from Morocco to replace him.[33] The deputy Abel Ferry was one of the first to transfer criticism of Joffre from the whispers of the parliamentary corridors to the Chamber itself:

All this, gentlemen, is the result of an initial error, because the government has assigned functions to the High Command which do not properly belong to it. General Headquarters ought only to be a Command post, but you have made it a ministry. Do you want that to continue? Very well! Yours will be the responsibility.[34]

Matters came to a head on 7 March when Galliéni read out a fifteen-page note on the high command to his cabinet colleagues. This amounted to an indictment of Joffre, particularly as regards his encroachments into civilian affairs. It concluded with three recommendations. The high command should be relegated to its basic function of the direction of military operations; the minister of war should recover his administrative control; and there should be a streamlining of the army with the elimination of inefficient generals unable to adapt themselves to the realities of the war.[35] Significantly, however, it was not Joffre but Galliéni who suffered from this *démarche*, since it was the latter who resigned ten days later, claiming that he lacked the confidence of the government.[36] The majority of ministers were clearly hesitant about dislodging Joffre from his pedestal, apprehensive of what the effect might be on public opinion and the army.[37] Thus Joffre emerged from this crisis, for the time being at least, stronger than before, even though both military and political leaders found fault with him and were beginning to blame him for the neglect of measures for the proper defence of Verdun.[38]

Such factors meant that Joffre would always be an unpredictable factor in the continuing Anglo-French dialogue over the future of the Salonika expedition. Robertson was never as fully in charge of the situation as his rhetoric sometimes suggested. On 6 March he set out his views to the British commander, General Mahon:

Until you hear from me you can take it that I am not out for any offensive operations in the Balkans. Such operations would be unsound from every point of view, and the day they are sanctioned I shall leave the War Office. I know the Balkans pretty well, I also know the Germans, and I know where a decision will be got, and that certainly will not be in the Balkans. I do not intend to have anything to do with British soldiers being engaged in killing Bulgars and getting killed themselves in return.[39]

At a conference of the allied chiefs of staff at Chantilly on 12 March the question of operations in the Balkans was fully discussed. It was agreed that for the time being it was not feasible to withdraw troops

from the Armée d'Orient or to reinforce it. Robertson asserted that
the whole issue of Salonika would have to be re-examined at a later
date and pointed out that it was difficult for Britain to make its forces
there more mobile while France, Italy and Russia were making calls
on its shipping in other theatres of war.[40]

The CIGS sensed that the argument was going his way. A month
earlier Joffre had been pressing him to send six divisions from Egypt
to Salonika with a view to taking the offensive in the Balkans. Now,
however, Verdun had 'brought him to his senses'.[41] Robertson prepared to push home his advantage. In a paper prepared for the War
Committee he argued that German activity in the west made it more
than ever important that the Allies should use all the men who could
possibly be sent there and not keep them 'useless and idle in secondary theatres'. He pointed out that a force of more than 200,000 had
now been locked up at Salonika for several months without exerting
any appreciable influence on the course of the war. It was time that
'an end was put to this ridiculous situation'. He wanted the British
government to inform the French that Britain intended to remove
one division from Salonika to the Western Front as soon as transport
could be made available and to follow this up with the removal of
further divisions once the reconstituted Serbian army arrived on the
scene.[42] The War Committee met on 23 March to discuss Robertson's
proposals. Despite the objections of Lloyd George and Balfour, who
suggested that these plans would have a demoralizing effect on Russia
and Romania, the committee accepted the CIGS's assurance that the
forces at Salonika were considerably in excess of the number necessary to secure the position there and soon adopted the general's
conclusions to put before the French at a forthcoming conference in
Paris.[43]

At the conference in late March the British delegation tried to rely
on Kitchener's prestige to win their case, with the war minister –
diminished in his domestic authority but still a valuable political asset
– expatiating 'in a hectoring manner on the inutility of the Salonika
Expedition'.[44] He announced that Britain intended to withdraw one
division and then Robertson disclosed that this would be preliminary
to the withdrawal as soon as possible of a second and a third division.
But Joffre had now swung back in support of the campaign and was
not to be outdone by Kitchener's performance. The French commander 'beat his chest, stamped about, said that W[illiam] R[obertson]

had promised this and that for the offensive, and now was going back on his promise, and made some cross remarks about the British Army generally'.[45] Knowing now the sort of arguments to which the British were susceptible, Prime Minister Briand concentrated on the diplomatic and political consequences of a withdrawal in present circumstances. His tactics worked. In the face of such arguments Asquith announced that he would not persist with the proposals put forward by the British military authorities.[46]

The CIGS was deeply disappointed that his 'heated discussion with Joffre in front of Asquith and Briand' had again failed to bring back any divisions from Salonika, and he remained convinced that Sarrail would 'get us into a mess there before he has done'.[47] From Robertson's point of view the conference had been typical of Anglo-French wartime gatherings for the way in which the British delegation had been outmanoeuvred by its allies. In later years he reflected that British ministerial opinion at such meetings had seldom been determined or unanimous. French ministers, by contrast, invariably presented a united front and came to the conferences well prepared, not just to meet British arguments against continuing with the expedition, but also to produce new ones for enlarging it. When, as was often the case, these arguments were of a political character, it was claimed that they were so important as to necessitate military considerations being overridden.[48] In fact, British ministers were particularly susceptible at this stage of the war to arguments about endangering the alliance. According to Lloyd George, the French view was that they were making all the military sacrifices, while Britain tried to preserve its trade and carry on an almost peacetime existence. This was very prejudicial to the alliance and Lloyd George believed that Britain should 'make strong efforts which will dispel this feeling'.[49] Asquith, Grey and Bonar Law were of like mind and it was in this spirit that, on 7 April, the War Committee agreed to the participation of the British Expeditionary Force in an offensive on the Western Front. As Asquith explained, 'M. Ribot [Briand's minister of finance] said definitely that, if France did not get the required assistance, she would not go on. She must put up the shutters.'[50]

The Salonika campaign received further consideration at a meeting of the War Committee on 28 April, but no final decision was reached. Two days earlier Robertson had thought it wise to remind Mahon of the limits of British policy in the Balkans. The British commander could hold the enemy under the threat of an offensive by moving his troops up to, but not over, the Greek frontier, but he should be careful to avoid taking any action which might commit his troops to offensive operations beyond the frontier, more especially as he was not properly organized for mountain warfare.[51] The upshot of the War Committee's deliberations was a decision that Robertson should produce a memorandum looking at future operations in the Balkans and the possibility of an offensive in that theatre. Deputizing for the foreign secretary, the enquiring Lord Crewe wished to know just what the military purpose of the campaign was. He received little satisfaction. Asquith lamely confessed that there did not seem to be any immediate strategic objective: the real justification was to influence the Greek and Romanian governments.[52]

Robertson's memorandum was duly prepared and discussed at the War Committee on 3 May. The general pointed out that Joffre had been expecting the intervention of Romania for more than a year now and that there were no good reasons for supposing that it was any nearer taking the field on the allied side than it ever had been. The intervention of Greece was a more realistic possibility, but the Greek army was deficient in munitions and equipment, which could only come from the Allies and which would entail a further strain on their shipping resources – a strain which would have been increased by their own action in taking the offensive in the Balkans. Moreover, Robertson believed that there was no justification for expecting any great success in the Balkans. Operations there would soon degenerate into a state of deadlock similar to that on the main European fronts. As regards the advantage of holding enemy forces in the Balkans, these would be restricted to the Bulgarian army and a small German force, and he could not see that this would have any material effect on the outcome of the war. Even Lloyd George seemed persuaded by Robertson's arguments. 'He was not in favour of [an offensive] because General Joffre simply asked for it.' More importantly, he did not believe that 300,000 men would be enough to make an impression in the Balkans and feared that a premature offensive would simply discredit the whole Balkan strategy.[53]

Yet Robertson himself now seemed to be coming under the influence of political considerations. He warned that, if Britain insisted on the forces of the Armée d'Orient remaining inactive, this would place it in an impossible position *vis-à-vis* the French and might seriously strain inter-allied relations. The only course, therefore, was not to reject any French proposals for an offensive but to do the utmost to ensure that the plan of operations was strictly limited and suited to the size, organization and equipment of the force available. In order to ensure that this was done, it was necessary that Mahon should, on the assumption of any offensive, revert to his original status as an independent commander – a position he had conceded to Sarrail at the end of 1915.[54] In the event, the War Committee merely decided that Robertson should discuss with Joffre the scope and plan of the proposed offensive in order that an estimate might be made of the liabilities involved in respect of men, munitions and ships before a final decision was reached.[55] To his predecessor Robertson confided his fears that the War Committee would eventually accept the French position *in toto* and that offensive operations would begin in June. In such an eventuality, however, he would insist on Mahon regaining his independence. He thought it likely that there would 'be a row with the French in this connection', but argued that it would be 'preposterous' to suppose that Britain should in any sense place its forces under Sarrail's orders.[56]

The position of General Sarrail himself was clearly becoming an important factor in the development of Anglo-French relations over the Salonika campaign. In the words of the official British historian:

> in the case of this theatre of war it is necessary, as in few others, to discuss the personality of an allied commander, because that of the French commander-in-chief had here an influence so important not only on operations but also on the relations between the French Headquarters and the British.[57]

Capable of arousing very different reactions from those with whom he came into contact, Sarrail was certainly strong-willed, sometimes to the point of impetuosity. He too readily gave the impression of looking down upon others and his personal manner was sometimes brusque. But there was no pretension about him and he was hard-working and blessed with a good memory and lively sense of humour.

From the outset Sarrail had attracted a continuous stream of critical comment from his British colleagues. The most pervasive complaint was that he devoted more time and attention to Greek politics than to military action.[58] The difficulty of working harmoniously with him was demonstrated at an early date. At the end

of 1915 General Mahon's intelligence service had been weaving a net
in which he hoped to catch all enemy spies and agents in one sweep.
The plan had been submitted to Sarrail, who offered no immediate
comment. But at 2.40 p.m. on 30 December Sarrail sent Mahon a
message to the effect that he intended to arrest all enemy consuls at
3 p.m. that day and adding that, if Mahon had any suggestions to
make, he should do so before then. Sarrail also invited the nominal
co-operation of a small party of British troops. To preserve a
semblance of allied unity Mahon sent these and the consuls were
duly arrested and taken to French headquarters. Mahon noted that as
a result of Sarrail's unexpected, independent action the capture of
enemy agents which was to be attempted later in the day was unlikely
to succeed. In the event the lack of allied co-ordination resulted in
many important enemy agents escaping capture.[59] In a similar incident
the following month Mahon learned in the early evening of 27 January that the fort of Kara Burun was to be occupied twelve hours
later by a French battalion and two batteries under the guns of French
warships. The garrison was to receive no warning and, if it resisted,
the fort would be taken by assault. The British were asked to station
two battalions east of Salonika to resist any attempt by Greek troops
to march towards the fort. In exasperation Mahon telegraphed to
London: 'I greatly regret this step and particularly the methods about
to be employed ... but I have not been consulted and the measures
are now too far advanced to attempt to modify them.'[60]

As 1916 progressed, it became ever more apparent that Mahon
was no match for the wily Sarrail. Robertson heard that Mahon had
entirely subordinated himself to the 'masterful personality' of the
French general.[61] In view of the increasing gravity of the situation
Mahon was replaced by the more senior and experienced General
George Milne at the beginning of May. Milne was an old colleague
of Robertson's, having served with him on Lord Roberts's staff in
South Africa and in the Intelligence Division at the War Office. The
new commander assumed his duties without enthusiasm: 'A bitter
blow as I hate the whole thing and am only too anxious to be out of
it ... I spend an unhappy evening ... The difficulties ahead are great
and there are too many rocks to be rounded.'[62]

Robertson lost no time in making his views clear to the new
commander. He admitted that Britain would have to co-operate with
its ally to the fullest extent possible, but this would not justify

undertaking 'futile and costly operations'.[63] Above all, he wanted Milne to know that Britain was in no sense committed to offensive operations.[64] In reply, Milne pointed out that Sarrail had received definite instructions to attack when ordered, but Milne had made it clear that he was not bound by such instructions. He considered that a clear definition of future policy was essential if Britain were not to be drawn into unforeseen operations based on the term 'limited offensive'.[65]

Developments in Paris now began to quicken the course of events. On 11 May the French cabinet decided to ask Britain to send two divisions from Egypt to Salonika.[66] Briand told Paul Cambon, the French ambassador in London, that for the second time the question of Salonika had arisen as a serious issue between the two allied governments.[67] The Armée d'Orient had already achieved diplomatic results sufficient to justify its continued presence in the Balkans but, with its fighting strength about to reach 350,000 men, there could be no question of its remaining idle at a moment when the Allies were about to attempt concerted action on all other fronts. The French government therefore requested that the British forces should be supplied with all necessary material. Moreover, a reserve of 50,000 men would offer the prospect of much greater success than was likely with existing forces and would probably succeed in pulling Romania and Greece into the conflict. So Cambon should urge the need to divert two British divisions, originally destined for the Western Front, from Egypt.[68]

Having obtained more precise details from Joffre as to the scope of the proposed offensive, Robertson prepared a further paper for the War Committee. He now stated categorically that the campaign should not be undertaken. He did not think that Joffre himself believed that the allied forces were strong enough to achieve success. The CIGS added, 'with full respect to the Committee', that he could take no responsibility in regard to the plan and that he considered it 'entirely unsound from every military point of view'.[69] When the War Committee met on 17 May Robertson was even more emphatic. Any man who was attempting to get 350,000 men to attack 300,000 in a restricted and highly entrenched terrain was 'a madman'. He was therefore most anxious that Milne should be placed on the same independent footing as Haig on the Western Front.

Robertson's arguments were readily accepted and it was decided to inform Milne that he should continue to comply with Sarrail's orders for the defence of the town and harbour of Salonika, but that as far as offensive operations were concerned the British general was in every respect an independent commander, not bound by any instructions except those received from Robertson.[70] At the same time a memorandum based on Robertson's paper was drawn up for presentation to the French government. This document pointed out that Joffre himself had previously laid great stress on the inevitable impact of the prolonged fighting at Verdun on French reserves and the consequent need to strengthen the Western Front, and that the British government felt that the security of the Franco-British forces in the autumn might demand the services in France of every available man. The British authorities were convinced that it was not feasible to undertake such a stupendous task as a campaign in the Balkans at a time when the entente forces were so vitally committed on the main front. The general policy in the Balkans must therefore be defensive and the allied force at Salonika be reduced to the size needed for the defence of that place.[71]

Robertson confessed that he found it 'very difficult to deal with people like the French'. He expected 'rather serious trouble about this matter', but felt that 'we really must stick to our ground on this occasion'. If Britain embarked upon a Balkan campaign, the result might be extremely serious in relation to the war as a whole.[72] Sure enough, the War Committee heard on 26 May of the 'great emotion' caused inside the French cabinet by the British attitude.[73] Briand let it be known that Britain's stance was likely to cause a parliamentary crisis in France. He stressed that Joffre completely shared the view of his government as to the necessity for a vigorous offensive and that he, Briand, was ready to defend the French project at a conference of the two allies.[74] Robertson now conceded that the issue was no longer one for military opinion, since the two countries clearly disagreed. The solution rested with the governments. The War Committee agreed on 30 May that it would be necessary for the leaders of the two governments to meet once again.[75]

Pressure, however, was building on the French government to force the British to agree to an offensive. On 2 June Joffre reminded Briand that the longer a decision was delayed, the more difficult the ensuing operations would become because of the opportunities afforded to Bulgaria to reinforce its defensive positions.[76] On the same day Briand himself gave an undertaking to the Chamber Foreign Affairs Commission that he would insist on the British sending their two divisions from Egypt to Salonika.[77] The British attitude, however, showed no immediate sign of weakening, as far as the French could tell. But while the British government maintained an outward show of resolution, the actual discussions of the War Committee revealed a return of that overriding concern for the stability of the French political situation which had so paralysed British diplomacy at the end of 1915.[78] Asquith pointed out that Briand would be arriving at the inter-allied conference knowing that his ministry would fall if he failed in his mission. Politically, the Salonika offensive was a matter of life and death for the French. Balfour voiced the opinion that Joffre and Briand – indeed the whole French people – must be mad. Rather more acutely, Grey commented that, for their own political purposes, the French were prepared to force a disaster. As Lloyd George explained, the men who were criticizing Briand were the friends of General Sarrail and 'if Briand went then General Joffre would go too and then General Sarrail would have the command in France'.[79] Such a prospect was sufficient to send a chill down the spines of most British politicians.

There was no doubt that the whole French politico-military command structure was in a state of crisis. Verdun, symbolic of so much in France's war effort, had become crucial to the survival not only of Joffre but of Briand's government itself. The premier must have feared the effect upon public opinion of reports of the slaughter at Verdun. It was only a matter of time before eyewitness accounts of the carnage received widespread publicity. Briand, moreover, held the responsibility for having accepted Joffre's assurances that all was in a state of readiness to repel the German attack. In the event of Verdun falling, a parliamentary crisis would be inevitable, with Briand's own position in jeopardy. In this unpromising situation Briand began to see in Joffre the scapegoat to ensure his own political survival. Paul Cambon was confident that an article critical of Joffre, which was published in *Le Matin* on 10 May, could not have appeared without Briand's approval and concluded that, with the prime minister now turning against him, Joffre's days were numbered.[80]

At the beginning of June, for the first time in the war, the Chamber met in secret session. The days of automatic parliamentary acquiescence were at an end. Briand now reverted to his earlier stance of solidarity with Joffre. Perhaps realizing that their fortunes were inextricably linked, particularly over the Verdun defences, Briand came to Joffre's defence as the Chamber vented its feelings against the high command in no uncertain terms. Paul Cambon was contemptuous of the whole exercise. 'They will make a few vague statements to which Briand will reply with a few vague answers and the Cabinet will be saved.' He concluded that the prime minister was safe because of the lack of an obvious successor.[81] Inside the Chamber Abel Ferry charged that the high command had sacrificed the best of the French army in useless, piecemeal attacks. Some deputies claimed to have seen, but could not now produce, copies of damaging letters between Galliéni and Joffre and of the famous memorandum of 7 March. But in the heated atmosphere of parliamentary debate, Briand was at his best. Scoring repeated oratorical triumphs over his opponents, he skilfully made some concessions to his critics by agreeing to a parliamentary commission being attached to the army and to the reorganization of Joffre's headquarters at Chantilly.[82] Joffre himself was not happy with these concessions: 'Once the door was open for Parliamentary investigation, no one could say where it would end ... I began to feel more and more hampered in the exercise of my command.'[83] But they were the price he had to accept for the continuation of the increasingly uncomfortable Joffre–Briand axis which had been the linchpin of France's wartime government for the previous eight months, accentuated by Briand's governmental decree of 2 December 1915, by which Joffre's already extensive jurisdiction was extended to the Salonika front. As a later commentator put it, 'the first nail in "Papa" Joffre's coffin had been hammered home by the Chamber'.[84]

Nor was parliament Briand's only focus of political concern. Increasingly, as the year progressed, the French premier needed to keep one eye on the unity and loyalty of his own cabinet. The absence of formal minutes makes the task of the historian of the Third Republic in charting the deliberations of its supreme policy-making body more difficult than that confronting his British counterpart. But fragmentary evidence does exist.[85] From this it is clear that, Sacred Union notwithstanding, Briand's was a deeply divided government. The question of the Salonika expedition and the associated issue of policy towards Greece were at the heart of the prime minister's troubles. Briand was, of course, a declared supporter of the Balkan campaign. For the military competence of General Sarrail, on the other hand, he felt considerably less enthusiasm. But the support which Sarrail enjoyed inside the Chamber of Deputies was mirrored within Briand's cabinet. Appointed minister of public instruction in October 1915, Paul Painlevé rapidly emerged as the most ardent champion of both the campaign and its commander inside the French government. Painlevé epitomized the feeling in some left-wing circles in wartime France that victory on the battlefield might be the prelude to a right-wing, even clerical, *coup d'état* by the victorious generals, which would effectively sign the death warrant of the Republican regime. This normally retiring man, in private life a distinguished mathematician, could be roused to outbursts of considerable emotion in his defence of General Sarrail.[86] For a man like Painlevé, Sarrail held a crucial importance as a general whose adherence to the principle of republicanism was as ardent as his own.[87]

In his support for Sarrail Painlevé developed a series of channels of communication with him. A direct correspondence existed between the two men, but because of the military censor matters of extreme delicacy could be included in this only if the letters were entrusted to an intermediary travelling between Paris and Salonika. Sarrail had, after all, been forbidden to correspond with the government except through Joffre.[88] To circumvent the censor Painlevé therefore secured the appointment to Sarrail's headquarters staff of Paul Fleurot, a municipal councillor in the fifth *arrondissement* of Paris, which Painlevé represented in the Chamber.[89] Acting as Sarrail's mouthpiece, Fleurot then proceeded to correspond in code, but through the normal postal service, with Painlevé's trusted private secretary, Jean Bourguignon. Painlevé and Sarrail were thus able, at one remove, to maintain a regular exchange of information and ideas. 'Thanks to the secret code which Bourguignon and I have established,' noted Fleurot, 'it is easy to circumvent the postal censorship and to say many things.'[90] Painlevé was also kept up to date on events in the Balkans through frequent visits from Louis Leblois, brother of Sarrail's subordinate general and right-hand man.

Sarrail had greeted Painlevé's appointment to Briand's ministry with undisguised enthusiasm – on behalf of France, the republic and the Armée d'Orient – and lost no time in pointing out that his great need was for reinforcements, which he hoped Painlevé would help him secure.[91] Before long Sarrail was complaining to Painlevé that

General Joffre seemed to have set his face against sending any more men to the Balkan front.[92] Responding to Sarrail's complaints Painlevé developed into a persistent thorn in Joffre's side. As early as February 1916, General Pellé of the Grand Quartier Général was requesting that Painlevé should be stopped from presenting plans of operations to the Council of Ministers without Joffre having had prior notice of them.[93] By the early summer Painlevé was finding his position inside Briand's government more and more uncomfortable. In sum, the Sacred Union was still holding but showing increasing signs of strain.

It was against this complex background that Briand, Joffre and War Minister Roques came to Downing Street on 9 June. The chances of full agreement were obviously not good. Joffre argued that it was unacceptable that at Salonika alone, of all the theatres of war, the allied forces should remain idle. He did not want to increase the number of troops there, but believed that those which were there should be used. Briand recalled that it was the British government which had asked France to press for Italian troops to be sent to Salonika. Evidently it was contemplated making some use of them. He begged the British government to join in action in the Balkans and to furnish its troops with the necessary supplies. But Asquith countered that unsuccessful or indecisive action would have a bad effect and the British military authorities were convinced that failure was more probable than success. Joffre suggested that a local success was possible with only a minimum risk, but Balfour believed it was criminal to dissipate energy at Salonika when every other theatre was crying out for reinforcements in men and material. For Robertson the question was not one of merely local importance but of general policy. He thought the operations were not likely to succeed and questioned the possibility of a 'limited' offensive. Lloyd George spoke as a supporter of the Balkan campaign in principle, but he believed that unless there was a fair chance of success, which he doubted, an offensive would be fatal. Asquith conceded that there was no question for the present of any withdrawal from Salonika, nor of any reduction of troops as had been suggested at Paris in March. In full oratorical flight Briand had pointed to the absurdity of keeping 350,000 men idle, but, insisted Asquith, this was not a true description of the situation as they were immobilizing the whole of the Bulgarian army, 100,000 Turks and some Germans and Austrians. Briand retorted that it was not a question of oratory. The opinion he had expressed was the deliberate, considered and fixed opinion of the French government, based not only on political but on military considerations. The French had prepared an offensive, Sarrail had taken his measures. Briand urged the British to think again. He could not conceal the extremely delicate position in which the British attitude was placing him.[94] But British resolve had perhaps been strengthened by receipt of Bertie's opinion that a refusal to join in a Balkan offensive would not have 'any evil effect on entente between France and England'.[95]

A situation of complete impasse thus existed when the conference broke up. Haig was 'surprised and sorry' that after all the talking the Salonika question had still not been settled. He urged Robertson to 'stick to it', assuring him that he would win in the end.[96] Before long, however, under pressure from Paul Cambon, Grey accepted French amendments to a British memorandum on the Downing Street conference which substantially undermined the stance taken by his government. Cambon secured the insertion of paragraphs to the effect that the British government would not at a future date refuse to examine the question of an offensive from Salonika as soon as circumstances allowed, and that it would hasten the equipment of its army with a view to such operations.[97] This addition obviously gave encouragement to French advocates of an offensive since it now appeared that the British government rejected it not on general principles but for temporary, technical reasons. Robertson considered that it 'knocked the bottom' out of the War Committee's memorandum of 17 May, which had given the impression of opposing the offensive because it was fundamentally unsound.[98] He was not therefore surprised when the French 'at once weighed in' with a memorandum which suggested that they would be ready for an offensive in July and that they proposed to send orders to Sarrail to the effect that he should move his troops up to the frontier to be ready for the offensive. This, complained Robertson, was not at all the sense of what had passed at the conference.[99]

Understandably enough, Robertson felt that the time had come to strengthen the British government's resolve and, in a further paper drawn up for the War Committee, pointed out that the British memorandum of 17 May had argued that allied troops at Salonika should be reduced to the number required for the defence of that place. The latest British communication, however, had given Joffre the impression that Britain had more or less accepted French policy and that the proposed offensive was merely deferred for the time being. Robertson thought it desirable that there should be no further misunderstandings. France was unlikely to agree to any reduction in forces unless it was made clear that there was no prospect of Britain being ready for an offensive for several months to come. It would be little less than a crime to maintain more troops at Salonika than were needed for defence at a time when Haig was crying out for all available assistance on the Western Front. So Robertson sought the War Committee's assurance that preparations for an offensive in the Balkans were not to be undertaken until the results of the offensive on the Somme were known and the general situation could be reconsidered.[100] The War Committee agreed that Grey, in concert with Robertson, should draft a further communication to Cambon, stressing that the British government had never yet accepted the principle of taking the offensive in the Balkans and that in any case the British forces could not be fully equipped for offensive operations for some months.[101] What the effect of this communication would be Robertson could not guess, but 'the whole of the fat [was] in the fire once more'.[102]

The French government was nothing if not persistent and on 28 June Cambon suggested to Lord Hardinge, newly appointed as permanent head of the Foreign Office in place of the ailing Nicolson, that, the diplomatic and military situation having changed, the moment had come to examine again the question of an offensive from Salonika. Cambon reminded his government that it would be necessary to work on Robertson, whose influence pervaded the British government, to convince him of the reasonableness of the French case.[103] The formal French communication of 30 June stressed that the situation had been changed by a Russian victory and an Italian counter-offensive, and that it was during the attack on the Somme that allied action in the Balkans would be most effective.[104]

Robertson, however, was quick to act to cut the ground from under this latest French initiative. Commenting on Cambon's memorandum, he argued that nothing had happened to charge his long-held view that a Balkan offensive, before the conditions essential for success had been realized, would be a 'useless and unjustifiable sacrifice of British lives and wasteful expenditure of war material'. He noted that French tactics had changed in recent weeks and that they were now trying to argue on military grounds and were suggesting that his opposition alone stood in the way of offensive operations. Robertson hoped that the government would make it clear that the views conveyed to Paris were not only those of the General Staff but of the entire War Committee.[105]

But the now genuine prospect of Romanian intervention was adding a new dimension to the situation. On 4 July the entente heard that Romania was ready to join the struggle provided that Sarrail's army offered protection in the form of a prior attack on Bulgaria. This seemed to undermine Robertson's contention that Romanian entry into the war would be the result of successes obtained by the Russians and 'not due to any efforts at Salonika'.[106] At all events, the War Committee, while agreeing with Robertson that recent developments on the main fronts had not created such a new situation as would justify reversing its previous decisions, concluded that the actual entry of Romania into the war would create such a situation.[107] On 20 July Robertson was instructed to discuss and conclude a military convention with the French regarding the operations of the Salonika armies, with the significant modification of earlier statements that the British government would be prepared, as soon as Romania had definitely entered the war, to authorize the British forces to co-operate with their allies in such action as might be necessary to contain the Bulgarians on the Greek frontier.[108] After further hesitation on the part of Romania, the new war secretary, David Lloyd George, agreed at the French Foreign Ministry on 11 August to a revised protocol regarding Romanian intervention and the launching of an offensive.[109] The Treaty of Bucharest was signed on 17 August. Romania would declare war ten days after the opening of an allied offensive, though Robertson wanted it known that all he would consent to Milne's army attempting was to do its best to hold the Bulgarian forces where they were.[110]

Under pressure Robertson conceded that Milne's mission was to support and co-operate with Sarrail in containing the Bulgarian forces so as to facilitate the action of the Romanian army against Austria-Hungary, 'without prejudice to any further objectives which [might] present themselves for consideration later, having regard to available resources including transport'.[111] But at heart Robertson remained as doubtful as ever about the whole operation. He insisted that Britain had no more troops available for the Balkans. To take a division from Egypt would be to take the only one available for despatch, if needed, to India, while to take one from Britain would be to leave the home defence forces unduly weak. This was irrespective of the cardinal need to send every possible man to the Western Front. The whole Salonika expedition, Robertson reflected, was a French enterprise from start to finish and the French ought to see it through.[112] He complained that he did not dare turn his back on the politicians, for in a moment they would be sending out another expeditionary force – if they could find one. It was 'a queer business' for him to conduct but, with some exaggeration, he assured Haig that he had 'no difficulty in getting [his] own way', even though the situation demanded eternal vigilance.[113]

The intervention of Romania raised spirits in the allied capitals. For perhaps the first time since the outbreak of hostilities the entente seemed to be directing the strategic course of events. Momentarily, the chimera of a Balkan coalition reappeared once more. But Sarrail's offensive and the intervention of Romania proved equally disappointing. By mid-September the advance of the Romanian army had been halted by the Central Powers. Recalling what had happened the previous autumn – or, as Robertson put it, suffering from 'the Servian fit again'[114] – Lloyd George called for additional forces to be sent to save the Romanians from the fate which had already befallen Belgium and Serbia. But the CIGS insisted that the best way to help Romania was by pounding away at the German line on the Somme.[115] Robertson made it clear to Asquith that he could not accept responsibility for a Balkan strategy of which the General Staff disapproved. With Lloyd George absent inspecting the Western Front, the War Committee endorsed Robertson's position on 12 September.[116] But the debate smouldered on throughout September. When von Falkenhayn's Ninth Army launched its offensive against Romania at the end of the month, Lloyd George renewed his appeal. At the War Committee on 9 October he reported that Milne believed that he could break the Bulgarian front if he received an extra eight divisions. Robertson countered that these could only arrive too late and that, in all conscience, he could not advise the government to send more troops to the Balkans.[117]

Lloyd George's appointment to the War Office, following Kitchener's death on board HMS *Hampshire*, had clearly changed the balance of power within the War Committee. Robertson was not accustomed to this strength of opposition from his political colleagues and, hinting at resignation, he accused Lloyd George of showing 'want of confidence' in his advice by raising the question of re-inforcements at the War Committee. Lloyd George, however, was not to be intimidated. 'You must not', he replied, 'ask me to play the part of a mere dummy. I am not in the least suited for the part.'[118] Ultimately it was agreed to sanction the despatch of about 21,000 reinforcements so as to enable Milne to sustain and intensify the offensive action he was then taking, but, Joffre was told, this was the utmost that could be done.[119]

Frances Stevenson's description of events was certainly seen through Lloyd George's eyes:

> being a soldier [Robertson] does not look at the political side, nor does he realise what loss of our prestige following upon such a catastrophe would mean to the conduct of the war ... Robertson came to him almost in tears this morning, very upset by D[avid]'s letter. However, they made it up and compromised on the subject of the Balkans, D assuring Robertson that he did not wish to hinder him in his work and Robertson promising to send 2 divisions to the Balkans to help to keep the pressure off Roumania.[120]

In reality, Robertson found the new situation of having to resist the pressure not only of the French, but of his own war minister, a taxing one. It had been only 'with the greatest difficulty' that he had managed to get his own way and, he revealed to Murray, he had been obliged to write Lloyd George 'a straight letter', indicating that he could no longer carry on in his post unless his advice was accepted. These tactics had been successful, but he recognized that 'the same thing [would] occur again later'.[121] The stage was thus set for the regime of mounting mistrust which would characterize relations between the two men until Robertson's fall in February 1918.

A further allied conference was held at Boulogne on 20 October. Briand and Asquith agreed on the desirability of avoiding a Romanian defeat but disagreed as to the means of securing the same goal. As far as the British prime minister was concerned, the allied army in the Balkans was already doing its job by preventing the Bulgarians from diverting any of their forces to the north. Lloyd George rather embarrassed his colleagues by making a strong plea in favour of sending large reinforcements to Salonika, but the conference broke up without any firm agreement on this point being reached.[122] 'For once', noted Haig, 'the British Govt. stood firm and refused to be

blackmailed by the French.'[123] But Lloyd George was clearly disappointed by this result. He had done his best to secure a favourable
outcome at Boulogne, even making sure of the presence in the French
delegation of his ally, Albert Thomas – an 'absurd and transparent
subterfuge', thought Hankey – and was surprised that Briand had not
been more insistent for vigorous action in the Balkans.[124] A visit by
Thomas to London on 23 October raised the Welshman's spirits and
he went off to the War Committee the following morning 'full of
beans' and 'in a most Machiavellian state of mind'.[125] At the committee Grey reported that there would be a row in the French
Chamber if Romania collapsed and that all the blame would be put
on Britain. Even Robertson seemed ready to give ground. He said
that in purely military terms the sending of one more division would
have no impact. If, on the other hand, the committee considered that
it would have a good effect on Romania, he could send a division
from France and replace it later by one from Britain. According to
Miss Stevenson, Lloyd George 'pretended that it was too late, but the
more he pretended the more anxious they became to prove that it
was not, and they ended up by becoming quite enthusiastic about
the Balkan expedition'.[126] At all events, with political considerations
once again to the fore, the committee agreed to accept a French
proposal to increase the British contingent at Salonika to seven
divisions.[127] Indeed, the subsequent communication to Paris showed
the extent to which military arguments were being pushed into the
background, for it was now stated that the British government 'as a
proof of their desire to meet the wishes of the allies in every way
possible [had] decided to waive further consideration as to whether
this [would] produce useful military effects and to accept the French
proposal'.[128]

But Robertson still had 'no intention of adopting the Balkans as a
main theatre' and was anxious to enlist Joffre's support in this respect.
He felt that the Allies were undoubtedly winning on the Western
Front and that it would be folly to weaken their effort there in the
futile hope of gaining decisive results in the Balkans.[129] The War
Committee had been 'very good about the matter and quite realised
the uselessness of sending the division', but had been obliged to
weigh 'the military disadvantages against the political and moral
conditions'.[130] Shortly after the decision to increase the British contingent at Salonika was taken, Robertson drew up a careful review of

the whole war situation. As far as the Balkans were concerned, an addition of fifteen divisions would be necessary decisively to defeat the Bulgarian forces. Such a reinforcement was out of the question until the War Committee decided that the Balkans and not France was the main front. There was thus no satisfactory military alternative between continuing on approximately the present scale and making the Balkans the main theatre of war. Bad strategy, argued Robertson, had never yet proved to be good policy and he regretted the sending of another division to Salonika, while recognizing the reasons which had prompted this decision. He regretted it not only because of the wasteful dissemination of forces which it involved but because it had brought Britain a step nearer to embarking on extensive operations in the Balkans where, he believed, decisive results were impossible.[131]

At its meeting on 24 October the War Committee had also discussed the question of Sarrail's command. There was general agreement with Asquith's assessment that 'something curious' was going on in France. According to Lloyd George, some members of the French government were looking to Britain to press for Sarrail's removal in order to shift the responsibility for the general's dismissal on to their allies.[132] The presence of Léon Bourgeois at the Boulogne Conference was probably only explicable in terms of Sarrail's position. 'Bourgeois and his party', Lloyd George was informed, 'are the staunch upholders of Sarrail, who is essentially a political general.'[133] Certainly, Sarrail's command had once again become an extremely divisive issue within the French war directorate. Matters came to a head when Joffre attempted to send out his chief of staff, General de Castelnau, to Salonika on a mission of inspection, with the obvious aim of securing Sarrail's removal. Bertie heard that Joffre's first proposal, made on 25 August, had been thwarted when Painlevé objected to de Castelnau as a 'clerical'. General Gouraud had then been suggested as an alternative, but his nomination raised problems as he was considerably junior to Sarrail. Bertie understood that the compromise arrived at was that Gouraud should be kept in reserve for use if Sarrail did not hurry up his offensive.[134]

During October Joffre renewed his attempts to secure approval for a de Castelnau mission, but by the end of the month news reached Sarrail of how Painlevé had parried this latest and most dangerous initiative by the commander-in-chief. In the face of Joffre's insistence on de Castelnau, Painlevé had persuaded the French cabinet to accept the principle that the question of inspection should be the preserve of the government rather than the high command. The attribution of the mission to the war minister, General Roques, was thus Painlevé's idea and, according to Bourguignon, Joffre and de Castelnau were furious at the minister's success. Roques should therefore be welcomed by Sarrail with confidence and good humour.[135] Colonel Herbillon, Joffre's liaison officer at the Ministry of War, thought that Roques's impartiality was sufficient to remove all objections to his appointment, but the enthusiasm with which Painlevé and other Sarrail partisans viewed his mission would suggest that Roques, under Painlevé's influence, was as likely to report favourably upon Sarrail as de Castelnau would have been to recommend his recall.[136] Spirits at Chantilly were depressed by the conviction that Roques would fall victim to Sarrail's cunning.[137]

With something less than total frankness, Painlevé informed Lloyd George that he had full confidence in Roques's impartiality, that he had no idea what the war minister's first impressions were in Salonika and that he, Painlevé, would be bound by any report which Roques brought back to Paris.[138] Meanwhile Joffre's own liaison officer with the Armée d'Orient had returned to France and informed Poincaré, Briand and Joffre of his opinion that the direction of operations from Salonika could improve only if there were a radical transformation in Sarrail's character.[139] In practice the question of the command of the Armée d'Orient was no longer within Joffre's jurisdiction. In mid-November Briand received Roques's report which, predictably enough, concluded in favour of keeping Sarrail at Salonika. The war minister commended Sarrail's military ability, suggested that he enjoyed the support of the allied commanders in Macedonia and vindicated the part he had played in Greek politics. This was a serious blow to Joffre's position. Coming on top of Painlevé's success in making Sarrail answerable to Roques rather than an officer of the GQG, it effectively undermined the governmental decree of 2 December 1915, which had placed the Armée d'Orient under Joffre's control.

Whatever his feelings about Sarrail, Joffre continued to argue that Romania's entry into the war had given the Balkans an entirely new significance which the Allies would ignore at their peril. Robertson, however, remained unconvinced. Nothing, he told the War Committee on 7 November, could be worse than adding a few divisions to those already at Salonika and, while Joffre might talk in terms of an advance towards Sofia, there was no realistic alternative for the Armée d'Orient to its present limited role.[140] Inter-allied relations regarding the Salonika campaign were thus at their customary low ebb when the politicians of Britain and France assembled once more in Paris on 15 November. Yet in the course of the conference Asquith meekly accepted Briand's resolution that, for the coming winter, the Balkan theatre should be recognized as the principal front of the allied war effort.[141] This was a striking departure from the policy Britain had attempted to pursue since the very beginning of the campaign. At the same time the military chiefs were meeting at Chantilly. Here Robertson vainly tried to resist the pressure of the French, but ended by agreeing that, as part of the renewal of the combined offensive of the last campaigning season, the strength of the Armée d'Orient should be increased as soon as possible to twenty-three divisions, including seven British, with the aim of seeking the decisive defeat of the Bulgarian army.[142] Lloyd George found this outcome 'very satis-factory'. Robertson had 'been beaten in his strategy'. But the war secretary remained cautious. He knew from experience that the decisions reached at inter-allied conferences were 'never acted upon with sufficient vigour' and in any case feared that it was now too late to do much to save Romania.[143]

Certainly, Robertson was as yet unready to abandon his corner. By the beginning of December the CIGS was arguing that it would be incurring undue risks for the Salonika force to try to hold its present front against the sort of attack that might be brought against it. He therefore advised that a defensive front should be selected, appropriate to the size of the available forces. If this was done, and if the allied army was effectively commanded, then Robertson considered that it should be able to hold its own.[144] His argument seemed all the stronger when the forces of the central powers entered Bucharest on 6 December. The high hopes raised by Romania's intervention in the war only three months earlier lay in ruins. Robertson now wrote to Joffre that the collapse of Romania had altered the whole situation and invited him to consider what would happen to the Salonika army in the event of an attack by Bulgaria, Germany, Turkey and Austria, combined with hostile action on the part of Greece.[145] But the French government was thinking in altogether different terms. On 5 December the Council of Ministers had decided that in view of the worsening situation in Greece, where a group of French soldiers had been ambushed, the total strength of the Armée d'Orient should be raised to nine British divisions, eight French and five Italian.[146]

For Briand the Athens ambush represented the low point of his policy towards Greece, the evolution of which must be reviewed at this point. The allied position in Greece, which after all remained a neutral state, was an inherently difficult one. The Armée d'Orient was in practice occupying that neutral state, an act for which the sole legal justification derived from the Allies' capacity as guarantors of Greece's nineteenth-century constitution.[147] The possible deposition of the apparently Germanophile King Constantine was seriously discussed in French political circles from the first days of the military campaign. Denys Cochin recommended such a course following his return from his mission to Greece as early as November 1915.[148] But Briand's constant excuse for failing to pursue so radical a course was the need to take account of the susceptibilities of France's allies, particularly Britain.[149] In meetings of the French cabinet, Briand often found himself Constantine's sole defender, resisting the efforts of his ministerial colleagues and the president of the republic to open his eyes to the Greek monarch's duplicity. Against such an onslaught the French premier had but one line of argument: Britain's hostility to any energetic measures in Athens and the overriding need to maintain the entente.[150] As he explained to the Chamber Foreign Affairs Commission: 'do not forget that we are dealing with two monarchies [Britain and Italy] and an absolute empire [Russia] and they have all told me, "If you harm the dynasty we shall no longer follow you".'[151] But a growing body of opinion was reaching the conclusion that what really dictated Briand's policy – much softer than that urged by the rest of his government – was his intimate relationship with the Greek princess Marie, sister-in-law of the king.[152] As one angry observer put it, everything was being done to save Constantine, to the detriment of French interests, simply in order to earn the caresses of her royal highness.[153] The lady herself admitted that her affair with Briand had become the talk of Paris.[154]

Only when Briand's own political survival seemed threatened, as when probing questions were asked in the Chamber of Deputies, did he really make a show of urging strong action upon the British government.[155] For the most part Briand treated the promptings of his ministerial colleagues with measured disregard. Soon after receiving a

warning from Admiral Lacaze that the Greek situation was deteriorating rapidly and required a firmer policy, Briand told Guillemin that
the despatches coming from Greece were far too prejudiced in their
hostility to the Greeks and their calls for action.[156] Poincaré, on reading
this telegram to Athens, immediately protested to Briand that he
drew a completely different conclusion from the prime minister.
Briand once more attempted to convince Poincaré of Constantine's
sincerity, but without success.[157] Within a few days Briand was again
castigating Guillemin for his criticisms of the policy of the French
government, when in practice the majority of the government wanted
to see the implementation of the very measures which Guillemin
proposed.[158] Jules Cambon found himself obliged to intervene on
Guillemin's behalf, believing that, if there were excesses in the
minister's telegrams, these were less dangerous than Briand's blind
faith in Constantine's loyalty.[159]

The bewildering effects of this lack of consensus inside the French
government came to the surface at the end of August 1916. In conference at Calais Briand informed the British representatives that he
was in agreement with them that rumours of a German invasion of
Greece were unfounded and that he did not consider that any special
military or naval counterstroke was needed. The British authorities
were therefore astonished to learn that Admiral Dartige du Fournet
had been ordered to proceed to Salamis Bay with his fleet, while
Sarrail was to prepare the transport of troops, and that British co-
operation had been requested.[160] What had happened was that, in
Briand's absence, Poincaré had nerved the Council of Ministers to
declare for firm action, leaving Briand to face a virtual *fait accompli* on
his return.[161] In the end the British War Committee agreed to allow a
squadron to be despatched to act under the French admiral, but Grey
succeeded – with little difficulty – in persuading Briand to give up the
proposal to land troops. Briand, as usual, was very willing to seize
upon British hesitations as an excuse to stop all action.[162] The dispute
within the French government rumbled on, however. There was even
a suggestion that a hostile demonstration at the French legation in
Athens was deliberately engineered in a desperate attempt to force the
government in Paris to take some action.[163] It seemed to Poincaré that
Briand was prepared to tolerate unending insults and affronts from the
Greek government rather than do anything which might upset the
Greek king – 'in short he seemed quite resolved ... to do nothing'.[164]

Only when the British War Committee decided in September that strong action was needed in Greece was the ground cut from under Briand's feet. The French premier was obliged to admit that the situation had completely changed. This was a moment to be savoured by his opponents and Albert Thomas even moved a resolution in the French cabinet 'welcoming the British attitude and expressing readiness to follow the British government in any course proposed by them – however drastic'.[165] As Paul Cambon noted – and he was exceptionally well placed to understand the position and annoyed that Briand had blamed him for failing to persuade Britain to follow the French lead – the British had for too long believed that Constantine could be accommodated, but now 'the throne of Greece has only one prop and that is Briand'.[166] By October 1916, therefore, it appeared to be France, or at least Briand, who was placing a restraining hand on Britain in allied policy towards Greece, rather than the other way around.[167]

At the beginning of October the Greek Liberal leader, Venizelos, succeeded – with the evident connivance of Sarrail and the French naval attaché, Commandant de Roquefeuil – in establishing a provisional government, favourable to the Allies, based on Salonika. Such a development may not have been wholly pleasing to Briand who, according to Paul Cambon, was more anti-Venizelist than Constantine himself. It was said that the French premier never tired of uttering abuse against the Greek leader.[168] In conference at Boulogne on 20 October Britain and France agreed that the only way in which the official Greek government could convince them of its good intentions would be by an immediate declaration of war against Bulgaria. But Briand saw to it that no French pressure was put on the Greek king to declare war, for the Boulogne decision was effectively reversed as a result of conversations between Constantine and the little-known French deputy, Benazet, undertaken while the Allies were still in conference. According to Briand, Benazet had no official mission but was merely acting for the Chamber Estimates Committee on an inspection of the health facilities of the Armée d'Orient.[169] Yet Briand seems to have summoned Benazet to see him before the deputy left Paris and told him to make contact with France's agents in Athens.[170] Indeed, many believed that Briand had commissioned Benazet to negotiate with the king behind Guillemin's back in order to bring about a pro-Constantine policy.[171] The bargain struck in these

mysterious negotiations, undertaken without the knowledge or consent of the British government, was that Constantine should hand
over the war potential of his army and fleet in return for allied respect
for his country's neutrality in the war.[172] More importantly, the effect
was to delay the chances of the Venizelist movement gaining complete control of Greece, at the very moment when it seemed to be in
the ascendancy. Constantine had once more been reprieved and the
chimera raised of a reconciliation between the king and Venizelos,
although by this stage many questioned the desirability of such a
reconciliation.[173]

In practice the Benazet negotiations failed to produce the results
which had been promised.[174] Grey told the War Committee that
Benazet did not appear to have brought about very much of consequence and that he, Grey, had taken it upon himself to inform
Paris that the time had come for the Allies to take more drastic
measures.[175] But Briand merely replied that he was confident that the
negotiations would succeed, that he remained convinced that the
unity of Greece could be brought about only through the reconciliation of Constantine and Venizelos and that this was the final
solution to be sought.[176] As the initial optimism surrounding Benazet's
negotiations evaporated, Admiral du Fournet made a formal request
to the Greek government on 16 November for the surrender of
armaments equivalent to those already taken from the Greeks by
Bulgaria. Following a direct refusal by the Greek government, the
French admiral demanded the surrender of the weapons by 1 December, failing which he intended to land allied detachments in Athens.
Blindly confident that the Greek king would give way before a show
of force, du Fournet led the allied contingent into a carefully prepared
ambush in which more than 200, mostly Frenchmen, were killed or
wounded.[177]

Briand's opponents naturally hoped that his position would be
shaken by Constantine's latest performance and by the miscalculations
of the French admiral.[178] It was certainly unfortunate for the French
premier that this incident coincided with parliamentary and governmental crises in France. At the very moment that du Fournet marched
his men to their deaths, the frustrations and only partly hidden
divisions of the French political system were coming to the surface in
a second secret session of the Chamber of Deputies. Here, freed
from the glare of publicity, deputies had the opportunity to probe

deeply into the inconsistencies of Briand's conduct of affairs and to voice their misgivings about the command structure on the Western Front. Compounded by war weariness, discontent now spread far beyond the political Left from which Sarrail drew his support.

The secret session began well enough for Briand. On 29 November the Radical deputy Abrami voiced the disappointment felt by Sarrail's supporters at the government's conduct of affairs. Briand, he said, had established his own credentials as an 'easterner', but had then thrown everything away with the decree of 2 December 1915 by placing the future of the Balkan campaign firmly in Joffre's unsympathetic hands. 'In reality, that day you committed a grave error and it is the country which has had to pay for it.' The Chamber, he insisted, still had confidence in Briand, but the names of Joffre and Chantilly no longer evoked the confidence they once had.[179] At this stage, however, Briand appears not to have been unduly worried at the progress of the secret session. His own two-hour speech on the opening day had created a good impression and Bertie heard that the intrigue against him might collapse, but that 'there may be some Ministerial changes as sops to the Radicaux Socialistes'. Even after Abrami's onslaught Bertie was confident that Briand would 'pull through all right'.[180] The line of argument which the French premier pursued on 30 November reflected the apparent strength of his position. He blamed Britain for the failings of allied policy in the Balkans and seemed to have no intention of using Joffre as a scapegoat.[181]

Even so, Briand was clearly looking for a readjustment of the politico-military balance, as was evident when he lunched with Joffre on 3 December. As Joffre later recalled, to his surprise Briand told him that he was much troubled by the parliamentary situation and that the only way to restore calm was to effect a drastic reorganization of the high command. If this were not done, the government would fall and chaos ensue since no other political combination could be made to work. Appealing to Joffre's sense of patriotism, Briand pleaded with the general to accept the modifications which he proposed, since if he could not announce them to the Chamber the following day his government would collapse. Briand's scheme was that Joffre should give up day-to-day control of the French military effort on the Western Front and instead become technical adviser to the government, in which capacity he would exercise an overview over both the Western Front and the Armée d'Orient.[182] Before Briand could place this scheme before the Chamber, the situation changed dramatically as news arrived of events in Greece.

In seeming to confirm Constantine's duplicity the events of 1 December in Athens served also to destroy Briand's policy of trying to effect a rapprochement with the Greek king. Bertie heard that the Chamber was 'talking of demanding King Constantine's head or Briand's'.[183] In addition, General Sarrail's positive reaction to the developments in Greece reflected badly on Joffre, since it was well known that he had wished to recall Sarrail. Sarrail's recent capture of Monastir – the most important success of his whole command – further strengthened his position *vis-à-vis* the commander-in-chief. Clearly, Briand and Joffre were now both vulnerable to renewed parliamentary attack in a way that could not have been anticipated when the secret session had opened only a few days earlier. Joffre seems to have appreciated this, since he was not slow to add his weight to Sarrail's demands for positive action to avenge the Greek king's treachery.[184] The changed atmosphere was very evident when Briand attempted to sell his scheme of reorganization to the Chamber on 4 December. Bertie's information was that Briand had 'a bad day' and that he would 'have to do some fresh Jonah-throwing'. Joffre would be 'elevated out of authority and power'.[185] Worse was to come on the following day, which the Chamber devoted to a bitter attack upon Joffre and the prime minister's proposed reorganization. The left-wing deputy Pierre Renaudel argued that Joffre no longer had the competence to lead the war effort. As spokesman for the Radical Socialist group, Joseph Noulens demanded clarification of Joffre's new status and in particular of the extent of his authority over Sarrail and whoever now became commander on the Western Front. Briand replied that directives would be issued by the government, but that Joffre would assist in determining these orders. He implied that Joffre's new position would be accepted by France's allies and that the general would become president of a sort of inter-allied control council.[186]

Briand's position was now shakier than at any time since his assumption of the premiership over a year earlier. But at least when the Chamber focused its attention on the high command it deflected its critical gaze from the affairs of Greece where Briand was evidently more culpable than Joffre for the collapse of French policy. In the days which followed, Briand came to the conclusion that, if his parliamentary majority were to be maintained, his recent agreement with Joffre would have to be jettisoned. Viewing the crisis from the British Embassy, Bertie was convinced that 'Joffre *has* to go, whether he resign or not'.[187] Briand's survival now necessitated the effective removal of Joffre from the higher direction of the war and a governmental reshuffle to inject some new vigour into his regime. The premier's guiding motive was simply the salvation of his own government and to this everything else was subjected. As one hostile critic savagely put it, 'Let France perish rather than M. Briand.'[188]

There was plenty of evidence that the Chamber was not impressed by Briand's manoeuvres. On 7 December Pierre Forgeot bluntly told the prime minister that his oratorical mastery was not enough. At the head of the government, as at the head of the army, Forgeot exclaimed, France needed leaders – and it had none.[189] Briand ultimately obtained his vote of confidence at the end of the secret session, but the strength of the government's bloc inside the Chamber had diminished by 100 deputies since the first secret session in June.[190] The following day Briand received a letter from the former deputy Joseph Reinach, warning him that the Chamber's impression was that he had simply improvised solutions throughout the course of the secret session.[191] This feeling was widespread and hampered Briand's attempts to streamline his government. Significantly, Paul Painlevé refused to serve in Briand's reconstructed cabinet, demanding a more radical reorganization of the command structure and an assurance that Sarrail would be made answerable to the War Ministry alone.[192] In addition, it was evident that Robert Nivelle, chosen as Joffre's successor, would not assume command on the Western Front until his complete freedom from Joffre's tutelage was assured. The latter's position was in fact rapidly becoming untenable. Before the month was out, Joffre had been relieved of his posts, compensated with the prestigious but largely empty title of Marshal of France.[193]

This then was the background to the latest French request to increase the strength of the Armée d'Orient. But Britain too was in a state of political crisis, where the supersession of Asquith by Lloyd George delayed an immediate response to the French proposal.[194] When, however, Lloyd George's new war cabinet did meet on 9 December, Robertson was as emphatic in his opposition as ever and ready to deal with this 'difficult business'.[195] Owing to the defeat of Romania and the hostile attitude of Greece, he argued, the situation in the Balkans had undergone a complete transformation and the plan agreed upon at Chantilly to knock Bulgaria out of the war no longer made sense. In a *tour de force*, which epitomized the attitude he had unfailingly held throughout the year, Robertson summed up his advice by saying:

> none of the objects for which we went to and remain in the Balkans can now be attained. It is impossible to maintain and employ there a sufficient force to exert a decisive effect on the war in our favour. We ought therefore to withdraw altogether from the country, but as this proposal is probably not practicable for the moment for political reasons, we should at the most definitely adopt the policy of holding Salonika defensively.[196]

At the conclusion of the meeting, Paris was merely told that difficulties of transport and supply were such as to rule out acceptance of the French proposal.[197]

Once again, Robertson had been successful in withstanding French pressure to carry out plans which he regarded as militarily nonsensical. But, as throughout 1916, his success had been at best partial, his so-called dictatorship incomplete. In general Robertson had been able to win the argument with his political colleagues in London, but the point about the Salonika expedition was that, as often as not, the last word in allied strategy lay on the other side of the Channel. 'Allies', concluded Robertson after nearly a year of attempting to co-operate with France in the direction of the Balkan campaign, 'are a tiresome lot.'[198] If Robertson's will had been final, the Salonika campaign would not have been allowed to drag on for as long as it did, involving ever larger numbers of British troops, with no obvious advantage to the ultimate determination of the conflict. As he later reflected, Britain had never had any real policy, but had simply 'danced attendance on the French' with the result that the campaign had become a 'hideous nightmare'.[199] Unable to bring the British divisions home and shut down the front, Robertson had become embroiled in a wearing contest with Joffre and the French government over reinforcements and the prospects of an offensive. By the end of the year the campaign threatened to create an ever wider rift between the British civil and military authorities, especially when on 23 December the war cabinet discussed the matter at a meeting from which Robertson was deliberately excluded. 'The new War Cabinet are really up against it,' recorded Maurice Hankey. 'They don't believe in Robertson's "Western Front" policy, but they will never find a soldier to carry out their "Salonika" policy.'[200] With Lloyd George, always the most sympathetic of leading British politicians to an eastern strategy, now at the head of the government and with the French once again pressing for more troops to be sent to Salonika, the outlook remained, as 1916 drew to a close, as unclear as it had ever been.

CHAPTER 5

The Troubled Year

Nineteen seventeen was a year in which the whole complexion of the war changed. Before the year was out, the Russians had effectively withdrawn from the conflict, and the United States had become a belligerent. In the present context the most significant development was a clear shift in the balance of power within the entente coalition. By the end of 1916 the increase in its overall military contribution had given Britain greater claims to equality in the direction of the allied war effort. The attrition of 1916 had severely weakened the strength, and more particularly the offensive potential, of the French armies on the Western Front. The problem was to become only too apparent in the mutinies which beset those armies in May 1917 following the failure of the Nivelle offensive. By contrast, the introduction of conscription meant that the British army would reach its maximum strength in the course of 1917. In addition, the fall of General Joffre in December 1916 had removed the man whom the French had attempted, by virtue of their larger armed forces, to elevate into a position approaching that of 'generalissimo'. With the Russian military machine also faltering, Britain had the chance to emerge for the first time as the dominant member of the coalition. The possibility existed, at least in the period before the Americans had time to deploy their full strength on the Western Front, that Britain could steer the allied war effort in directions more congenial to its own aims and ambitions.[1]

Political changes in Britain and France also indicated that the period of French preponderance might be coming to an end. In Britain the accession of David Lloyd George to the premiership suggested a reassertion of civilian control over the British war directorate and a reversal of the trend, characteristic of 1916, in which the military, and in particular Robertson as CIGS, had exercised the dominant voice in the control of British war policy. Though Robertson remained a considerable power in the land, Britain's political leadership now seemed stronger than at any time since the outbreak of hostilities. By contrast, the position of the French prime minister, Aristide Briand, despite recent changes to his government, looked distinctly weaker. Even the sacrifice of Joffre to the latter's parliamentary critics had failed to quell discontent within the civilian government. As 1917 opened, Briand's parliamentary majorities rose and fell, but the general trend seemed to be moving against him. The two governments which had presided over France's destiny between the outbreak of hostilities and 12 December 1916 had enjoyed an average life of fourteen months. From December 1916 until November 1917 there were a further three administrations with an average duration of less than four months. During the course of the year, the Sacred Union, which was always best seen more as a temporary truce than as the definitive end of party political dispute, began inexorably to fall apart. Even before the end of January Briand was obliged to face a third secret session of the Chamber of Deputies. According to the British ambassador in Paris, it was only the French premier's persuasive oratory and his skilful political manoeuvring, together with the widespread fear that a crisis might lead to the succession of Georges Clemenceau, that kept him in power.[2]

Yet it was by no means clear that all these changes and developments would work to the detriment of the campaign in the Balkans. Lloyd George had long shown himself to be the most favourable of leading British politicians to the Salonika expedition. His small War Cabinet was thought to be sympathetic to the prime minister's strategic vision and would be an important factor in counteracting the views of Robertson and the General Staff. As Lloyd George reminded an inter-allied conference in Paris in May 1917, he had always supported the Salonika campaign, often in opposition to the entire British government.[3] When Lloyd George became prime minister, Douglas Haig, the British commander in France, immediately confessed that he was 'afraid honestly that he may squander our resources on side shows, i.e. Salonika'.[4] Much would depend on the outcome of the new premier's internal power struggle with the British military led by Robertson. As the latter later reflected:

the constant aim of the new Prime Minister was to take the military direction of the war more and more into his own hands and to have carried out military plans of his own devising, which, more often than not, were utterly at variance with the views of his responsible military advisers.[5]

Nor was the French situation entirely clear-cut. Briand, though politically weakened, may well have come to the conclusion that his own government's survival was now dependent on the maintenance of the campaign in the Balkans. In December 1916 he had been obliged to remove General Sarrail from Joffre's control; the following month he faced what was effectively a vote of censure on the military and diplomatic conduct of the French government in Greece since 1 December, the date when a number of French sailors had been ambushed and killed; and Salonika was almost inevitably the first subject of discussion when the Chamber again went into secret session at the end of January. The question of Salonika and Greece remained 'his weak spot'.[6] On the other hand, the replacement of Joffre by Nivelle heralded, as in Britain, the beginnings of a reassertion of governmental authority over the military – in the French case, for the first time since 1914. From the interaction of such conflicting, even contradictory, determinants would the fortunes of the Balkan campaign in 1917 be decided.

Not surprisingly, it was in an atmosphere of considerable uncertainty that delegates from Britain, France and Italy assembled in Rome on 5 January to attempt to reach an understanding on the future role of the allied Armée d'Orient and on policy towards Greece. The three-day conference revealed many of the inherent tensions in Anglo-French relations and also the on-going divisions between Britain's political and military authorities. There was certainly an element of *déjà vu* about the proceedings. 'More conferences were held ... in regard to [Salonika] than to any other military question,' Robertson later recalled.[7] That in Rome suggested that few lessons had been learnt from the experience of the fifteen months since the campaign had begun. On the first day of the meeting Lloyd George invited the delegates to accept the British contention, reached after exhaustive examination, that the grave shipping situation precluded the despatch of further British divisions to Salonika. He did not, however, rule out reinforcements from Italy, since the sea route from Italy to the Balkans was comparatively short and reasonably well protected.[8] In response Briand, in the course of a forty-five-minute oration, argued that the question of Salonika was not really a military matter but one for governments, and there were times when governments should by-pass their military advisers and judge for themselves. When it was merely a question of transporting two or three divisions the French premier refused to believe that it was a physical impossibility. If the British government were to insist upon it, he was sure that transport could be found. With unwarranted optimism Briand declared that, with three more divisions, victory on the Salonika front would be a certainty, but to continue in the present, half-hearted manner might lead to disaster.[9]

Briand's had been an exceptional performance. 'As a piece of oratory,' remembered Lloyd George, 'it was the finest exhibition I have ever heard at any Conference.'[10] The French prime minister's appeal to have the question of reinforcements decided by governments alone was clearly an attempt to circumvent the known opposition of Robertson to any increase in the allied commitment to the Balkans. In the interval before Lloyd George replied to Briand on behalf of the British government, the tensions within the British delegation came to the surface. Robertson dropped a broad hint that his resignation would follow from any decision which ran counter to his advice. He did not know what effect Briand's oratory had had on the prime minister 'in regard to the wretched Salonika business', but he thought it only right to warn him that he could never sign an order for the despatch of further British divisions to Salonika. He told Lloyd George this 'as a friend' and hoped that he would not be compelled to say it to him 'as Prime Minister'.[11] Understandably, Lloyd George was 'rather annoyed at this and described it as holding a pistol at his head'.[12] Yet precisely what impact this scarcely veiled threat may have had is difficult to assess, for Briand's appeal to ignore Robertson's advice must also have had its attractions for Lloyd George, anxious as the prime minister was to curb the general's authority. At all events, when the conference reassembled he announced that, if eloquence on its own could transport troops to Salonika, Briand's speech would already have accomplished the task. Sadly, however, boats were also needed and Britain had none to spare.[13]

Inevitably, therefore, the discussions ended in deadlock. No agreement was reached in Rome concerning the question of reinforcements, nor was a precise role for the Armée d'Orient in 1917 defined. Robertson remained uneasy about the whole situation in the Balkans:

> Salonika is doing more to prevent us winning this war than anything else and we spend more than half our time over the wretched place. We had the French Government over here the week before last urging us to send still more troops to the place and last week we were in Italy engaged on the same mission. Fortunately I managed to get my way. But at the same time there is not much prospect at present of getting anyone away. I only hope that we shall not have serious trouble there.[14]

To add to his difficulties a new axis had emerged in Rome which Robertson could not have anticipated.

This resulted from the favourable impression which General Sarrail – who, unusually, had himself been summoned to the conference – had made upon the British prime minister.[15] As Frances Stevenson recorded: 'D[avid] says he is a remarkable, fascinating character, handsome, impulsive, full of fire.' In a private interview the French general pleaded with Lloyd George to give him a free hand in the Balkans. 'His idea was to march into Greece and shoot every man who attempted to stop his army.' Though Lloyd George drew back from such a strategy, he does appear to have offered Sarrail some reassurance. 'I promise you that whatever happens in the Balkans, I and my colleagues will see that you get fair play.'[16] According to Robertson, Sarrail 'completely captivated the Prime Minister who has formed the opinion that he is an exceptionally good man'.[17] Sarrail also appears to have made a more favourable impact upon Briand than might have been expected.[18] As a result, the British agreed in Rome that Sarrail should henceforth serve as commander-in-chief of the allied armies at Salonika, with all the national commanders accepting his orders for military operations, but retaining a right of reference to their own governments.[19] Sarrail had not obtained all the powers he would have liked, but for the time being his command appeared to be out of danger. Despite all the criticism made of him over the preceding months he had won a renewed vote of confidence.

Yet it proved difficult for Lloyd George to maintain his favourable view of Sarrail in the face of an overwhelming weight of contrary opinion. Lord Granville, the British diplomatic representative accredited to the Greek provisional government at Salonika, whom Lloyd George had invited to Rome to express his views on the situation, was emphatic that Sarrail was much disliked by all the allies represented at Salonika. He wondered whether it might not be possible to persuade the French government to recall Sarrail, since this would 'very greatly improve conditions and prospects' in the Balkans and the relations between the different nationalities.[20] In the course of 1917, moreover, Lloyd George became increasingly disillusioned with the whole Salonika venture. Other fields of battle began to arouse his enthusiasm – Italy, Palestine and even, for a while, the Western Front itself. His growing alienation from the Balkan campaign inevitably drew him closer, on this issue at least, to Robertson. A diversion of British troops from Salonika to support General Allenby against the Turks was not perfect from Robertson's point of view, but at least such troops would 'enjoy a better climate and be under British control'.[21] The partial rapprochement between Lloyd George and Robertson was evident when the delegates of Britain and France met again, this time at the Hotel Terminus in Calais, on 26 February, and heard Robertson declare that he and the prime minister were anxious that the first thing to be settled should be the scope of Sarrail's mission. Robertson pointed out that Sarrail's present plans envisaged an advance to Sofia as an ultimate objective. He considered, however, that this was most unlikely to be achieved, since it had always been recognized that such an advance would have to be combined with an offensive from the north on the part of the Russians and Romanians. As this was not presently possible, Robertson proposed that the conference should accept that, for the time being, the decisive defeat of Bulgaria was not a practical objective and that the mission of the allied forces should be limited to keeping on their front those enemy troops already there. This formula was accepted by Briand and his war minister, General Lyautey, though the French insisted on adding that Sarrail should be left to take advantage of striking the enemy if the opportunity presented itself.[22]

Notwithstanding this conclusion, and illustrating how rudimentary the processes of allied decision-making remained two and a half years into the conflict, Lyautey told Sarrail on 9 March to be ready to launch an offensive around 15 April. Astonishingly, the British seem not to have been consulted before this step was taken. The secretary to the War Cabinet, when drawing up a summary of the whole campaign in July 1918, could not date this decision with any precision between the Calais Conference of late February and that at St Jean de Maurienne in mid-April.[23] In Paris, however, the French political scene was once again in a state of confusion. Briand's government had not really been strengthened by the reorganization of the previous December and was widely seen to be at the mercy of the first serious internal or external disturbance. The crisis came with the mishandling of a relatively unimportant parliamentary debate on aviation by General Lyautey, after which the minister of war resigned. Briand had hoped that Lyautey's prestige would strengthen his own position, but in government the general had proved to be politically inept. Briand fought desperately for survival, but had finally to admit defeat. On 19 March Alexandre Ribot, the elderly minister of finance in the outgoing cabinet, succeeded in forming a government. In this the key post of minister of war went to Paul Painlevé and there was a widespread belief that he and not Ribot would be the real master of the situation.[24]

Painlevé, of course, had long been the most ardent champion of both Sarrail and the Armée d'Orient inside the French Chamber. There was even speculation that he might now bring back Sarrail to replace General Nivelle as commander-in-chief on the Western Front.[25] Certainly, Ribot's government and its successor, in which Painlevé himself became prime minister, represented the high summer of Sarrail's command and the period in which he had least to fear from his opponents. Indeed, Painlevé proved to be the most sympathetic to Sarrail of all the incumbents of the rue St Dominique during the course of the Salonika expedition. The general's liaison officer at the Ministry of War, Commandant Decrais, reported that Painlevé's attitude towards the Armée d'Orient was excellent, that he would provide the maximum possible supplies for the army and that Sarrail had a true friend in the new minister of war.[26]

Robertson, however, had learnt to live with the vagaries of French politics and clearly believed that Britain must not be deflected from its task. He was now looking for support from the First Sea Lord, Sir John Jellicoe.[27] The beginning of the German policy of unrestricted submarine warfare in February had created a potentially disastrous situation for the Allies. In April, the worst month, 850,000 tons of shipping were lost. Though the adoption of the convoy system in May greatly eased matters, the shortage of shipping remained a key determinant of allied strategy for the rest of the conflict. To an extent an overland route had to be developed to replace the supplies hitherto shipped from Marseilles and Egypt. At the War Cabinet in late March Robertson suggested that the time might not be far away when shipping considerations would require a reduction in the Salonika force. There was general agreement inside the War Cabinet that the army should either be diminished or that much greater military activity would have to be displayed to justify its continued existence. Lloyd George now undertook to discuss the whole question with Painlevé.[28] Meanwhile Robertson, intent on following up the favourable reception which his views had received, drew up a fresh memorandum on the situation at Salonika in which he reminded the government of the allied policy that had been agreed at Calais in February. He insisted that the expedition had been a failure from the start. This had been foreseen by the General Staff at the time and he himself had never missed an opportunity to argue that the campaign had no military justification and would probably never produce results commensurate with the expenditure of men and equipment which it entailed. The Admiralty, he noted, found the strain on shipping resources unendurable and considered it better to leave the enemy established at Salonika than to have to provide the naval resources required for the maintenance of the allied armies. Seeking to make the most of Lloyd George's change of heart, Robertson argued that there was ample scope in Palestine for the profitable use of any British troops that could be got away from Salonika. Results to be obtained there were likely to contribute far more to winning the war than anything that could be achieved in the Balkans.[29] On 4 April the War Cabinet had a preliminary discussion of the possible effects of withdrawing some British forces from Salonika to reinforce the Palestine expedition, but it was agreed that no final decision would be taken until after Sarrail's impending offensive.[30]

As the days passed, however, the spectre of political chaos in Paris resulting from a British refusal to toe the French line was once again brought into play. The period of instability following Briand's fall from power rekindled the rumour, encouraged by Lord Esher, that Caillaux might soon gain office at the head of a government committed to a compromise peace.[31] Robertson was determined that this old argument should not be used once more to paralyse Britain's initiative. He sought the backing of General Smuts, soon to become a member of Lloyd George's War Cabinet and the member of the prime minister's inner circle whose views approximated most closely to Robertson's own. There was no sign of compromise now, as Robertson stated that the expedition had been wrong from the start and would be wrong until the end. It always had been and still was motivated by purely French political purposes. If Britain was not careful it might lose the war in a vain attempt to bolster up the French government. Ribot was not, he thought, likely to remain prime minister for very long and it would be folly to undertake further commitments in the Balkans merely to save him. For more than a year Robertson had been trying to get the government to take greater control over the war effort. To 'attempt to win the war by constantly giving in to unsound French proposals was folly'. The best solution would be to come away from Salonika altogether. This, perhaps, was not possible for the moment, but there was no need on that account to increase British liability still further.[32]

Robertson was not sure what to expect from Lloyd George, but his own tactics were clear. When Sarrail launched his offensive and when, as Robertson confidently predicted, this failed to achieve very much, he, Robertson, assured of the support of the Admiralty, would then 'go bald-headed for a reduction of the forces in Salonika'.[33] The problem, as he recognized only too well, was that the British were 'tied to the tail of the French'. Robertson refused to believe that the French nation attached the sort of importance to the campaign which its government claimed. 'It has been a government blunder from the start and I have no doubt it will be the end of the government.'[34] When the War Cabinet met on 18 April it was reported that Painlevé had taken steps to speed up Sarrail's arrangements and that an attack should be anticipated in the near future. From the Admiralty, Jellicoe provided the sort of support which Robertson was looking for when he argued that the submarine danger in the Mediterranean made it impracticable to continue to supply the Salonika expedition with stores or to evacuate the sick and wounded. Jellicoe recommended the immediate reduction of the British contingent and advocated a complete withdrawal if the government anticipated the war continuing beyond 1917.[35] The War Cabinet therefore decided that, after the impending attack, Britain should withdraw its forces from the field of operations and fall back on a defensive line in the vicinity of Salonika.[36]

Even Lloyd George had come to regard Sarrail's forthcoming offensive as the last chance which could be given to the Armée d'Orient and on the following day, in conference at St Jean de Maurienne, he informed Ribot that, if considerable success were not achieved, the British government would have to give serious thought to a reduction of troops because of the gravity of the shipping situation.[37] In the discussion which followed, Ribot and Painlevé showed less opposition to this statement than Lloyd George had anticipated, but they were clearly looking for a *quid pro quo* in terms of British assistance to clear up the situation in Greece, involving if necessary the removal of the supposedly Germanophile King Constantine from his throne.[38] The British prime minister formed the opinion that a bargain could be struck along these lines to ensure a reduction in the British forces in the Balkans.[39] In the end it was agreed that the whole question should be considered again at a further conference to be held in Paris in two weeks time.

For the first time Robertson was optimistic that this would result in getting some troops away from Salonika, 'if not all of them in due course ... The great thing [was] to make a start.'[40] He reminded the War Cabinet that, as it would take six or seven months for Britain to withdraw all its troops from Salonika, it was advisable to begin the process at once. He proposed that at the next conference the French government should be informed that Britain could not possibly maintain its present forces at Salonika and that it intended to bring away two brigades of mounted troops and one division immediately, this to be followed by the whole or greater part of the remainder as soon as the shipping situation allowed. Anxious lest his political colleagues should once more fall victim to French persuasiveness, he suggested that the preliminary shipping orders for these moves should be issued at once. Lloyd George, however, preferred to act more circumspectly. He pointed out that it would be very difficult for the British delegation at the Paris Conference to have to insist on the withdrawal of troops on whose presence the French had always placed such importance, unless they were able to offer some compensation to the French government. Probably the most acceptable compensation from a French point of view would be a free hand to deal with King Constantine as they thought fit. But opinion in the War Cabinet remained divided and it was not possible to reach a firm conclusion at this meeting.[41]

The following day brought a meeting of the full Imperial War Cabinet, the body created by Lloyd George to allow for representation by the dominions in the higher management of the British war effort. Here the prime minister explained that he and the junior foreign office minister, Lord Robert Cecil, were going to Paris to attempt to arrive at a clear understanding with the French on the subjects of Salonika and Greece. Cecil revealed the extent to which the machinations of French policy had baffled British observers when he confessed that he was not sure what the objectives of successive French governments had been. There seemed to be a faction in France which aimed at utilizing the war to secure some special financial or political position in Greece. This was matched by a real unwillingness to restore peace and harmony to Greek affairs. Whenever there had seemed to be an opportunity to get matters back on to a more satisfactory footing, it had somehow been lost. But Cecil had come round to Lloyd George's position that, if Britain intended to press for the withdrawal of some of its forces from the Balkans, it would be necessary to offer the French an appropriate *quid pro quo*. Unless the British could give the French some satisfaction on the Greek question, an estrangement might result which could react on the general prosecution of the war. Tentatively, Cecil suggested that France could be offered complete political control in Athens, subject to a definite undertaking that it would embark on no extreme or wild policy towards Greece. He thought that by placing the whole responsibility on the French, with a clear understanding of the kind of line to be pursued, it might be possible to secure a more moderate and successful policy from them than under existing conditions. The members of the Imperial War Cabinet assented to this policy and so Lloyd George and Cecil set out for Paris, ready to give up Britain's independent voice in Greek affairs.[42] Cecil, however, still hoped that France would be prepared to give Constantine one further chance, whereas Lloyd George was now convinced that the Greek king's deposition was the only possible solution which the French would contemplate.

Almost certainly, Lloyd George's was the more accurate assessment. Briand's perceived weakness towards the Greek regime had been an important factor in the erosion of his own power base in France and there had been a widespread expectation that the arrival of a new government in Paris would lead to a stiffening of policy in Athens. French agents in Greece, frustrated by Briand's long months of hesitation, were now able to predict a new policy and urge the prompt removal of Constantine from the Greek throne.[43] By his authority and persuasiveness Briand had kept opposition to his policy within limits, but once he left office 'it was as if the lid had been taken off the pot'.[44] The Ribot government itself made it clear that the previous policy of undue moderation towards Constantine would now be abandoned.[45] The major determinant of Ribot's attitude towards Greece was undoubtedly the insecurity of his own parliamentary position. The new French prime minister had already told Lloyd George that public opinion in France was very disturbed about the whole question of Greece. There was an intense feeling against Constantine and something drastic would have to be done when the Chamber met on 24 May, otherwise no French government would be able to survive the likely storm of indignation.[46] Paul Cambon judged that, in moving towards Constantine's deposition, Ribot was as always thinking in terms of what would make himself popular – 'everything in order to attract the applause of the crowd' – for his mind was too preoccupied with retaining power to encompass broader issues.[47] Meanwhile, there were clear indications of the movement of opinion inside France. A series of articles was appearing in the press almost daily calling for the dethronement of Constantine and the establishment of a Greek republic.[48]

For once, therefore, the British delegation seemed to hold most of the diplomatic cards when representatives from the two countries gathered in Paris on 4 May. Over the next two days Ribot seems to have been thoroughly outwitted by Lloyd George and Cecil. Britain's willingness to accept French diplomatic control in Athens had, of course, already been accepted by the Imperial War Cabinet, but Cecil, in raising the question of unified political action, suggested that the single diplomatic representative should be British. When, therefore, Painlevé and Ribot protested that it would be difficult to have a French military command and a British political one, Cecil and Lloyd George were able to present the proposal of a French diplomatic chief as a concession granted as a result of the conference discussions. The French now agreed to recall Guillemin and replace him with a man of 'exceptional position' acceptable to the British government, while the latter undertook to withdraw Elliot and substitute a chargé d'affaires or diplomat of subordinate status. The Italian and Russian governments were to be invited to consider similar action.

From this 'concession' Lloyd George was able to turn the discussions to the question of the withdrawal of the British forces at Salonika. He argued that the essential shipping needs of the allied populations could be met only if the Salonika force were reduced to that required to hold an entrenched camp surrounding the harbour. The method of reducing the army could be settled later, but Britain considered it imperative to make immediate arrangements for the withdrawal of one division and two cavalry brigades beginning on 1 June. Only if Sarrail achieved an overwhelming victory would the situation be reconsidered. Predictably, the French delegates raised the political consequences involved. They urged the impossible position that the French government would be in *vis-à-vis* its parliament and people if British troops were withdrawn leaving French troops where they were. For once, however, the British remained firm and their resolutions were reluctantly accepted *ad referendum* to the French cabinet.[49] Thus the conference accepted in general terms the very bargain which the Imperial War Cabinet had identified as its tactical goal a few days earlier, but which Lloyd George now described as 'the maximum concessions towards the French point of view that he and Lord Robert Cecil ... could make'. In return for abdicating responsibility in Athens, where the situation appeared distinctly unpromising, Britain had taken a first tentative step towards the evacuation of its forces from the Balkans – a policy for which the General Staff had long pressed and which Lloyd George had now come to accept, convinced as he was that the Armée d'Orient no longer offered prospects of material success in the war.

The usual roles of the Allies in their wartime diplomacy had thus been reversed. The French had been presented by Britain at an inter-allied conference with a *fait accompli* in terms of a decision reached prior to the meeting. Not surprisingly, the Grand Quartier Général did not like this trend and warned that, if it were repeated, it might lead to the political direction of the war passing increasingly into the orbit of the British government.[50] Yet the French themselves had some cause for satisfaction in terms of their control over the situation in Greece, where their plans for acting against Constantine were in fact already well advanced. General Pétain rather let the cat out of the bag, much to the dismay of his civilian chiefs. When the conference discussed the question of withdrawing troops from Salonika, Pétain mentioned that this would be very difficult granted that the French government contemplated sending a force into Thessaly and also one to Athens. 'Upon hearing this,' noted Robertson, 'they all jumped up like Jack-in-the-boxes and tried to make out that they had intended no such thing.'[51]

Much now depended on the outcome of Sarrail's offensive. Given the limited resources available to him and the ability of the enemy to counter any increase he might receive, the prospects of success did not look good. Undeterred, Sarrail proceeded to make his greatest military effort of the whole campaign. In the event, his spring offensive proved a complete failure, reducing still further his tarnished military reputation. At the cost of about 14,000 casualties, no appreciable territorial gains were made. British losses were disproportionately high – something like a quarter of the total casualties suffered by British troops in the entire campaign. 'Nowhere was it found possible to drive the desired wedge into the Bulgar front.'[52] Though this seemed like a minor setback when placed against the magnitude of Nivelle's defeat on the Western Front, Sarrail's position looked less secure than for many months. At all events it was clear that the impetus to withdraw British troops would now be reinforced.

Meanwhile, French plans for military action against Greece continued apace. War Minister Painlevé instructed Sarrail to prepare for joint operations in Thessaly and Athens. If Britain objected to this, Sarrail was to go ahead with the Thessaly operation and prepare for the Athens expedition in case that in Thessaly provoked incidents in the capital justifying French intervention. The two operations would thus take place either simultaneously or consecutively, depending on Britain's attitude.[53] A visit to Paris by Painlevé's opposite number, Lord Derby, persuaded the War Cabinet that a further meeting of the two governments was necessary to find out more about French policy.[54] Robertson remained concerned that his political masters would agree to the French proposals and leave the French to carry out the occupation of Greece by their own means and in their own way. He warned that the French plan involved gambling on the collapse of Greek resistance – a gamble which, if it did not come off, might involve Britain in unforeseen military operations.[55]

Delegates assembled for the latest inter-allied conference, this time in London, on 28 May. At an informal meeting between Cecil and members of the War Cabinet just before the conference opened, it was agreed to support a demand for Constantine's abdication in favour of one of his sons.[56] But at a preliminary meeting with Ribot,

Lloyd George urged that France should not insist on British support for the proposed march on Athens as this would split the War Cabinet.[57] The chief point at issue in the conference itself turned out to be the manner in which the will of the Allies could best be put into effect. The British, anxious for a peaceful outcome, thought that if the king refused to abdicate voluntarily the country should be starved into submission. The French, by contrast, pressed for an immediate occupation of Athens which, as the British saw, was more likely to involve armed conflict with Greece. In the event it was substantially the British proposals which were accepted. Sarrail would establish those military posts in Thessaly which were necessary to secure control over the Greek harvest in the most unprovocative manner possible. Once this was done, the Allies, through their designated representative, the former French minister and governor-general of Algeria, Charles Jonnart, would demand Constantine's abdication and withdrawal on the grounds of his continuing violation of the Greek constitution. If he refused, a complete blockade would be established to secure his submission. If he moved his troops to resist the Allies in Thessaly, Sarrail would be at liberty to occupy the isthmus of Corinth, with Britain contributing a nominal contingent.[58]

Lloyd George seemed well content with the outcome of the London Conference, though Robertson had less cause for satisfaction. As Frances Stevenson, the prime minister's mistress, recorded:

> The French departed today, and D[avid] is very pleased with the result of the Conference. They have decided to depose Tino, and establish a republic in Greece – this much against the will of our military people, but D overruled them. Robertson was inclined to be nasty, but D turned on him roughly. 'We are entitled to your military advice, General Robertson', he said sternly, 'which you have not yet given. The *policy* is ours.' D said he crumpled up, and was as meek as a lamb for the rest of the Conference.[59]

Doubts about Sarrail's suitability for so delicate a mission in Greece persisted. Inside the British Foreign Office Harold Nicolson produced a survey of the recent complaints that had been made against him. The Russian foreign minister considered Sarrail untrustworthy owing to his political ambitions; the Serbian prime minister had stated that all the Allies were critical of his conduct of the recent offensive; and the Italian commander-in-chief regarded him as a serious threat to 'a situation already sufficiently grave'.[60] Not surprisingly, though, it was Robertson who raised the matter at the War Cabinet, pointing out that the consensus of opinion was that Sarrail had concerned himself more with the political aspects of the campaign than with the actual conduct of military operations. The War Cabinet concluded that, whatever instructions he might receive from the French government, Sarrail could never be relied upon. It was agreed that his removal should be demanded in exchange for British acquiescence in the deposition of King Constantine. Lloyd George now undertook to write to Ribot to express the War Cabinet's unanimous view that Sarrail should be replaced in the command of the Armée d'Orient.[61] The British premier noted that reports received on the recent offensive reflected very gravely on his fitness to lead a great force. Competent judges on the spot believed that, with proper leadership, an excellent opportunity had existed to deal a heavy blow to the enemy. Yet the operations appeared to have been a fiasco.[62]

Ribot discussed Lloyd George's despatch with the president of the republic, admitting to Poincaré his own lack of confidence in Sarrail and suggesting a readiness to relieve him of his command once the operation in Thessaly – the necessary military preliminary to the deposition of the Greek king – had been carried out.[63] The French War Committee considered the problem on 7 June. As usual it was Painlevé who sprang to Sarrail's defence, stressing the difficulties which any general would have faced if placed in command of troops of differing nationalities, but even he agreed that the matter would have to be re-examined after the Thessalian operation.[64] In response to Lloyd George, Ribot stressed that it would be politically inexplicable for Sarrail to be replaced at the very moment when the allied agreements on Greece were about to be put into effect and when the commander of the Armée d'Orient needed all of his authority.[65] Painlevé went further. Through unofficial channels he impressed upon Lloyd George that, in the wake of widespread mutinies in the French army on the Western Front, the British prime minister had chosen the worst possible moment to present an ultimatum to the French which, if it were accepted, would bring the Ribot ministry crashing down and the alliance with it. Painlevé insisted that once the Greek question had been settled the situation might be very different. The French government could then claim that Sarrail's mission had been accomplished and that he could now be withdrawn without disgrace.

Yet it may be surmised that what Painlevé really envisaged was Sarrail's triumphal return to Paris to take over some higher position than the command of the Armée d'Orient.[66]

Little then had changed since the very beginning of the campaign. In June 1917, as in the autumn of 1915, the internal politics of France were being allowed to determine the course of allied policy in the Balkans. Now as then, Lloyd George was among those prepared to let anxious cries about the dangers to the alliance override military considerations. On 11 June the War Cabinet agreed to express the British government's satisfaction at Ribot's willingness to transfer Sarrail from the Macedonian command, but to accept that this move should not take place until after the existing critical situation in Greece had passed.[67] But, as the British ambassador in Paris warned, the course of events mapped out by Ribot was by no means assured. If, when the acute phase of the Greek crisis had passed, the French government acceded to the British demand, there would be a great outcry from the political Left in Paris that the general's successful handling of the situation was being rewarded by his recall. It was just as probable that the French were merely playing for time and that, when the Greek affair was over, they would find another excuse for not bringing Sarrail back.[68]

In the event, Constantine's deposition was effected more smoothly than might have been expected, though not without the imposition of further strains on the Anglo-French alliance. Cecil now heard that the French government had decided to demand the Greek king's abdication by means of a note to the Greek government, giving the latter only one day in which to reply, and that this demand would be enforced not by the seizure of the Greek harvest but by the landing of troops at the port of Piraeus, adjacent to Athens. Urgent representations were made to the French government to revert to the London decisions which had made no mention of an occupation of Piraeus under any circumstances.[69] Cecil reminded Ribot that the resolutions of the London Conference contemplated one course and one course only in which the Allies were to use force and that was if troops were moved by Constantine in order to resist the Allies in Thessaly.[70]

Ribot was running a high-risk strategy, but his parliamentary position left him little alternative. He had promised Constantine's head on a charger to the Chamber of Deputies and had cut his own line of retreat, so that if the Greek king did not give way peacefully it would be impossible for Ribot to back down. Viewing the situation from London, Paul Cambon was unimpressed, judging that Ribot's vision was restricted to the corridors of the parliamentary Chamber, at whatever cost to the alliance. He was appalled by his own government's lack of frankness and embarrassed at having to convey Ribot's assurances to the British government that no landing was contemplated at Piraeus at the same time as he was hearing from his brother that this was precisely what had been arranged between Painlevé and Sarrail.[71] The British War Cabinet was left very much in the dark. It was not clear whether troops were being landed or not, nor indeed what was happening. The news coming out of Athens was continually contradicted by assurances from Paris. But some British ministers perhaps preferred it this way, and it was suggested that, whether or not French actions were entirely in line with what had been contemplated at the recent inter-allied conference, they might none the less be the most efficient means of dealing with the situation.[72] So it proved. Constantine gave in and quietly surrendered his throne.[73]

Where then did this leave Sarrail? The British War Cabinet, meeting after the Greek king's deposition, conceded that this was a move which Sarrail had consistently recommended. No steps would therefore be taken for the present to remind the French government of its undertaking to transfer the general from Salonika.[74] An attempt by the Foreign Office to present the French with a lengthy indictment of Sarrail's military incompetence was blocked by Lloyd George.[75] It looked, therefore, as if British policy might simply be allowed to drift. After Constantine's deposition and the return of Venizelos as Greek prime minister, the cabinet's newly formed War Policy Committee argued that the changed situation, with Greece converted from a questionable neutral into an active ally, meant that it was no longer necessary to cling to the policy of withdrawing to an entrenched camp surrounding Salonika.[76] But could the allied forces achieve anything more constructive than hitherto? Robertson declared himself ready 'to carry out any policy that may be laid down', but felt 'quite sure that there is no reasonable prospect of a military success in the Balkans unless the Bulgars crumple up in a manner which at present we have no reason to suppose they will do, or unless the Russians put in a really big attack from the north'.[77] Senior ministers felt uneasy about the lack of clarity in the British position. Lord Milner for one was concerned that Lloyd George should not go to France for the next inter-allied conference before the War Cabinet had formulated a more precise policy. If he were to go 'without our knowing our own minds', he would be 'as wax in the hands of any French minister'. As far as Milner was concerned, the whole matter was still 'the most hopeless impasse and muddle imaginable'.[78] Major-General Webb Gilman, Milne's chief of staff, was brought back to London to give evidence to the War Policy Committee. Robertson, Gilman reported to Milne, wanted 'me to bring out that our military forces in Salonika are materially assisting French and Italian commercial and political aims without any corresponding gain for ourselves'.[79]

Largely under Milner's influence, the War Policy Committee now recommended that British policy in the Balkans should aim at the gradual withdrawal of British divisions from the fighting line with a view to the formation of a reserve either to be used to support a great offensive in conjunction with a Russian attack on Bulgaria, or preferably for transfer to some other theatre. No opposition should be offered to any French proposals for the withdrawal of part of their Balkan army for independent operations in Syria or elsewhere, provided this did not involve the use of British troops or shipping.[80] This policy, including the immediate withdrawal from Salonika of one division as a reinforcement for the British Expeditionary Force in Egypt, was adopted by the War Cabinet on 20 July.[81]

The British delegates were thus more than usually well prepared when the inter-allied conference assembled in Paris five days later. Discussions centred almost entirely upon the question of the immediate withdrawal of a British division. Robertson stressed that the Allies were making poor use of their resources. There were 600,000 allied troops in the Balkans and only 400,000 of the enemy. He surveyed all the ground which had been covered by the War Policy Committee and stated that an offensive from Salonika would have no practical advantage unless it was combined with a Russo-Romanian attack from the north, of which there was now little prospect. In reply Ribot reminded the British that when the question of removing a further division had arisen at an earlier conference, it had been agreed that a French division would be withdrawn first. Deadlock now ensued and all that could be agreed was to postpone a decision until yet another conference had been held in London.[82] Sarrail's command was not even discussed. Private conversations before the conference opened between Painlevé and the British representatives had the effect of excluding all formal consideration of this issue.[83]

This outcome inevitably came as a serious disappointment to Robertson. The CIGS stirred himself to one further effort. The only policy he had discerned at Paris was to hold the ground currently held at Salonika, keep all troops there and wait until the following year to see what would happen. This was 'a poor apology for a policy' and he begged the cabinet to try to arrive at a clear strategy for the future in the Balkans. He could only repeat his long-held conviction that the Salonika force would never materially contribute to the winning of the war, but that the entente might lose it if it failed to maintain sufficient strength on the Western Front and sufficient shipping to meet all requirements. If the apparent Russian collapse continued, the Allies must be ready to put more men on the Western Front 'where undoubtedly the issue of the war will be decided'.[84] Robertson's patience was clearly wearing thin. Scathingly he noted that at the most recent Paris Conference forty-three men had talked about the Salonika issue for three days, arriving at no decision except to have another conference. He did not think it an exaggeration to suggest that the generals and politicians of Britain and France had spent at least half their time in the war worrying over 'the wretched matter'.[85] Additionally, Robertson remained convinced that Sarrail's continued presence at the head of the Balkan army was a fundamental problem. While ministers protested that Sarrail's removal would provoke a serious crisis, leading possibly to the fall of the French government, Robertson persuaded the War Cabinet to reverse an earlier decision and ensure that the question of Sarrail's replacement was definitely raised at the next conference.[86]

At the London Conference the two sides rehearsed old arguments. Lloyd George announced that the British determination to withdraw one division for use in Palestine had not wavered. Ribot countered that the French government too had not changed its mind. If Britain acted against French advice, he would be obliged to reveal this to the Chamber. Would a serious dispute between the two governments, he asked, be justified by the single division in question? Astonishingly, Ribot announced that he would prefer Britain to reinforce its armies in the Middle East at the expense of the Western Front rather than Salonika. In the face of British resolution, however, the French premier

gradually shifted his ground and pressed for an undertaking that no
more British troops should be withdrawn beyond the one division
presently under discussion. On the suggestion of Lloyd George, the
conference adopted the conclusion that the British government,
recognizing the need to maintain the strength of the allied forces at
Salonika, undertook not to withdraw any further British troops unless
unexpected events occurred, in which case the matter would be
submitted for further discussion.[87] Thus the Salonika question had at
last been in some way settled. The withdrawal of the British division
had been agreed to, but in order to secure this concession the British
government had effectively committed the remainder of its forces to
the Balkan theatre for the duration of the war. Sarrail, moreover,
remained in place. Lloyd George had not 'found an opportunity' to
raise the question of his replacement with the French ministers while
they were in London.[88] Robertson could not disguise his disappointment with his political masters:

> The conference lasted two days. It was of the usual character and resulted
> in the usual waste of time ... [Lloyd George] is a real bad'un. The other
> members of the War Cabinet seem afraid of him. Milner is a tired,
> dyspeptic old man. Curzon a gas-bag. Bonar Law equals Bonar Law. Smuts
> has good instinct but lacks knowledge. On the whole he is best, but they
> help one very little.[89]

After the May offensive no further operations of much account
were attempted during the remainder of Sarrail's command. This
was the result of the heavy fighting in Flanders and Italy during the
late summer and autumn, the collapse of the Russian front and the
intervention of the United States in the war, which all combined to
fix the final trial of military strength more and more on the Western
Front. The whole Macedonian theatre once more lapsed into a state
of stagnation.[90] While the allied forces continued to outnumber their
opponents, their effective strength was lower than it had been for
fifteen months.[91] Until his dismissal in December, moreover, Sarrail
remained a major obstacle to the smooth running of the campaign.

The fall of the Ribot government in September made it still more
difficult to broach the question of Sarrail's position, as Painlevé now
became president of the Council. Even Robertson suggested that it
would be best to wait until the French political situation became
clearer.[92] Painlevé hinted to Lord Derby that an unofficial approach

by Lloyd George might lead to Sarrail resigning 'of his own accord',[93] but no mention was made of this subject, at least in the formal discussions, when British and French delegates, including Lloyd George and Painlevé, consulted at Boulogne towards the end of the month. Indeed, Sarrail heard that Painlevé's private interviews with Lloyd George and General Cadorna of Italy had produced a most favourable effect. 'The Allies once more found in him [Painlevé] the faithful defender of the Armée d'Orient and its head.'[94] Sarrail himself now clearly wanted to return from Salonika to be rewarded with a prominent position on the Western Front, perhaps at the head of a combined Franco-American army. Painlevé's failure to secure this outcome caused the general's political supporters considerable disappointment. Suggestions that Sarrail should return to France were greeted with the reply that it was imperative to keep him where he was. Painlevé must have known that, while he probably had the power to save Sarrail's existing command from British attacks, to have elevated the controversial general to a more senior posting and to have placed a left-wing general at the top of an essentially conservative army hierachy would have been to court political, and possibly military, disaster.[95]

For their part the members of the War Cabinet remained wary about doing anything which might disturb the French political edifice. Granted that Painlevé's eventual replacement, Georges Clemenceau, was an avowed opponent of both Salonika and Sarrail, this might seem strange. But it is striking that a Clemenceau ministry was not the outcome envisaged by British observers – almost until it happened. Back in June the War Policy Committee had determined to avoid anything which might threaten the stability of the existing French government, since the only alternative 'was M. Caillaux and his advent to power would mean peace'.[96] Ambassador Bertie was convinced that too much animosity existed between Clemenceau and President Poincaré to permit the former to become president of the Council. If, by any chance, Clemenceau did succeed in forming a government, he had 'so many personal enemies ... that any ministry formed by him would not last any useful time'.[97] Logically, Clemenceau's prospects in the context of a left-inclining Chamber did not look good. As late as mid-October the British liaison officer, Edward Spears, mapped out possible future developments on the French political horizon without mentioning the Tiger's name:

> There is great talk of the possibility of a Briand Ministry in which
> M. Viviani would enter, which would mean the reinstatement of the
> Malvy Party ... The general opinion is that M.Painlevé is quite incapable
> of remaining President of the Council owing to his great weakness in the
> debate. I am told that in the Chamber, when making a speech, he looks
> like a Parson expounding a text which he, himself, does not understand.[98]

On 11 November, just two days before Painlevé's government collapsed, Lloyd George, fearful of the possible implications for the
future of the entente, tried to persuade his friend, Albert Thomas, to
join Painlevé's cabinet and urged the French premier to attempt to
form a new coalition on the model of his own, with Thomas as
minister of war and Briand playing the part of 'the French Bonar
Law'.[99] But in practice President Poincaré knew where his duty lay.
Having exhausted the available candidates of the Third Republic and
eschewing the suggestion that he should take the unprecedented step
of combining the presidency with the premiership, Poincaré had no
alternative but to turn to Clemenceau.[100]

In Britain the last months of 1917 saw a waning of the influence
of Sir William Robertson. His fortunes sank steadily, like those of the
western offensive of this time, into the mud of Passchendaele, and
he came increasingly to be outshone by the former director of
military operations, Sir Henry Wilson. As Robertson's long-term
struggle with Lloyd George moved ever more in the latter's favour,
the most consistent and vehement opponent of the Salonika campaign was gradually pushed into the wings. But for the time being no
one was prepared to countenance the resumption of major operations
in the Balkans and, with the French army and nation drained by the
disastrous Nivelle offensive on the Western Front, Painlevé defined
the mission of the Armée d'Orient as to protect conquered territory
against any enemy attacks.[101] For the most part, the close co-operation
between Painlevé and Sarrail was such that the general's actions at
Salonika were shrouded more than ever in mystery. 'In fact,' complained Robertson, 'he seems to be allowed to do as he wishes and
apparently no soldier dares to interfere with him.'[102]

The whole outlook changed with the fall of Painlevé's ministry on
13 November. His government had proved to be the weakest in the
history of wartime France and it was the only one which fell as a
direct result of an adverse vote in the Chamber of Deputies, this
despite the fact that he had done much to enhance his reputation by

his role in the re-establishment of stability in the French army following the spring mutinies. Painlevé had shown some skill in the game
of political and parliamentary manoeuvres, but perhaps did not have
the stature needed for the highest office, especially in time of war.
'He lacks the qualities of a prime minister,' judged Paul Cambon.[103]
More importantly, Painlevé's government had been constructed on a
narrower political base than any since the declaration of the Sacred
Union. The Union's ultimate demise had been heralded by the
resignation back in August of the right-wing Catholic Denys Cochin,
who claimed that his presence in the cabinet gave it 'an inaccurate
appearance'.[104] At the formation of his own ministry, Painlevé's determination to retain the services of the outgoing premier, Alexandre
Ribot, as foreign minister had been enough to ensure the non-
participation of the Socialists. As a result his ministry of nineteen
ministers and eleven under-secretaries was drawn almost exclusively
from the Republican Socialist and Radical Socialist groupings. In the
end his government was submerged beneath a mounting tide of
political scandal in which it was clear that Sarrail himself was implicated.[105]

Inside the British War Cabinet the hope was now expressed that,
in the event of Clemenceau succeeding in forming a ministry, it might
be possible to approach the French once more with a view to Sarrail's
removal.[106] Shortly afterwards, with rumours circulating of an impending enemy attack on the Armée d'Orient, the War Cabinet
agreed to send the French government a copy of Lloyd George's
letter to Ribot of 6 June requesting Sarrail's replacement and to
indicate that the views of the British government had not changed in
the meantime.[107] Lloyd George himself wrote privately to Clemenceau, as soon as the new French government was installed, to point
out the mistrust with which Sarrail was regarded in British army
circles.[108] In the French Council of Ministers Clemenceau read out
the correspondence exchanged between Ribot and Lloyd George in
June and expressed a willingness to satisfy British demands by recalling Sarrail. Henri Simon, the minister for the colonies, warned of
possible difficulties in the Chamber of Deputies, but in the end the
council left Clemenceau free to tell Lloyd George that Ribot's promise
would now be honoured.[109]

In practice Clemenceau had little choice. By this time the extent of
Sarrail's involvement in French political intrigue had begun to enter

the public domain. Back in August, while in London for an inter-allied conference, Ribot had received an urgent despatch from his minister of justice, René Viviani, informing him that a series of confidential documents and private letters relating to the Salonika campaign had been found in the safe of the spy known as Almereyda.[110] Poincaré learnt that Almereyda had received the documents from an officer on Sarrail's headquarters staff, who had Sarrail's authorization to hand them over in order to create a campaign inside France in favour of the Salonika expedition. Sarrail, however, was not apparently implicated in the second stage of the process, by which the documents had passed into enemy hands.[111] The pieces found in Almereyda's safe, which all dated from 1916, included several letters from a Captain Mathieu on Sarrail's General Staff to his friend Charles Paix-Séailles, who was a clerk in Painlevé's ministry. In these letters Mathieu had sought to show how Sarrail was being persecuted by both Joffre and Briand.[112] Among the politicians whom Paix-Séailles was instructed to contact, in order that they might use their influence to counteract the hostility and distortions of Joffre and Briand, were Caillaux and Painlevé.

The arrest of Almereyda had proved an immediate embarrassment to Painlevé and posed a considerable threat to Sarrail. Commandant Decrais kept the general in close touch with the development of the scandal in Paris. He advised caution in a delicate situation and warned that matters would become serious if Paix-Séailles and Mathieu were brought to trial. If they were not charged, Sarrail would have to cover Mathieu or mete out some nominal disciplinary punishment.[113] Under pressure from Painlevé the government had repeatedly put off a decision on the matter. In late August he protested forcefully against the attempts that were being made to link Almereyda and Sarrail.[114] But by early October Painlevé did not think it would be possible to delay judicial proceedings against the two men much longer.[115] Sarrail seemed less aware of the gravity of the situation and suggested that it would be unjust to punish Mathieu.[116] He was 'completely indifferent' to the whole affair and suggested that his enemies would have to find a more effective stick with which to beat him.[117] By the beginning of November, however, such accusations were being bandied about in the French press that the government had no alternative but to bring Paix-Séailles to trial under the espionage law of 1886.[118] The feeling was gaining ground that the whole administration was riddled with corruption and that only a complete overhaul of the government could refurbish its tarnished reputation. It was very much on this basis that Clemenceau returned to power. With pressure also mounting for action against Caillaux and the former interior minister, Louis Malvy, whose indulgence towards left-wing pacifism had long been a cause for concern, Sarrail's fate was all but sealed.

Ironically, then, this major irritation in inter-allied relations in the Balkan theatre was on the point of resolution when the Allies made their first substantive step towards the creation of a unified command structure. The setting up of the Supreme War Council, based at Versailles, at least provided a forum for continuous dialogue. Here on 1 December Clemenceau frankly conceded that all that was known about the situation at Salonika was that nothing was known. He had asked Sarrail for a report on the situation, but had received only a brief reply which was in no sense a report. The French government proposed to make important changes in the command, but as these were not finally settled and were of purely French concern, he could not discuss the matter further.[119] Even with the prospect of fruitful developments now that Clemenceau was in power, Robertson became irritated as soon as the discussion moved on to Balkan affairs. To Henry Wilson he passed a scribbled note: 'we always get on to this subject and waste all our time over it.'[120] It was the cry of a soldier who had long seen the prosecution of the war compromised by the intrusion of politics and politicians. Perhaps, even now, he could not bring himself to believe that any French government could actually dispense with Sarrail's services. Be that as it may, Sarrail was recalled a week later.

The resolution of Clemenceau had thus succeeded in doing what countless inter-allied conferences had failed to achieve. After two bitter years Sarrail's command was at an end. The changing balance of power within the coalition, which had probably left Britain as the senior partner overall, had not enabled it fully to dominate the diplomacy of the Balkan campaign. The French meanwhile had continued to view the expedition primarily in terms of their domestic politics. Not until the end of 1917 did the French government accept that it could not expect whole-hearted co-operation from Britain at Salonika while as distrusted a commander as Sarrail remained in post. Strikingly, Sarrail's recall resulted in none of the dire political consequences which had for so long been predicted. Indeed, the general's dismissal produced hardly a ripple on the surface of French politics – though this reflected above all the entirely different regime which Clemenceau's arrival in power entailed.

The lasting impression of 1917 is of the waste of time involved in periodic meetings of the leaders of the two countries. At conference after conference the same issues had been raised with no meeting of minds and no means of resolving the resulting deadlock. As Paul Cambon put it after one such occasion: 'The discussion was interminable. It was the same with Briand last year and with Ribot two months ago. No decision was reached.'[121] As Lloyd George had come to realize, these gatherings were not really conferences at all, but meetings of people with preconceived ideas who desired only to find a formula which could superficially reconcile them. They were nothing but 'tailoring' operations at which differing plans were crudely stitched together.[122] Be that as it may, as the war entered its final year the Salonika campaign was still a serious impediment to the smooth functioning of the wartime alliance between Britain and France.

. . . .
Underlying Motives

I t was certainly galling for British political and military leaders to
know that their participation in the Salonika expedition was largely
a function of the requirements of French politics. But even if, as
William Robertson argued, 'the whole thing is a French political rant',
this situation was still capable of rational analysis and justification.[1] If
it was indeed the case that any attempt to withdraw troops from
Salonika or even to replace General Sarrail, let alone to terminate the
whole campaign, might precipitate a governmental crisis in France,
this was not a matter to be taken lightly. The ending of France's
wartime political truce might lead to an entirely different type of
government emerging – one which might not be willing to sustain
the country's war effort. British observers were understandably
alarmed at such a prospect, since France's withdrawal from the war
would have made it virtually impossible for Britain to continue the
fight. This was particularly the case in 1917 when Russian commitment to the common cause came increasingly into question, while
America's contribution remained largely a matter of potential rather
than reality. Thus, as Kitchener had pointed out to the Dardanelles
Committee as early as October 1915, Britain was not really faced by
a simple choice between what was politically expedient for France
and what was militarily desirable for Britain. The question was altogether more complex.[2]

As the campaign progressed, however, a further and even less
comfortable realization dawned on British observers: that France
might be using its presence in the Balkans to further long-term aims
for the postwar world. France, after all, was not in a position where
it could afford to deploy its military resources indiscriminately. In
terms of strict logic it had less choice than Britain as to where the

war should be fought. The paradox must be faced, however, that for three years France maintained a large army in the Balkans, whose military activity was severely limited in both scope and effect until the last few months of the war, while at the same time many of its national departments were under constant enemy occupation and German forces seemed within striking distance of Paris. France stuck steadfastly to its Balkan strategy even though half its coalfields, the iron ore of Briey and Longwy and a large proportion of its overall industrial capacity had fallen into enemy hands. British perceptions of what their French allies might be up to were vague and ill-defined, based more on instinct than concrete evidence. Typically, Robertson had felt since the beginning of the expedition that there was 'something behind the French mind in regard to their policy in that part of the world', but what it was he had never been able to discover.[3] Gradually, however, the belief mounted that in some way or other the French were not really playing the game, or at least that they were engaged in a very different game from the British.

Lord Kitchener was perhaps the first British leader to voice his misgivings. In March 1916 he warned his colleagues on the War Committee that the French were using the war for purposes of future expansion in the East.[4] The following week he suggested to Douglas Haig that France was aiming to develop its influence in the Eastern Mediterranean and would not now fight actively to beat the Germans in France.[5] Robertson had heard that there was 'a great deal of Finance as well as Politics mixed up in this French enterprise', which explained why the French would not think of coming away from Salonika if they could help it.[6] He believed that France and Italy had 'conflicting aims in that part of the world' and that they refused to make concessions 'for reasons other than those they give'.[7] By October Lord Hardinge, the permanent under-secretary at the Foreign Office, while admitting that he still did not 'quite know what the French were up to in Greece', judged that they had some 'ulterior object in view' which amounted perhaps to an aspiration to 'a sort of position of eventual protector of Greece in the Eastern Mediterranean'.[8] Such views developed during the course of 1917. As Lord Robert Cecil told the Imperial War Cabinet in May, there seemed to be 'a section in France which aimed at utilising the war in order to secure for France some special political or financial position in Greece'. He sensed a real unwillingness to restore peace and harmony to Greek affairs.

Whenever there had seemed to be an opportunity to get things back on to a better plane, it had somehow been prevented.[9] Reviewing the problem for the Cabinet Committee on War Policy in the summer, Lord Milner concluded that the French were 'playing a game of their own', but he did not believe that they themselves quite knew what they wanted, except to exercise a predominant influence in Greece and to get some economic advantage out of it in the future. The policy was one of 'indefinite grab' and Milner believed that Sarrail was its living embodiment, being interested only in 'schemes of future exploitation'.[10] Even the king voiced concern about what was going on and was informed by Foreign Secretary Balfour that 'the Italians suspect the French and the French suspect the Italians of entertaining schemes (vague perhaps but not negligible) which will enable them respectively to use Greece as a pawn in the game of rivalry which they are playing in the Eastern Mediterranean'.[11]

The lack of precision in these British interpretations of the motivation of their leading ally is striking. It reflects above all the inadequate understanding with which the French political structure was viewed in London during the course of the war. No one seemed really sure where the ultimate direction of French policy lay, nor what its purpose was. As late as July 1918 the usually well-informed secretary to the War Cabinet, Maurice Hankey, could confide to his diary only that 'there are and always have been subtle influences, possibly of a financial character, behind the French attitude to the Salonica expedition'.[12]

Observers on the spot believed that they had a better under-standing of French motives in the Balkans. From Salonika itself the British commander, General Milne, focused attention on Sarrail's personal role, suggesting that the French general was doing all he could for French interests in the Near East after the war.[13] Such concern with the postwar world was evidently galling for Milne, who argued that it was costing Britain a good deal in men, money and material, with no compensatory advantages, to place Greek affairs entirely in French hands with a view to future French supremacy in the Eastern Mediterranean. The British commander wondered how long this process of Britain being made a catspaw was going to go on. He would have had no objection to these French activities if they were helping to win the war, but in practice they seemed to have little to do with the main issues.[14]

By far the clearest evaluation of the long-term aims of French diplomacy in the Eastern Mediterranean was enthusiastically conveyed to the Foreign Office in March 1917 by Sir Francis Elliot, the British minister in Athens. It came from the head of Britain's intelligence activities in Greece, Compton Mackenzie.[15] Attempting to explain the French position Mackenzie argued that it was scarcely surprising that once Sarrail had secured the military safety of Salonika and realized, as he must have realized in the face of the prevailing consensus, the impossibility of a serious advance, that the French brain should have started to look around for something to do. The reproach often levelled against Sarrail of being too political a general accorded, Mackenzie thought, with the lazy British way of thinking he was 'up to something', without trying to find out what it was. Yet it might be assumed that the whole of Sarrail's policy since the British refusal to consider an advance from Salonika had been dictated by nothing but political considerations, even though Sarrail had always been clever enough to mask French political ambitions under the plea of military necessity. Throughout the tortuous negotiations with Greece the safety of the Armée d'Orient had always been an effective excuse for any action the French had taken and it was only now being realized that French policy in Greece had nothing whatever to do with the army's well-being. Yet even now, to Mackenzie's irritation, the explanation of French policy in the Near East was that Sarrail, as a member of the 'Financial Democratic Party', was engineering a scheme for French Jews to make money, that his personal dislike of King Constantine had unreasonably coloured his whole outlook, or even that he aimed at a military coup in France itself, after the style of General Boulanger. It seemed to be generally assumed that it was Sarrail who was dictating the policy and that, if Sarrail were removed, the policy would change. Mackenzie, on the other hand, believed that the contrary view – that Sarrail was but the agent of his own government's schemes – was equally possible.[16]

Mackenzie argued that political schemes of a far-reaching nature had been behind the arrival of the French naval mission under Commandant de Roquefeuil in January 1916.[17] As early as February Venizelos had been approached with a view to creating a revolution in Greece and by April the occupation of the country by French forces had been definitely envisaged. De Roquefeuil's ambition was 'to make Greece the halfway house to a French domination of the

Levant'.[18] Any action the French wished to take in Greece had been facilitated by the attitude of the British government which, throughout 1916, had consistently allowed them to take the lead in every matter connected with Greek politics. At the time of Mackenzie's memorandum, March 1917, the French were still persevering in their efforts to occupy Greece and the moment had now come, he believed, to decide on British policy. The French now wanted to occupy Greece in order to thwart Italian aspirations in the Near East. The reason they hung on so tenaciously to Salonika was probably their nervousness over their own claims to Syria. 'Salonika was the expression of their aspirations in the Near-East.'[19] It was time, Mackenzie concluded, to stop British policy any longer being the rubbing rag of the ill-considered aspirations and unreasonable ambitions of two rival Latin nations.

Mackenzie's analysis was just what Elliot had been waiting for. The previous November he had warned Foreign Secretary Grey of the way in which France was determined to obtain complete control over Greece so as to be able to use that country as a stepping-stone between Marseilles and Syria.[20] Now, with the Foreign Office in new hands, Elliot reiterated that the French had a definite policy to bring Greece under their exclusive or at least predominant influence.[21] 'Both the French and the Italians', he argued, 'are constantly looking to the future and to the partition which is to come after the war, while we are devoting our whole faculties to the one object of winning it.'[22]

Inside the Foreign Office Mackenzie's report seemed initially to have a less conspicuous impact. George Clerk, head of the War Department, minuted that it was 'worth reading', but commented that Mackenzie lacked knowledge of the general political position of the British government. But the memorandum was clearly in the minds of Foreign Office officials as they reacted later that month to a despatch from Bertie in Paris, which indicated that the recent fall of the Briand government was likely to precipitate a stiffening of French policy in Greece. Harold Nicolson now argued that an early opportunity should be taken to discuss with the French the essential objects of allied policy in Greece and to discover what they were really aiming at in the Near East. Discussions had previously been limited to the local problems of the moment, but Nicolson thought it clear that the French saw matters in broader terms and that Greece was to play an important role in their future Mediterranean policy –

a policy to which, on imperial grounds, Britain could not remain indifferent. The essential question, he concluded, was whether or not Britain was going to allow France to assume a protectorate over Greece and the Eastern Mediterranean. Despite his earlier reservations, George Clerk also now showed the impact of Mackenzie's analysis. He argued that the time had come, not only for a frank discussion with the French government about Greece, but also for Britain, when met as it would be by old arguments, to insist that the question of Greece was vital for Britain and that it would no longer tolerate the lines of present French action.[23]

With Foreign Secretary Balfour absent in the United States, Harold Nicolson now drafted a long and detailed despatch to Bertie in Paris. After amendments by Hardinge and Balfour's deputy, Lord Robert Cecil, it was signed by the latter. The despatch argued that there was an urgent need for a full and frank discussion of the attitude to be adopted towards Greece. Though there was no specific indictment of French as opposed to British policy, the whole tone of the telegram was critical of French actions and suspicious of French motives. It was argued that the behaviour and language of several French agents in Greece had created the suspicion that an influential section of French opinion was keen to use the Balkan campaign to secure something like a permanent protectorate over Greece.[24] Had this telegram been despatched, it is possible that Britain and France would have gone some way towards sorting out their long-standing, but sometimes scarcely spoken, difficulties over the Salonika campaign. Bertie, however, had no opportunity to put the Foreign Office's observations before the French government as Prime Minister Lloyd George was still unwilling to risk a political crisis in the alliance. On his intervention the despatch was never sent.

British perceptions of French motivation were clearly an important determinant in the shaping of the wartime alliance, but the reality of that motivation must also be explored. More than three decades have now elapsed since the appearance of Pierre Renouvin's pioneering article on French war aims in the Great War.[25] In that time much important work has been published to supplement Renouvin's analysis.[26] But some of the difficulties and deficiencies of documentation to which Renouvin drew attention remain an impediment to a full understanding of France's aspirations for the postwar world.[27] In one important respect at least, historians have confirmed the perceptions of contemporary British observers. The decision-making processes of the Third Republic were extremely confused and confusing. French politicians may have secured a domestic political consensus on the need to repel the enemy invasion, but this did not extend to agreement on what the fruits of victory over Germany and its allies should entail. By the beginning of 1917 there existed a 'shambles of faction-fighting and parallel policies', a development which enabled France's representatives abroad 'to indulge their taste for independent action with disconcerting results'.[28] 'In effect,' writes Anthony Adamthwaite, 'an organized anarchy prevailed, with key decisions reached informally in huddles of senior ministers.'[29] Even during the three-year history of the Salonika campaign the distribution of power at the top of the French government and therefore the policy-making process itself varied considerably. Officials at the Quai d'Orsay enjoyed greater latitude under Briand and Pichon, Clemenceau's foreign minister, than they did under Delcassé and Ribot; within the Foreign Ministry the influence of individual functionaries varied according to the political master they served and did not always match the nominal career hierarchy of the Quai d'Orsay; until November 1917, but not significantly thereafter, Poincaré used the presidency of the republic to exercise a considerable if not easily defined influence; prime ministerial power was at its greatest under Clemenceau. 'Thus', writes David Stevenson, 'the exact locus of power varied with the personalities concerned.'[30]

The pressure for territorial and commercial expansion in the late nineteenth and early twentieth centuries was not, however, restricted to a few policy-makers at the heart of the French government. It grew, as research in the colonial sphere has shown, from organized pressure groups of parliamentarians, soldiers, businessmen and missionaries.[31] A recent study of France's military war aims in western Europe suggests a similar model, 'in which a series of close-knit and interlocking groups, many of whose members held important positions in government, were in a position to formulate policy'.[32] It was thus more from a ferment of ideas than from a set of agreed policies that French war aims emerged. This poses problems for the historian, not least as a result of the common French practice of filing memoranda in archives with little indication of who wrote the document, still less of who read it.[33]

What then did the French hope to get out of their commitment to the Balkans? When David Lloyd George visited Paris in February 1915 he received an interesting indication of the motivation behind Aristide Briand's enthusiasm for a Balkan campaign – at a time, of course, before the expedition had got under way and before the whole idea became inextricably bound up with the political position of General Sarrail. As Lloyd George reported, the French were very anxious to be represented in any expeditionary force. Briand thought it desirable that France and Britain should establish a right to a voice in the final settlement of the Balkans by having a force there. He did not want Russia to feel that it alone was the arbiter of the fate of the Balkan peoples.[34] In a future which might see Russian power enhanced, it was important that Greece, Serbia, Bulgaria and Romania should realize that Russia was not the only country to interest itself in their welfare. Indeed, they should be so constituted as to form a barrier to Russian omnipotence and possession of Constantinople, and to all the exclusive advantages which that possession would offer.[35] As will be seen, Briand's anxiety about Constantinople was highly significant in the light of subsequent events.

To an extent Briand appears to have been responding to pressure groups within and outside the Chamber of Deputies, which were clamouring for the protection of French interests, especially economic ones, in the Mediterranean. Relatively early on in the war the Chamber voiced its concern at the Mediterranean situation. When the question of Italian intervention came up for discussion in April 1915, Georges Leygues, a future president of the Chamber Foreign Affairs Commission, reminded his colleagues that France had vital interests in this area. When the war was over France would need a period of economic reconstruction. This could be secured only if France used the war to acquire and safeguard bases and lines of communication without which industrial and commercial prosperity would be impossible. Such considerations needed to be borne in mind in any diplomatic negotiations with Italy concerning the Mediterranean.[36] A few months later similar concern was expressed at the damage which would result to French interests if Germany were allowed to pursue its political and economic ambitions 'en Orient' and thus create an immense economic powerbase extending from Hamburg to the Persian Gulf by way of Constantinople, and from the North Sea to the Indian Ocean.[37]

With the Salonika expedition under way Briand revealed that his own strategy and diplomacy were largely determined by comparable considerations. In the course of the first secret session of the Chamber he argued that, in recognizing the Balkans to be an essential theatre of the war, he and his colleagues had been acting with an eye to the future. States like France could not allow their prestige in the countries of the east to be lost, and it was as a result of the decision to remain at Salonika that such a catastrophe had been avoided.[38] Later in 1916, when appearing before the Chamber Foreign Affairs Commission to give an account of the Balkan expedition, Briand revealed the overriding importance which he attached to the area when he stated that the age-old Eastern Question, in its broadest sense, would remain the vital issue even after the war was over. The countries which had assured for themselves a preponderant voice in its solution would be masters of the world.[39]

As the war progressed, the propaganda agency established under the direction of Briand's *chef de cabinet*, Philippe Berthelot, became increasingly concerned with economic expansion in the Balkans.[40] From Bucharest his agent at the French legation, Edouard Tavernier, argued that if Romania entered the war it would be necessary to gear French propaganda towards the replacement of the central powers by France in the postwar Romanian market.[41] As Tavernier noted, 'our future political influence should be a function of our economic influence'.[42] If, after defeating the enemy on the field of battle, France found itself vanquished on the economic plane, it would be as if nothing had been achieved: 'On the contrary, we should leave this terrible conflict, completely diminished and impoverished.'[43] Within the Quai d'Orsay the political director, Pierre de Margerie, added his weight to the idea of a campaign of economic and political propaganda in Romania, to make that country an outpost for France of the Latin civilization, protecting it against both German and Slav expansion, while providing a counter-weight to the growing Italian influence in the area.[44]

The conclusion seems inescapable. The development of French propaganda in the Near East, encouraged by agitation in the Chamber of Deputies, assumed a deeper significance than simply influencing indigenous peoples to win their confidence so as to help defeat the enemy in the current war. It was inextricably bound up with the preparation of France's position in the postwar world – a position in which the Eastern Mediterranean was seen to occupy a crucial role. In the light of this underlying motivation the continuing French commitment to the Armée d'Orient takes on a new importance.

France's interest in the Near East was, of course, no new phenomenon. Its connections with this part of the world were centuries old. As long ago as 1535 a treaty had been concluded with the sultan, Suleiman the Magnificent, which granted France far-reaching rights and concessions – the so-called 'capitulations'. By the nineteenth century, France, as the leading creditor nation of the prewar era, held the bulk of Turkey's public debt, controlled the Imperial Ottoman Bank and administered the *régie des tabacs*. Similarly, in Syria, France had acquired a virtual monopoly of transport facilities and was in control of all but two railway lines when the war broke out.[45]

'Constantinople in short was the heart of an Empire enmeshed by immense French political interests and financial investments amounting to 3,000 million francs.'[46] French investment in the Ottoman empire by 1914 was more than three times that of Germany, the next largest investor. French organizations, interested in the affairs of the Near East, had understandably proliferated and were constantly alert to anything which might undermine French predominance in the area. It was the apprehensions of such groups which were voiced in the Chamber during 1915 and 1916 and to which Briand and others proved responsive. In this general Mediterranean strategy Greece occupied an important but not overriding position. French trade with Greece had increased substantially since the end of the nineteenth century and stood at the outbreak of the war at around 24 million francs *per annum*. Even so, France occupied only the fifth place among Greece's trading partners and the volume of its exports to Greece was now tending to stagnate.[47] France, then, possessed interests in Greece which it understandably sought to safeguard and augment pending the ultimate decision of its conflict with the Central Powers.

As the war progressed, however, Greece came to assume an importance out of all proportion to France's prewar interests there or indeed to the fact that allied troops were based in Greece's northern provinces. As a Greek scholar has put it: 'France was playing for infinitely higher stakes. Greece was merely the strategic stepping-stone to the Balkans and the Ottoman Empire where France hoped to preserve its immense pre-war economic interests, especially in Constantinople, and if possible to win additional concessions after

the war in Syria and Asia Minor.'[48] The key development was the
secret arrangement of March 1915 by which Britain and France jointly,
but largely at British insistence, agreed to the acquisition of Constantinople by Russia, providing the war was fought to a successful
conclusion. This would have represented a first key step in the dismemberment of the Ottoman Empire, a development which the
British had begun to envisage the previous November.[49] And for
Russia, possession of Constantinople and the Straits might be the
prelude to its ultimate supremacy in the Near East and the development of a Mediterranean naval capacity.[50] Hitherto it had been
France's traditional policy to defend its influence in the Ottoman
Empire as a whole rather than to seek the empire's destruction. For
years France had tried to check the slow disintegration of the 'sick
man of Europe'. Even in its participation in the Dardanelles Campaign
– necessary for national pride and its national interests – France had
not aimed to destroy the Ottoman empire.[51] Delcassé had hoped that
the taking of Constantinople by Anglo-French forces would be
compatible with the maintenance of the empire, which was necessary
'to safeguard France's political and economic interests'.[52] As the
diplomat George Picot wrote in instructions he prepared for himself
prior to those negotiations which led to the Sykes–Picot Agreement
of 1916, the partition of the Turkish Empire was to be deplored. Its
'feeble condition' had happily offered France 'limitless scope' for the
expansion of its moral and economic influence in the area.[53] Not
surprisingly, as rumours of the agreement with Russia began to reach
the Chamber Foreign Affairs Commission, considerable disquiet and
dissatisfaction was expressed. Many still hoped that British and French
forces would reach Constantinople before the Russians did.[54]

A cardinal principle of French foreign policy had thus been
breached – but with only the very reluctant consent of the government. Bertie reported the French view that the Quai d'Orsay would
have been ready to take a firm line towards Russia if the British
government had shown any disposition to support the French. But
the former had seemed to be in a hurry to yield everything to Russia.[55]
Delcassé's instinct had been to play for time but on 12 March the
French hand had been forced when Britain formally conceded Russia's
claim to Constantinople and the Straits subject to the war being
fought to a successful conclusion. Looking back on this event in May
1917, President Poincaré wrote:

I have regretted more than anyone, and I have not ceased to say so in the Council, that France was dragged along in the wake of Britain in a policy ... which gave Constantinople to Russia and of which I only knew what was explained to us at the end of 1914 and in 1915.[56]

French diplomacy had now to prepare itself for the dismemberment of the sultan's realm. Consideration of territorial war aims, in this part of the globe at least, could not be postponed until hostilities were over. France's existing perceptions of the Mediterranean balance of power had been dramatically overturned, and it could only acquiesce in Russia's proposed gains if it managed to secure comparable advantages. As Poincaré explained, 'everything is inevitably linked. We can only support Russia's claims in proportion to the satisfaction we ourselves receive.'[57] Clearly, France was now anxious to compensate itself elsewhere in the region. Its opportunity derived from the inclusion in the Constantinople agreement of a clause to the effect that the promise to Russia was dependent upon France and Britain realizing their own aims in the Near East and elsewhere. France's problem was that while Russia and Britain were well placed geographically to enforce their claims – the one on the shores of the Black Sea and the Caucasus and the other from Egypt – France as yet had no such base.[58]

In the first instance French claims were likely to focus on Syria and Cilicia, which were no more than 'the counterpart of and legitimate compensation for the considerable rights and interests which we have sacrificed to Russia'.[59] But it was also likely that France would look again at the whole question of its standing throughout the Eastern Mediterranean. In this situation Greece and the Balkan peninsula in general assumed a new importance. At the Grand Quartier Général the conclusion was reached that in future France would need the support of a strong and friendly Greece. It could no longer count on Turkey and if, after the war, France were to occupy Syria alongside British, Italian and Russian influence in the Levant, it would need an additional *'point d'appui'*.[60] When, therefore, at the beginning of 1917 Britain and France began tentatively to discuss the possible terms of a future peace, Berthelot reminded Paul Cambon that the Balkans were of direct interest to France and that their settlement was entirely a function of the cession of Constantinople to Russia.[61]

The promise made to Russia in March 1915 was one factor lessening French enthusiasm for the Dardanelles campaign. This expedition has been described as a bid 'for the last link in the British power chain encircling the future Levantine Empire from Cyprus and Suez to Aden and the Persian Gulf'.[62] As such it scarcely appealed to many French minds determined to use the war for the construction of specifically French spheres of influence. Before the attribution of Constantinople had taken place, the Senate Foreign Affairs Commission expressed its anger at the French government's acceptance of a secondary role in a region where France possessed the right of command.[63] Clemenceau insisted that British command at the Dardanelles meant 'the abandonment of our control in the Mediterranean',[64] but French interest in the operation inevitably waned as its chances of gaining anything tangible from it diminished. As the Salonika expedition got under way, the Grand Quartier Général urged that a French presence should be maintained at Gallipoli – but only because of the undesirability of leaving Britain in total control of the situation.[65] In practice France preferred Salonika as a base for the sphere of influence which it now sought in the Balkans.[66] There was perhaps more than nominal significance in the French governmental order of 7 October 1915 by which the announcement of the formation of Sarrail's Armée d'Orient was made. The Gallipoli force, previously known as the Corps Expéditionnaire d'Orient, was now reduced to the title of Corps Expéditionnaire des Dardanelles. The Salonika army thus became the expression of France's aspirations 'en Orient', while that at the Dardanelles, pursuing now an essentially Russian goal, was symbolically reduced in status.[67]

Developments in relation to Russia and the Ottoman Empire were not the only factors affecting France's standing in the Near East in the early stages of the war. After being wooed by both sides, Italy renounced its allegiance to the Triple Alliance and concluded the secret Treaty of London with the entente on 24 April 1915. By this Italy was promised the south Tyrol, Trieste and Istria, many of the Dalmatian islands and reversionary rights to Turkish possessions if there were to be a colonial partition. Italy would thus emerge at the end of the war as an Adriatic and Mediterranean power of the first magnitude. In view of its own growing interest in the Balkans, France came to regard the prospect of too great an Italian expansion with some apprehension. From Rome the French ambassador, Camille Barrère, warned that Italian motives for participation in the Balkan expedition were far from disinterested. Italy hoped that in raising its standard in the Near East it would stake its claim to rewards commensurate with its military effort.[68] French agents in Greece quickly reached similar conclusions. From Salonika the director of the *Mission Laïque*, Lecoq, argued that France needed to create a strong Greece to act as a barrier against further Italian ambitions.[69] Greece was indispensable, reasoned de Fontenay, the former French minister in Albania, for the equilibrium of the Mediterranean. Greece stood as the obvious counterpoise to Italy and its ever-growing appetite for territorial expansion.[70] Was France, he asked, going to sacrifice its vital Mediterranean interests in order to satisfy present friends who, in the not too distant future, would once again become rivals? With Serbia requiring a long period of reconstruction at the end of the war, only Greece could provide France with the support which it would need.[71] The Balkans thus focused a power struggle between France and Italy for the right to exert a preponderant influence in the postwar situation. In some despair Sir Francis Elliot noted that both nations were constantly looking to the future and to the partition which would come after the war, while Britain alone was devoting its 'whole faculties to the one object of winning it'.[72]

The ambitions of two of France's current allies – Russia and Italy – thus exercised a marked effect on the way France viewed its own position in the Near East, a position which had been materially altered by the claims and aspirations of these two powers. But French policy in the Balkans was also determined by its appreciation of the war aims of its current enemy, Germany. Both Britain and France were conscious of the underlying expansionist push eastwards which helped fashion German strategy in the war. For Britain this posed a threat to its continued presence in Egypt, to its interests in the Near and Middle East and to the route to the Indian empire. The British mind, however, never really saw the Balkan campaign as a barrier to German expansion. It was understood that the Salonika expedition might make it more difficult for Germany to draw upon the resources of the Ottoman empire by blocking its path to Constantinople, but few British observers regarded the Balkans as the theatre in which the future destinies of those great powers with interests in the Near East would be determined. The same, however, was not true of France. One French commentator gave a startling twist to the logical order of priority among his country's war aims:

Even in the case where Germany, exhausted and half-defeated, agreed to return Alsace-Lorraine to France and to grant Belgium its full independence, if she were still able to realize her ambitions in the east, she would have obtained such an advantage that there would only exist enough room in Europe for one great power – Germany.[73]

As the Grand Quartier Général concluded, the Berlin–Constantinople rail link was of vital importance to Germany, representing 'the most precious guarantee that she could obtain with a view to future negotiations, while waiting for it to become in her hands, once peace has been concluded, her most powerful instrument of domination over Asiatic Turkey'.[74] German aspirations in the Near East forced France to defend its own interests there. In engaging in military activity in the Balkans France was seeking not merely to defeat the central powers but to nullify specific German ambitions for the postwar settlement which ran directly counter to its own. The danger was that, if France did not act decisively while the war was still in progress, Germany would be able to renew its push to the east, with Greece as a base, once peace returned. What ends would then have been served, de Fontenay rhetorically enquired, by the Salonika campaign and the great sacrifices which it had entailed?[75]

For a variety of reasons, then, the war obliged France to re-examine the bases of its authority and influence in the Eastern Mediterranean and forced upon the French the realization that the postwar balance of power in this part of the world would be very different from that to which they had grown accustomed. Greece, in particular, came to acquire a new importance for France which it had never previously held. It is against this background that the presence of a French army in northern Greece must be viewed. The Armée d'Orient inevitably became as much an instrument of France's political and diplomatic ambitions as of its military policy. No one was more conscious of this fact than the chief agent of French policy in the Near East, General Maurice Sarrail. Writing after the war was over, Sarrail disclaimed all intentions beyond what were proper in a military commander: 'I was in the East not to build the postwar world but to attain, through the war, a military result.'[76] His line of conduct was simple: to carry out the policy of the Allies not for the 'after-war', but for the war itself. An examination of Sarrail's activities at Salonika, however, reveals that the general's ingenuous behaviour extended no further than the pages of his memoirs. Ineffective as a military commander he may have been, but as the leading architect of a planned invisible French empire for the postwar world he proved singularly adept. Moreover, it was this use of a military occupation during a war against the central powers to carve out for France a postwar sphere of influence which would exclude current enemy and current ally alike which was so abhorrent to Britain. While the British realized that, for strategic reasons, France could not simply ignore Greece, they viewed with distaste the subordination of the military aspects of the Balkan campaign to the fostering of France's postwar influence.

It was above all in the field of financial and commercial affairs that Sarrail was most active. The French military commander showed himself to be acutely interested in the economic well-being of Salonika and its hinterland. Salonika was by no means a poor choice as a base for French commercial penetration and expansion. Its crucial geographical position meant that it inevitably dominated the economic life of the Balkans and its influence radiated throughout the Eastern Mediterranean. The Society of the Port of Salonika, which had been responsible for its construction and exploitation, was Turkish in name but, because of overwhelming financial involvement, French in practice.[77] In addition, the Bank of Salonika, whose capital was almost exclusively French, was closely connected with the great French financial houses. As the French consul noted, 'its co-operation will be vital for us in the commercial expansion which is bound to result at the end of present events'.[78] Sarrail himself gave a clear view of his own thinking in a long despatch to Briand at the beginning of August 1916. He clearly wanted Macedonia to be treated separately from Greece. Because of its military presence, France exercised an absolute control over the imports coming into Salonika. Its situation in Macedonia was therefore unprecedented – tantamount to an economic sovereignty. The position of Salonika itself, with a quarter of a million inhabitants and the port of transit for the whole of the Balkan peninsula, offered particularly favourable prospects for French industrialists and merchants to replace the prewar Austro-German domination of a very sizeable market. In addition, Sarrail argued that when he was finally able to launch an offensive from Salonika, this held out the hope of bringing Serbian and Bulgarian territories within the orbit of the port. As far as articles not restricted by the blockade were concerned, French industry should be forcefully encouraged to export as much as possible so as to create, while the war was still in progress, 'the habit of buying French products and the taste for them'. The need was to draw the merchants of Salonika both politically and economically into the French orbit. Import permits should therefore be granted on a scale commensurate with the great economic future which lay open to France in Macedonia.[79]

Lecoq noted with satisfaction that Sarrail had a clear understanding of the role to be played by the army which he commanded in the extension of French influence. It was, Lecoq argued, entirely within the scope of the Armée d'Orient that it should assist in the founding of schools which would spread the French language and, by extension, French influence. Undoubtedly, the army had a primary military task to accomplish once the long-awaited reinforcements arrived and when the climate and the political situation in the Balkans permitted, but in the meantime it should not forget its duty to leave behind it in Macedonia traces other than those of blood. It should bequeath something permanent and durable in the form of increased economic activity with France. At the time that Lecoq wrote in July 1916, the army was busy drawing up a commercial dossier to put French and Macedonian merchants and businessmen in touch with one another. Special contacts had already been established with Lyons through the enthusiasm of its radical-socialist mayor, Edouard Herriot, with the result that Macedonian industrialists would be represented at the next Lyonnaise trade fair. Under the influence of his officer, Intendant Bonnier ('one of the most open and precise minds in the Armée d'Orient whose industry matches his clarity of thought'), Sarrail had put his signature to a circular letter which would be widely distributed among commercial organizations in France. Lecoq concluded that France must continue to interest itself in the Salonika market, which offered a potential commercial outlet whose extent Frenchmen had still to appreciate.[80]

Sarrail's thinking was entirely in line with these sentiments. The task of the Armée d'Orient was self-evident:

> We should prepare for the postwar world by the immediate introduction of our products and our brands in the areas reconquered by our armies. Thus we shall safeguard the interests of the populations which we must bring under French influence and the future of French industry and commerce whose expansion in the East, more than anywhere else, must follow the victory of our arms.[81]

The general's circular letter to the presidents of French chambers of commerce, dated 1 August 1916, described the organization at Salonika of a 'Commercial Bureau for French Importations'. Sarrail expressed the conviction that they would wish to be associated with an enterprise whose aim was the immediate creation of an outlet for French industry, and one which would greatly expand after the war. 'To develop French exports at the present moment is to prepare for victory and to assure ourselves in advance of its benefits.' Sarrail explained that the creation of the Commercial Bureau under Bonnier was a response to a unique situation in which the Macedonian market found itself devoid of goods and in which French suppliers faced no serious competition. So Sarrail proposed to act as liaison between French producers, who would write to inform him of the nature of their goods and the quantities they were able to supply, and potential buyers in Salonika. Once contact had been established, the two parties would be able to conduct their business directly. A sure and stable clientele would thus be built up for French manufacturers which would assure for France 'in the postwar world the first place in this market'.[82] At the Quai d'Orsay Berthelot commented that Sarrail was preparing for the economic conquest of Macedonia by profiting from the exceptional situation resulting from France's military occupation.[83]

At all events Sarrail must have been heartened by the response to his initiative in France. On 20 August Lecoq reported that his last postbag had contained thirty requests from French merchants wishing to start trading with Salonika,[84] and in under three months an increase in business in the order of 600,000 francs was recorded. Organizations such as the Salonika Commercial Bureau thus represented 'a precious hope for the future', and should be regarded as a model to be copied elsewhere.[85] Bonnier was encouraged by the success of the new initiative. In a fortnight he had received 300 letters from French industrialists whom he had put in touch with business houses in Salonika. His only regret was that the administrative authorities in France had sometimes been intransigent over the question of export permits. Bonnier hoped that such restrictions would be removed from all goods unrelated to warfare. All the efforts of France should be galvanized into facilitating the extension of its economic interests in the area, a basic prerequisite of increased French influence in the Near East.[86] Indeed, by the end of January 1917 Bonnier was noting with satisfaction that permits were now being granted by the Customs

Office in Marseilles instead of the Derogations Commission in Paris. This was calculated to speed up considerably the administration involved in the export of goods to Salonika and reflected 'the interest which the government of the Republic shows in the development of relations between France and the great port of the Aegean Sea'.[87]

As 1917 opened Bonnier sensed that a fresh spirit was animating French businessmen and industrialists. The chambers of commerce had responded splendidly to Sarrail's initiative and had given their full support. The example of Edouard Herriot in creating a permanent Lyons–Macedonia Committee had been followed in Dijon, Grenoble and Marseilles. In addition the chambers of commerce in Bordeaux, Rouen, Toulouse, Beauvais, Orléans, Angoulême, Nancy, Belfort, Besançon and Limoges were in the process of organizing regional committees, which would be grouped together in Paris. Initial results by which 75 per cent of goods arriving at Salonika were French were such as to promise the widest extension of French economic power in Macedonia and, by extension, throughout the Near East.[88] Apart from putting the two sides in touch with one another, the Commercial Bureau offered several more specific services. By building up a collection of French samples and catalogues open to inspection by local merchants, the Bureau was able to supply potential buyers in Macedonia with accurate information necessary to complete their orders. Then, by drawing upon the information provided by banks and private informers, the Bureau had built up a file on 1200 firms in Macedonia, the details of which were at the disposal of French traders. Bonnier guaranteed to provide information within three days on any Salonika firm about which he received an enquiry from France. The Bureau also published a monthly *Commercial Bulletin* which contained studies on the natural resources of Macedonia and the needs of the area in terms of manufactured goods.[89]

The first of these publications set out succinctly the aims of the economic activity of the Armée d'Orient. 'We must from now on create a business link-up between France and Macedonia, where the presence and prestige of our arms as well as the widespread use of our language have gained us a privileged position, enabling us to hope for a great future.' At the end of the war French commerce would find the way open and the route prepared, but at that moment it would not be just Salonika and Macedonia, but all the Balkan states which would be in need of supplies. The effort expended during the war would then bear fruit. To export to Macedonia while the war continued would have its immediate advantages, but above all it meant reserving the Balkan peninsula in advance for the French sphere of influence.[90] This theme was taken up in the November issue of the *Bulletin*, which stressed the need for French commerce and industry to interest themselves in the Serbian market. When Serbia recovered its territorial integrity, the population would be in need of almost complete re-equipment as a result of the devastations of war. This situation would offer particularly favourable opportunities to French suppliers, who at that time occupied only a lowly place among Serbia's commercial partners.[91] The crucial period in the struggle for economic supremacy would be that which would immediately follow the cessation of hostilities. Immense works of reconstruction would then have to be undertaken involving vast orders for manufactured goods. The country which would be able to seize these opportunities would be the one which offered its merchants favourable credit terms. The *Commercial Bulletin* therefore proposed the creation of a National Commercial Bank for the Near East which could offer extensive credit facilities. If France wanted its influence in the area to survive the passage of its soldiers, this influence must be based on concrete commercial interests and the provision of credit remained the basic and indispensable condition of all economic activity.[92]

Other issues of the *Bulletin* dealt with the need to provide adequate transport facilities between Macedonia and France, commensurate with the efforts being made at both ends of the route to develop French interests. The danger otherwise existed that commercial activity would be built up at Salonika for the benefit of others, for if the Greek merchant was obliged to receive his goods in Italian vessels he would soon reach the conclusion that it would be easier to place his orders in Naples than at Marseilles. Yet it would be dangerous to allow the French flag to be superseded in the Eastern Mediterranean – an area whose freedom was guaranteed by the presence of French arms – when that flag could and should occupy 'the position which no one is dreaming of taking away from it – the foremost'.[93] A further topic examined was the agricultural potential of Macedonia. The *Bulletin* concluded that Salonika could become, what it had been in ancient times, the granary of the southern Balkans.[94]

In all this preparation for 'l'après-guerre' Sarrail himself was deeply involved. It was the combination of these apparently inappropriate activities and his perceived military incapacity which made Sarrail so unacceptable to his British opposite numbers. British observers reported that Sarrail was a political general, not a military one, and that he knew that financial and economic success would better please his political supporters than would military progress.[95] It was noted that Sarrail personally passed or refused, and then signed with his own hand, every single application for a permit to export goods from the district. This was 'hardly the work for a Commander-in-Chief of allied armies in the field'.[96] Sarrail also made use of the postal censorship and by it learnt which local merchants sent their orders to France and which to other countries. The latter were not infrequently the object of thinly veiled threats and persecutions, inflicted with a view to persuading them to change their ways.[97] Such methods were not without success. With pride the general informed the then war minister, Paul Painlevé, in April 1917, that of a monthly total volume of 22 million francs in imports to Salonika 16 million were French.[98]

The reunion of Greece following the deposition of King Constantine in June allowed those interested in the subject to think in terms of applying to the whole of the country those aspects of French commercial penetration which had been so successful in Macedonia. Bonnier thought the time had come seriously 'to prepare for the development of economic relations between French industry and Greek commerce'. Even if some French industrialists were unable at that moment to export their goods, Bonnier felt it was still important for them to send samples to 'their Greek clients of the postwar world'. It was a question of basic French interests. After the war, if France was going to face its obligations and assure its prosperity, it would have to find new openings for trade. And nowhere, Bonnier argued, was more open to French economic activity than the Hellenic world, where France had just dramatically affirmed its authority.[99] But the underlying problems of transport remained, exacerbated by the German U-boat campaign, and were never fully overcome.

In the last weeks of his command Sarrail interested himself in the need for the reconstruction of the town of Salonika following the disastrous fire of 18 August. He reminded the War Ministry that the destruction of many Greek schools opened up the possibility of French institutions gaining a near monopoly of education in Salonika which was so important in the development of French influence.[100] But with the war still undecided and his work in preparing for France's situation at the coming of peace incomplete, Sarrail was of course recalled. Lecoq recorded that Sarrail had borne high the name of France and had never allowed its pre-eminence to be disputed in any field. Now the danger existed that Britain might use the occasion of Sarrail's removal to launch its own policy of extending its influence in Greece and the Balkans.[101]

The extent of France's strategic, political and commercial interests in the Near East in general, and of its more specific concerns in particular parts of the area, should now be apparent.[102] The war seemed to magnify and accentuate these in their wider context and in certain cases afforded France the opportunity to develop them. In both instances the Armée d'Orient became the expression of French aspirations. Its value therefore extended far beyond what it might achieve in winning the war – which proved to be of limited importance – to the role of determining what sort of victory France was likely to win. Sarrail's army encapsulated a French determination to ensure that the peace settlement would represent not only the defeat of Germany but also the victory of France – a victory which would be expressed in tangible gains, territorial, strategic, commercial and political. The abandonment of the Salonika campaign was thus unthinkable on the basis of purely French considerations, whatever might have been desirable in terms of the total allied war effort. 'If we re-embark,' wrote one parliamentarian, 'we thereby lose for all time our initiative in the East. The abandonment of Salonika would mean the end of France's role at the eastern end of the Mediterranean.'[103]

Salonika thus highlights the differing emphases in the war aims of France and Britain. For France the struggle against the central powers would determine whether Germany was to be allowed to establish its own hegemony in central and eastern Europe and the Near East. This was an issue in which France felt itself immediately and vitally involved. But while the prevention of an over-mighty power on the continent of Europe was a long-standing principle of British foreign policy, such considerations affected Britain less centrally than they did France, and it did not share the latter's overriding concern at the outcome of the war in the Eastern Mediterranean. British war aims reflected its own status as the world's leading naval, commercial and imperial power and centred on its desire to protect its existing empire. The defence of Egypt naturally entered into such calculations, but

Britain never really saw the Salonika campaign as a means of defending its postwar interests in the Near East and the route to India. The belief existed in France, on the other hand, that only through the maintenance of the Armée d'Orient could the French secure the right to a say in the postwar arrangement of the Near East. The physical presence of its army was seen to bestow the right to a commanding voice at the final peace settlement. Moreover, because of the ambitions and encroachments of France's present allies but likely future rivals, it was seen that the Armée d'Orient was based on a country where France would need to interest itself to a far greater degree than in prewar days. The war increased the importance of Greece to France, just as its military presence there increased the temptation to use this country as a foothold for wider Mediterranean ambitions.

France had certain territorial designs in the Eastern Mediterranean. In the first instance these involved the acquisition of Syria and Cilicia, and also included, at least in the first half of the war, Palestine.[104] But the possession of Syria merely reflected a deeply-held conviction that France's future was inextricably bound up with its standing in the Near East. It masked, therefore, a broader aim to carve out as wide a sphere of influence as possible in the whole area. While campaigns on the Western Front might enable France to win the war, those in the East would play no less important a role in helping it to win the peace. In a strategic sense, then, the Salonika expedition was a lever for French ambitions in a wide area. More immediately, it came to be used as the vehicle by which France would acquire direct commercial, and hence political, influence in the area closely affected by the presence of the Armée d'Orient. French industry would find itself in a difficult position at the end of the war. The vast plant which had been employed in the manufacture of armaments would have to be converted to peacetime production if serious unemployment were to be avoided. But to cope with this inevitable increase in production France would require new markets and the Balkans, which would be in great need of agricultural equipment and manufactured goods, were ideally suited to fill this role.[105] So the Armée d'Orient fought a commercial war for France in addition to the efforts it made on the battlefield, and its opponents in the two struggles were not necessarily the same, since that for economic supremacy involved 'a peaceful struggle against our allies'.[106]

All of this made it most unlikely that Britain and France would be able to co-operate fully in the Salonika venture, especially when there were few advocates in Britain even for the military possibilities of the campaign. France's underlying strategic motivation inevitably cut across British interests in the Mediterranean balance of power, while its commercial and political aspirations in Macedonia and Greece ran counter to British policy which, in this part of the world at least, seemed more concerned with winning the war as quickly as possible. What is difficult to determine is the extent to which what may be loosely described as 'French ambitions' permeated the whole of the governmental hierarchy – whether in fact they may be seen to represent government policy rather than the sectional, vested interests of pressure groups in France and of French agents in Athens and Salonika. It has been written that 'only Clemenceau, the strongest prime minister of the Third Republic, possessed the power and determination to shape Middle East policy according to his own design'.[107] What seems beyond question is that French agents on the spot, and in particular those closely associated with the Armée d'Orient, were almost unanimous in championing at least some of the non-military advantages of France's participation in the eastern theatre. While no coherent and precise governmental policy ever seems to have emerged, this understanding of the situation was apparently shared, to varying degrees, by the changing governments in Paris. Not surprisingly, it emerges that Paris and its agents in the Near East were most closely in accord on this matter during the ascendancy in 1917 of those politicians most sympathetic to General Sarrail himself.

. . . .
The End of the Campaign

No one can look at the documents relating to the last year of the Salonika campaign without realizing that radical changes had occurred since the beginning of the expedition in 1915. The divisive problems which had so frequently threatened to tear the Anglo-French alliance apart were no longer to the forefront, replaced – perhaps for the first time – by a genuine assessment on both sides of the Channel of the military prospects of the campaign. No longer was the diplomacy of the Allies fatally hamstrung by domestic political considerations. As political intrigue receded into the background, attention focused instead on the actual military struggle against the enemy. Nor did the problem of Greece any longer occupy the centre of the stage. The British government's decision to accede to the deposition of King Constantine and to leave to France the directing hand in allied diplomacy in Athens had effectively removed this particular bone of contention. As the Quai d'Orsay concluded in February 1918, 'the affairs of Greece give rise to minor problems, but have now ceased to occupy the important place in the preoccupations of the allies which they held for so long'.[1] This changed situation is explicable above all in terms of personalities. The succession of Clemenceau to the presidency of the Council in France and the removal of Sarrail from the command of the Armée d'Orient were of the highest significance in the history of the campaign.

The diplomatic instructions personally given by the new foreign minister, Stephen Pichon, to General Marie-Adolphe Guillaumat before the latter left Paris to take up his new command contained a tacit admission that Sarrail's presence as commander-in-chief had been one of the principal causes of the lack of inter-allied co-operation on the Salonika front: the British 'have always begrudged the help which they have given us. Your assumption of the command will, I hope, bring about the disappearance of those divergences of view which are so out of place and harmful to our joint efforts.'[2] Almost from the beginning of the campaign no other single factor had so impeded Britain's whole-hearted co-operation as the fact that the allied army was under the command of a general whose primary interests appeared to lie away from the battlefield. Whatever Sarrail's military worth – and he was not without his admirers – British politicians and soldiers were almost unanimously convinced that no good could be done at Salonika while he remained in charge. With the arrival of Guillaumat, therefore, a fresh wind blew through allied headquarters at Salonika which was bound to be beneficial. On 12 December 1917 the British War Cabinet heard that the new commander was a 'plain, blunt soldier' who had commanded at Verdun after Nivelle had become commander-in-chief, and that he was regarded by Clemenceau as 'a first-class man'.[3] Within days of Guillaumat's arrival Milne was insisting that the new appointment would 'tend to ease the situation as far as this theatre of war is concerned'. After 'two years of uncertainty' Milne found it refreshing to have someone with a definite plan, even if that plan was a purely defensive one.[4] Early in the new year Milne concluded that Guillaumat was 'essentially a soldier' and that, in marked contrast to Sarrail, he looked upon the situation from a purely military point of view. He seemed to be a firm believer in thorough organization and was willing to listen to the opinions of others, while at the same time having very clear views of his own.[5] Guillaumat made a similarly favourable first impression on Lieutenant-Colonel Plunkett, who reported regularly to the British government on the situation in the Balkans. Plunkett heard that the new commander had spent a fortnight at the French War Office getting acquainted with the situation and that he had been particularly warned against becoming influenced by, or too interested in, political and economic considerations. Guillaumat had been instructed to confine himself to the command of the allied armies and was urged to get on good terms socially with the other allied generals and their staffs.[6]

As important as the changeover between Guillaumat and Sarrail was that between Clemenceau and Painlevé, or rather between Clemenceau and the political system which Painlevé represented and to which, to one degree or another, the ministries of Viviani, Briand

and Ribot had all conformed. Clemenceau's was a new type of government, different in kind rather than degree from its wartime
predecessors. Its arrival involved far more than the shuffling of ministerial portfolios, which usually characterized a change of government
in Third Republic France. Clemenceau regarded Viviani, Briand, Ribot
and Painlevé with varying degrees of contempt and there was no
place for any of them in his administration.[7] The new prime minister
preferred what was in effect a cabinet of 'obedient underlings'.[8] As
Bertie put it to Lloyd George: 'the Tiger did not invite individuals to
be members of his cabinet in order to hear what they might have to
say but to carry out his views. It is practically a one-man ministry.'[9]
The fact that Sarrail's recall did not give rise to the great outcry
which might have been expected was in large measure due to the
forceful personality of the new French premier. As one observer put
it: 'General Sarrail comes back, everything stays calm and his return
has no effect.'[10] For perhaps the first time in the war France found
itself with a government which could govern without undue concern
for the fluctuating votes of the Chamber of Deputies or for the party
political intrigues of the parliamentary corridors. In one sense
Painlevé's fall represented the final act in the long-running conflict
between government and parliament which had begun in 1915. But it
was a Pyrrhic victory for the Chamber. With the formation of Clemenceau's government France accepted what amounted to a ministerial
dictatorship and, after initial trials of strength in the Chamber and
Senate had revealed that the premier could command a comfortable
majority, the French parliament relapsed into the sort of secondary
role which it had not occupied since the early months of the war and
the ascendancy of Joffre. The possibility now existed, therefore, that
the Salonika campaign would be viewed in Paris on its intrinsic merits,
removed from the web of political complications in which it had
hitherto been enveloped. With as dominant a figure as Clemenceau
completely overshadowing the men who surrounded him – 'of course
he is the only man in the Government', concluded the British ambassador in Paris[11] – the future of the Balkan venture lay very much
in the hands of one man. And Clemenceau's views on the Salonika
expedition were likely to place him nearer to the point of view of his
British allies than any of his predecessors had been.

Ever since October 1915 there had been no more ardent or vociferous critic in Paris of the French government's conduct of the

Balkan campaign than 'the tiger'. Ruthlessly attacking what he regarded as a waste of effort, Clemenceau had launched a series of bitter assaults on those who championed the Salonika front through his celebrated newspaper *L'Homme Enchaîné*. Frequent clashes with the censor had failed to lessen the severity of his critique. An article written in May 1917 epitomized the attitude which Clemenceau had held throughout:

> I continue to wonder whether these hundreds of thousands of men sent to the east, and their precious supplies, would not have had a more decisive impact for us on the Western Front. We shall have to pay until the bitter end, and in too many ways, for Briand's master-stroke.[12]

Sarrail later argued that Clemenceau had subjected successive French governments to flagrant blackmail in order to prevent them from sending the reinforcements which were indispensable to military success. In office, however, Clemenceau seems to have concluded that it was now too late in the day to pull out from Salonika and 'on my successors in the East he lavished co-operation and support – the reinforcements he had defied successive governments to grant me even piecemeal'.[13] This was an exaggeration. To the end of the war Clemenceau remained a convinced westerner. As he told the Chamber Foreign Affairs Commission in May 1918: 'Je ne suis pas très "Saloni-quais".'[14] But he was not now prepared to abandon the expedition when it had already consumed so much in terms of energy and resources. General Franchet d'Espérey, who succeeded Guillaumat in the summer of 1918, was probably near the mark when he argued that 'M. Clemenceau has never liked the east but, as a great Frenchman, he appreciates the important interests which are at stake there'.[15] At the very least, with Clemenceau in power, Britain could be confident that political factors would no longer dominate the direction of the French war effort, even at Salonika. In February 1918 Guillaumat reported: 'France and Britain alone concern themselves with the war. The other powers think only of the postwar era.'[16] What was significant in this was not that other countries, above all, presumably, Italy, were still concentrating on the postwar settlement, but that France could now be counted among those states which put the war against the enemy to the forefront. Clemenceau came to office obsessed with the war itself and with a determination to fight it to a victorious conclusion. Any other policy was, for him, tantamount to defeat and treason. This primacy of military considerations was implicitly recognized in the choice of Lord Derby to replace the ailing Bertie at the British Embassy in Paris in April. As Lloyd George put it, there was 'not very much diplomacy required in Paris'. What was needed was a representative who was in close touch with the views of the British government on the innumerable questions, essentially of a military character, which arose from day to day between the two countries.[17]

These crucial changes in personnel were accompanied by significant improvements in the allied direction of the war as a whole, resulting from a regularization of the relationship between the political and military authorities within Britain and France and between the two countries. The task of co-ordinating the activities of the allied armies, which for the first two years of the war had – almost by default – been left to the French high command, had, owing to the replacement of Joffre and the catastrophic failure of his successor, gradually fallen out of French hands. Nevertheless, the groundwork for a more satisfactory arrangement had been carried out while Painlevé was at the French War Ministry. On 29 April 1917 there were created for Pétain the functions of military technical adviser to the Comité de Guerre which Joffre had performed for a single week in December 1916. Furthermore, the disastrous Chemin des Dames campaign, by making the removal of Nivelle inevitable, had the compensating advantage of harmonizing relations between the French high command and its government to a greater degree than at any time since the opening months of the war.[18] Painlevé's nomination of Foch and Pétain to the two highest offices in the French army proved to be the first step towards the creation of a unified allied control of the war. Upon the prestige of Foch it would be possible to build a unified command structure. When Clemenceau took over the premiership he was thus able to follow the paths already charted by his predecessor.[19]

As Painlevé later put it, though his own role in the Salonika affair added irony to his words, 'for victory to be possible, it was necessary to establish a mutual confidence, a reciprocal desire to understand one another and a total loyalty between the allies'.[20] He had begun preliminary talks with the British on the ticklish question of a unified command on the Western Front as early as August 1917, but Lloyd George and Milner had advised caution in any attempt to secure the appointment of Foch as chief of an inter-allied General Staff.[21] But the Italian disaster at Caporetto in October demonstrated the urgent need for action and Painlevé hurried to London for renewed consultations. From these discussions there emerged the so-called Supreme War Council – a body to be made up of the prime minister (whenever possible) and a permanent military representative from each of the countries to be included.

> The Supreme War Council did not supersede the Commanders-in-Chief but gave them for their guidance an expression of the definite policy of the Allied Governments. It was not to act as a Commander-in-Chief, but an agency for the adoption and maintenance of a general policy for the Allies in the prosecution of the war, consistent with the total resources available and the most effective distribution of those resources among the various theatres of operations.[22]

It remained for Clemenceau at the Doullens Conference of March 1918 to secure for Foch functions which amounted to those of commander-in-chief of the Anglo-French armies. In this task he was greatly assisted by Lloyd George's continuing lack of confidence in the abilities of Sir Douglas Haig.[23] Thereafter, Foch's title and powers expanded with the course of events. In the Supreme War Council, however, the Allies found a far more satisfactory means of conducting the Salonika campaign than the series of *ad hoc* conferences of the preceding two years, which had so often damaged rather than improved inter-allied relations.

In addition to these developments, politico-military relations in Britain were placed on a more stable footing with the appointment of Sir Henry Wilson to succeed Robertson as CIGS on 18 February 1918. This step represented the final triumph of Lloyd George in his long-running struggle with Robertson. Wilson was no particular friend of the Salonika expedition, though back in 1915 he had preferred it to the campaign at Gallipoli.[24] During the remaining months of the war, however, the situation on the Western Front was such that Wilson had little time to devote to Salonika. At all events, Salonika never became for Wilson the key issue it had been for Robertson. This development too was likely to aid the cause of Anglo-French co-operation.

What then of the last year of the Salonika expedition? Upon Guillaumat's appointment Foch defined the mission of the Armée d'Orient as first and foremost to prevent the conquest of Greece by the enemy. When defensive arrangements had been finalized, it would be up to the new commander to study the possibility of offensive action according to the circumstances of the moment.[25] These instructions differed materially from those issued to Sarrail and implied that it was more important to cover Old Greece than Salonika, which might in case of need be left as an isolated fortress while the allied armies found new bases elsewhere.[26] Even now, in what was supposed to be a new era of co-operation in Anglo-French relations, these important changes were made without reference to the Supreme War Council or consultation with the British War Cabinet.[27] Fortunately Guillaumat's instructions corresponded almost exactly with the suggestions of the permanent military advisers to the Supreme War Council.[28] The overriding military consideration, though, lurking ominously in the background, was the defection of Russia from the allied cause. This might at any moment enable Germany to throw the weight of its forces against the Western Front, thus necessitating at least the partial evacuation of secondary theatres by the allied armies.[29] This, however, was a bridge which would be crossed if and when the need arose and a proposal made by Haig at a military conference in Compiègne in January 1918 that all British and French forces in Macedonia should be brought back to France received little support.[30] Even so, as divisions of the Greek regular army became available for the forward zone, they were eagerly counted by the British War Office which hoped that they would eventually allow for the complete withdrawal of British troops.[31] For the time being, however, the Balkan campaign would remain 'a considerable drag' for Britain. If the town of Salonika were abandoned, a great mass of stores would have to be destroyed, as there was such a collection there that it would take about nine months to clear the place even if all available military and shipping resources were used for the purpose.[32]

Guillaumat's initial inspection of the troops under his command revealed severe shortcomings and difficulties. While the British and Italian contingents were in relatively good condition, the French forces were short of supplies, suffering from hunger and 28,000 men below strength.[33] But the Germans too had withdrawn forces from the Balkans, with the result that something approaching numerical equality existed between the two sides.[34] From the Supreme War Council Brigadier-General Studd reflected on how far the Balkan campaign now was from producing the sort of easy victory which had been envisaged by some optimists at the beginning of 1915. For some time military activity had been confined to the type of trench warfare which had plagued the fighting on the Western Front. At the beginning of 1918 reinforcements for an offensive were even less likely to be available than before. Moreover, Studd concluded that no offensive in the Balkans, however successful, would have any decisive effect on bringing the war to a conclusion. To fritter men away there could only reduce those forces available for a decisive attack in France or Flanders.[35] But the British War Cabinet agreed in March that for the time being none of their divisions should be brought back to France since, although up to strength numerically, they had become severely weakened by malaria.[36]

It was inevitable that some anxiety would be expressed in the French Chamber at the inactivity of the Armée d'Orient,[37] and in March Guillaumat told Foch that he could undertake a modest operation along the Vardar and the Struma.[38] But when Lloyd George and Wilson met Clemenceau and Foch at Beauvais in early April, it was clear that the British government's attitude had changed significantly. The prime minister now pressed for the withdrawal of British troops. Foch retorted that, as far as the French government was concerned, the possibility of reducing the allied forces was to be envisaged only in the event of a military setback.[39] All the same, the French were not prepared to upgrade the Salonika front. Clemenceau reminded Guillaumat that, with a German offensive under way on the Western Front, the decisive act of the war appeared to have been engaged. In such circumstances there could be no question of reinforcements for the Armée d'Orient and Guillaumat could count only on the resources already at his disposal.[40] At the same time it was his duty to ensure that no enemy forces could be withdrawn from the Balkan theatre for use in the offensive in France. In such circumstances it was indispensable that the Armée d'Orient should be ready to take the offensive if the situation demanded it.[41] Wilson was understandably concerned at this suggestion of an offensive and proposed that allied policy should be to develop the Greek army and use it to draw French and British troops into reserve. With enemy forces steadily withdrawing, an allied offensive at Salonika would achieve no good purpose.[42] Clemenceau, however, would not countenance Wilson's suggestion that twelve battalions should be withdrawn from Salonika to reinforce the

Western Front.[43] He was determined to do nothing which would weaken the Macedonian front or lessen the possibility of minor offensives there and he secured Britain's agreement to having the matter decided by the Supreme War Council.[44]

Meeting at the beginning of May in Abbeville, the Supreme War Council reached conclusions which were broadly satisfactory to the British. Because the allied Salonika force was being reinforced by the addition of Greek divisions, the Council argued that it ought to be possible to transfer some battalions to the Western Front, where every man was urgently needed. It was agreed that no transfer should take place without consultation with Guillaumat, although attention was drawn to the general's suggestion that Indian battalions could be substituted for British troops withdrawn to the Western Front.[45] In fact, Guillaumat was becoming much less cautious and his staff were preparing for a powerful offensive on both sides of the Vardar, with Greek attacks on the Struma and a Serbian diversion further to the west.[46] Yet at the end of May Wilson informed the War Cabinet that the French were removing about 12,000 of their troops from the Salonika front. This was surprising in view of their attitude at Abbeville, but Wilson felt that no action was necessary as the arrival of Indian forces would also make possible the withdrawal of a few British battalions.[47]

The War Cabinet was still anxious about the general nature of the Allies' defensive policy in the Balkans. Guillaumat had been repeatedly asked for his plans in the event of a retirement, but these had still not been obtained. If, as there was reason to fear, there were no proper plans, it was quite possible that a disaster would ensue. Wilson suggested that the problem was taking on a new aspect, since he understood that Guillaumat was being recalled from Salonika to be replaced by General Franchet d'Espérey, whose name had been mentioned when the possibility of a Balkan expedition had first been canvassed at the beginning of 1915.[48] It was assumed that, with the crisis on the Western Front at its peak, Guillaumat was to take over the military governorship of Paris. Then, if the Allies suffered a reverse, he would be at hand to replace Pétain or even Foch.[49] The departure of Guillaumat was viewed with particular regret in London. Though not everything had run smoothly since Sarrail's dismissal, Guillaumat's actions and influence had had an extraordinarily beneficial effect upon the Salonika command and upon relations between the various contingents. Franchet d'Espérey had to feel his way towards the confidence of the allied armies in the face of their almost universal regret at his predecessor's recall. Something of a scapegoat for recent setbacks on the Western Front, d'Espérey's reputation did not stand very high at the time of his arrival in the Balkans.[50] But at least the British representative at the Supreme War Council was able to assure his government that Guillaumat's recall was dictated solely by military considerations and did not portend a change in French policy at Salonika.[51] Indeed, Guillaumat continued in Paris to have an influential voice in the determination of France's Balkan strategy.

On 22 June Clemenceau informed the newly installed Franchet d'Espérey that the general military situation required the assumption of offensive action by the Armée d'Orient.[52] It was essential to relieve the Western Front by going over to the offensive in the outer theatres and the Allies should therefore try to crack Bulgaria's defences with a concerted attack. Five days later the military representatives at Versailles declared that it was indispensable for the allied forces, within the limits considered possible by the commander-in-chief, to contribute to the common action against the enemy by offensive action. In a revision of the instructions given to Guillaumat, it was now stated that the retention of the Salonika base was of the greatest importance for the Allies, although bases and communications in Old Greece should also be developed.[53]

Lloyd George, however, was not happy at the way in which these changes had been carried out. As Lord Derby recorded on 3 July:

> I think there will be a row this afternoon as apparently the change of command at Salonika from Guillaumat, who is decidedly a good man, to Franchet d'Espérey, who was unstuck for really bad work at the Chemin des Dames was done without any reference to our people at home and now he has received an order to take the offensive equally without any reference to our people at home and in direct contravention of what had been settled at the last Versailles Conference.[54]

The Supreme War Council that day did indeed witness a 'terrific, sudden and extremely violent' outburst by the British premier against the French for appointing d'Espérey to the Salonika command and for issuing orders for an offensive there without consulting the Council. Maurice Hankey found the whole situation rather strange since Clemenceau, as he asserted during the course of the meeting, had always been and still professed to be an ardent opponent of the whole expedition. Part of the difficulty lay in the vaguely defined position of General Foch. The instructions issued to d'Espérey and only later communicated to the allied military representatives had been sent by Foch and counter-signed by Clemenceau. Foch and Clemenceau had not been over-tactful in this matter, since Foch's authority did not extend beyond the Western and Italian fronts and Clemenceau ought not to have approved instructions to an allied army in another theatre without consulting the governments concerned.[55] The French prime minister managed to extricate himself from a difficult situation by arguing that, with his record of opposition to the campaign, he could not now be suspected of wishing to launch a major offensive in the Balkans. But the progressive arrival of American troops on the Western Front had made it possible to reconsider the decision to transfer allied soldiers from the Balkans to France, while giving force to the instructions issued to Guillaumat as early as December 1917 that he should at least study the possibilities of offensive action.[56]

The whole episode inevitably revived old anxieties in Britain and concern was expressed at the Imperial War Cabinet on 9 July at the French tendency to take matters into their own hands without regard for the views of the Supreme War Council.[57] Two days later the military and diplomatic representatives of Britain and France meeting at Versailles determined that, while it was necessary to study the question of a general offensive in the Balkans, it would not be desirable to carry out this offensive unless it led to a victory of more than local importance.[58] Guillaumat, present at Versailles, developed his plan for an offensive designed to keep up the morale of the Serbians and Greeks and to undermine that of the Bulgarians, but he now argued that the offensive should not take place before October.[59] For once, however, it was the British commander at Salonika who now believed that the Armée d'Orient's moment might finally have arrived. With the Bulgarians becoming war-weary, the Austrians in difficulties in Italy and the Germans held up in France, Milne suggested that the time was approaching when the Salonika army would be able to act 'possibly with far-reaching results' and that it should be ready to do so when the necessity arose.[60] Franchet d'Espérey gave every impression of being less cautious than his predecessor and by the end of July the

British commander reported that d'Espérey was contemplating a more ambitious project than his original instructions had authorized.[61] As a result the Supreme War Council agreed at the beginning of August that preparations for an offensive should be pushed ahead with all speed and that d'Espérey was to be left free to launch this offensive when he thought fit, unless new and unforeseen circumstances arose.[62] The one proviso was that preparations for a Balkan offensive should not in any way weaken the Western Front.[63] At the beginning of September the French government sent Guillaumat over to London for discussions with British political and military leaders. The general put before Lloyd George, Milner, Cecil and Wilson the reasons in favour of the early resumption of offensive operations and secured their agreement to British participation.[64] The aim of the operations was to defeat the enemy armies and remove them from the conflict, to invade Bulgaria and occupy Sofia.[65]

The advance began in the middle of September and produced an immediate débâcle in the now disintegrating Bulgarian army.[66] Short of manpower and supplies, and with no assistance forthcoming from Germany, the Bulgarians were anxious to give up the struggle. Bulgarian emissaries approached Milne who, reasonably enough, referred them to d'Espérey as supreme commander in the Balkan theatre. Briand, the foremost architect of the campaign since its inception, sadly noted the irony of seeing Clemenceau, 'the unremitting opponent of the expedition', at the head of the government at this moment of triumph.[67] The success of the operation took just about everyone by surprise. Certainly, there had been too many false dawns in the war to date for the allied leaders to suppose that a Bulgarian collapse might, within six weeks, contribute to the defeat of the entire enemy alliance, as proved to be the case. The British ambassador in Paris captured the mood:

> Macedonia going extremely well. Far exceeding any of our most favourable hopes and the question is now not how far we shall get on but how far we can allow our troops to go on. Clemenceau tells me that Guillaumat will go out at once to take over command for six weeks but not to really command in the battle but in view of our great successes to see how far they ought to be pushed. Clemenceau seems to anticipate a great effect from this victory.[68]

Clemenceau, in fact, was almost embarrassed by the success of the Balkan offensive and feared that he might become too involved in it. He confided to Poincaré that he had supported the offensive with the aim of then bringing back to France a part of the French contingent. If the Allies now marched on Sofia this would not be possible. Clemenceau remained as convinced as ever that it was in France and not in the Balkans that the war would be decided.[69]

Franchet d'Espérey took matters very much into his own hands and it was he who laid down the terms upon which an armistice was concluded with Bulgaria. For one last time the Salonika campaign threatened to create friction between Britain and France. Lloyd George was 'very excited and said that the French were trying to get everything in their own hands and concealing anything from us'. In all probability, however, Clemenceau himself had not been consulted about the armistice terms.[70] The course of events dragged the French premier along and he was obliged to authorize d'Espérey to go on to the Danube as quickly as possible in order to cut off supplies from the enemy. Lloyd George, however, preferred that Milne's troops should turn east towards Constantinople with the aim of bringing down the Ottoman empire. The British War Cabinet assembled on 1 October amid considerable uncertainty as to the true state of affairs. But there was general agreement that the allied governments would have to be consulted before any further military operations were authorized and that this consultation could take place only at a meeting of the Supreme War Council.[71] This ignorance in Britain was mirrored in the French press, where the government imposed a silence on reports of the Allies' successes on 2 and 3 October. Some believed that Clemenceau, even at this late date, was reluctant for it to be known that the Salonika campaign was, after all, playing its part in the determination of the conflict.[72]

If the French were intent on settling the affairs of the Balkans on their own, Lloyd George determined that Britain would be predominant in the former Ottoman empire. 'Britain had won the war in the Middle East', he told the War Cabinet on 3 October, 'and there was no reason why France should profit from it.'[73] At all events the British prime minister seemed ready for a further crisis in Anglo-French relations. At the Supreme War Council on 7 October, Lloyd George rejected out of hand a proposal for a triumphal march into Constantinople led by French troops. The British and French premiers 'spat at one another like angry cats'.[74] A compromise was reached whereby Lloyd George agreed to drop a scheme to place Milne's army under General Allenby and allowed it to remain under d'Espérey, provided Milne was permitted to command the section which marched on Constantinople.[75] As the war drew to a close it was the turn of the British to act unilaterally. Lloyd George resisted Clemenceau's claims for a French voice in negotiating an armistice with the Turks, making it plain that this was an issue upon which he was ready to break the entente.[76] On 30 October the British commander, Admiral Calthorpe, negotiated an armistice with the Turks off the Aegean island of Mudros. At the Supreme War Council that day Clemenceau and Lloyd George 'bandied words like fishwives, at least Lloyd George did'.[77] But the French prime minister's line soon softened. Once the armistice with Germany was signed on 11 November he seemed keen to cede to Britain the primary role in the Middle East. This was a key factor in his strategy to secure British support for France's altogether more important war aims in Europe.[78] His sights were now fixed firmly on the Rhine. But it was an odd conclusion to the French war effort in the east.

How important had the late flowering of the Macedonian campaign been to the allied victory in the war as a whole? The German generals gave credence to the notion that the strategy of 'knocking away the props' had indeed been crucial to their country's ultimate defeat. On 3 October Hindenburg noted that 'as a result of the collapse of the Macedonian front and the weakening of our Western reserves which this has brought about ... there is, so far as can be foreseen, no longer a prospect of forcing peace on the enemy'.[79] Ludendorff's memoirs confirmed that what brought him to the point of insisting that his government should make peace was the impossibility of securing Germany's eastern and southern approaches after the collapse of Bulgaria and Turkey.[80] 'Side-shows' had really been decisive, suggested Lloyd George at a working breakfast on 17 October. 'He attributes great things to the belated though brilliant results of the Salonika campaign.'[81] But it is necessary to sound a note of caution. As Trevor Wilson points out, Ludendorff's self-indulgence in suggesting that he was not over-anxious about the Western Front itself is excusable but hardly deserves the endorsement of historians. 'The German forces in France had been experiencing defeat for nearly two months before the Bulgarians acted on the awareness that the cause of the Central Powers was truly lost.'[82]

With the premiership of Georges Clemenceau the Salonika campaign had inevitably decreased in importance. It was not possible, however, that the interests of France in the area, which had provided an underlying motivation behind the expedition while feeding the suspicions of its allies, would vanish overnight. The optimism shown by Milne in the wake of Sarrail's recall, that military considerations would now predominate, had faded by the summer of 1918. In July he judged that 'the French are playing their cards in this theatre solely for their own purposes, and that the British army ... is merely one of the cards'.[83] The French government maintained a strong interest in the commercial and financial affairs of Greece throughout 1918. As Foreign Minister Pichon stated in March, the Quai d'Orsay's support was assured for all enterprises which aimed at the development of French economic activity there.[84] French consuls in Greece continued their attempts to use the war situation to foster trade between France and the towns and districts in which they were posted. In February 1918, for example, Dussap sought Pichon's assistance in favouring the importation of French products into Epirus 'with a view to creating a business link between our country and this region'.[85] Similarly, to facilitate the large-scale purchase of French goods by the Greek government, a special office was created in Paris with the title 'Service des Travaux Publics en Grèce'.[86] From Athens de Billy urged that Greece should be disabused of the idea that at the end of hostilities it would be allowed to resume the unrestricted commercial intercourse with the central powers which it had enjoyed in the years before the war. It was unthinkable that the financial assistance afforded by France and Britain had not imposed obligations and restrictions on Greece in this respect.[87] De Billy even seemed worried that the Greek government might have enough money to pay off its debts to the Allies, since this would deprive France of its power of control.[88] The French military attaché in Greece called for the country to be made the point of departure 'for all our future network in the Balkans and in Turkey'.[89] Similarly, the French consul at Salonika, Graillet, repeatedly emphasized the need to preserve the Commercial Bureau set up by Sarrail and Bonnier in 1916. It had provided France with the opportunity of acquiring a preponderant position in the commerce of the area and must be retained after the departure of the army under whose auspices it had flourished.[90]

The fostering of French trade could not, however, in the circumstances of 1918, occupy the central role which men such as Sarrail and Bonnier had attempted to give it in 1916 and 1917. With the German offensive on the Western Front of the spring of 1918 France faced the most serious crisis of the war and, in the words of Jonnart, appointed by Clemenceau as minister of blockade, 'the question of creating new commercial links can now only play a secondary role in French economic policy; it is a question of ensuring the country's survival'.[91] Bonnier was therefore informed not to arrange for Greek purchases in France without first being sure of the resources available on the French market. The tonnage crisis, moreover, became so acute that in April 1918 it was found necessary to halt all French commercial services between France and Greece.[92] The French commercial attaché, Bargeton, warned that if this situation continued the commercial future of France in Greece would be gravely compromised. In no other country were preparations for postwar economic expansion more justified than in Greece, where it was imperative 'to profit from those circumstances which presently cut the country off from the Central Powers'. The needs of the hour would obviously impose a reduction of French exports, but French manufacturers and Greek merchants could easily be discouraged if all means were refused them of carrying out the transactions which 'should be the basis of strong economic relations after the end of the war'.[93] But Bargeton did not receive from Guillaumat the sort of support which Bonnier had come to expect from Sarrail. The new commander insisted that, although the expansion of French influence in the Near East was an entirely legitimate goal, he could not spare space on ships arriving at Salonika and Athens for purely commercial traffic: 'Before preparing for the postwar era, we must face up to the requirements of the present time.'[94]

France simply did not have the resources to replace German commerce in areas from which the latter had been excluded as a result of the war. The French Commercial Bureau in Athens therefore received a list of those products which France could provide and another of those for which Greece should look to other markets.[95] It was a choice of compromising the supplies of the Armée d'Orient in favour of French commercial interests – 'perfectly legitimate in themselves, but impossible to reconcile with military necessity' – or of sacrificing these same commercial interests to the benefit of the security of the French forces in the Balkans. In such circumstances no real choice existed and the decision imposed itself.[96] The consequences in Greece were inevitable and one French agent complained of the daily visits he received from Greek merchants, frustrated in their attempts to place orders on the French market.[97] By the beginning of 1919 the French Military Mission in Greece was noting sadly that France was not well placed to benefit from the important orders being placed by Greek merchants. The devastation caused in France itself by the German invasion would occupy the country's attention for the foreseeable future, leaving to France's 'allies' unrestricted opportunities in the Greek market.[98]

If anything, France's interest in Greece generally and Salonika in particular declined rather more than did its interest in the Near East as a whole. The 1919 peace negotiations on the future of Greece saw general Anglo-French co-operation, with Britain taking the lead in framing a settlement.[99] The reasons for this are probably to be found in a reversal of those peculiar circumstances which had given the area a crucial importance for France in the first instance. As early as May 1917 the Russian provisional government had declared that it had no territorial designs and that it proposed to conclude a peace without annexations. That July the Russians specifically renounced their interest in Constantinople since this city was not Russian. The implications for France of the Russian Revolution and the withdrawal of the Soviet government from the war, finalized by the Treaty of Brest-Litovsk in March 1918 but apparent for some months before, were considerable. The whole question of the settlement of the Near East, which had appeared to be determined by the attribution of Constantinople to Russia in March 1915, was now reopened, giving France a second chance to assert itself in an area from which it had come to feel excluded. With victory over Bulgaria assured in October 1918, Guillaumat insisted that this had to be viewed in conjunction with the eclipse of Russia: 'The Eastern Question appears in a completely different light from that which comparable success two years ago would have given it.'[100] As a result Greece and the port of Salonika, which had never been more than a second-best in France's quest for a 'point d'appui' in its aspirations in the Eastern Mediterranean, resumed the secondary role in French thinking which they had occupied until 1915.

With Bulgaria finally eliminated from the conflict in October 1918, Lloyd George was aware that the French government wanted to have full control over an attack on Constantinople.[101] As has been seen, however, under pressure from Britain Milne was given command of the Constantinople operation, much to Franchet d'Espérey's dismay.[102] When Britain began to exploit this situation to its own advantage, the cry was raised in Paris to transfer d'Espérey's headquarters to Constantinople. The struggle for commercial and political domination thus began to shift eastwards. The military victories in the Balkans could not be ignored, but in the overall plan of French expansion in the Near East Salonika would no longer be the central point of radiation.[103] When Charles Meunier urged the Chamber Army Commission to follow up the commercial activities of the Armée d'Orient, he was no longer thinking only in terms of Greece or even of the Balkans, but of Turkey as well.[104] Even the Salonika Commercial Bureau began fixing its horizons further afield than Macedonia and Greece. As the *Commercial Bulletin* pointed out in the autumn of 1918, Romania, Bulgaria and Turkey were going to become a vast plain of economic activity, where France should seek a leading role. Circulars were sent to the French consuls in these countries immediately after the conclusion of the armistice to inform them that the Salonika Bureau was now at the disposal of merchants in these states. The important thing was to act straightaway before German and Austrian commerce had had time to recover.[105]

By March 1919 d'Espérey reported that each of the Allies was pursuing its own aims in Asia Minor, exploiting the situation to the best of its ability in support of individual political and commercial interests.[106] The head of the French legation at the Turkish Ministry of War concluded in July that French interests required the maintenance of a large Turkish Empire.[107] All the signs were that France might revert to its traditional policy, which it had been forced to abandon in the three years following the secret treaty with Russia in March 1915. In December 1918 Foreign Minister Pichon had joined the call for the Armée d'Orient to be based on Constantinople. The choice of Salonika had been imposed by circumstance but was now becoming increasingly inappropriate.[108] But France lacked the resources at the end of four years of unprecedented military effort, and perhaps also its leaders lacked the political will, to pursue a new struggle in Asia Minor, and as the months passed it became increasingly clear that the predominant influence in the area was now that of Britain.[109] Britain's armies in the Near and Middle East gave it a position of strength which France, with what was becoming only a token contingent, could not hope to challenge.[110] By February 1919 Franchet d'Espérey was complaining bitterly at the systematic demobilization of French troops in the Armée d'Orient and the government's failure to replace them. By contrast the British had reinforced their contingents by taking men from their armies in Syria and Egypt. D'Espérey found the means at his disposal ridiculously insufficient when compared with those of his rival.[111] A Quai d'Orsay note prepared for Pichon reflected sadly on France's failure to follow up its military triumph with a political one – that is, on the failure to achieve what had always been seen as an underlying purpose of the Salonika expedition: postwar French domination of the Near East.[112]

The ousting of France as the dominant influence was particularly noticeable in Greece. As the Chamber of Deputies had heard as early as March 1918, it was Britain and not France which was ingratiating itself with the new Greek government: 'Our government seems to disinterest itself from the question, the Greek government congratulates itself and the British take advantage of the situation.'[113] Pichon was told in May that French interests were no longer spoken of except to sacrifice them to the insatiable appetite of Italy or to the requirements of Britain.[114] The British were profiting from Venizelos's tenderness for their country and there was already talk of placing an English prince on the throne of Greece in place of the present king, who had failed to win the affection of his subjects.[115] It was a sign of the times that the Greek premier was constantly accompanied by the British naval attaché, Commander Talbot.[116] The post of French commercial attaché, whose holder had been changed three times in two years, was allowed to lapse in the summer of 1918, whereas the head of the British Commercial Bureau had his staff substantially increased. The British Bureau seemed to know more about Greek trade than did the native government and was soon preparing an industrial exhibition in Athens.[117] A group of Greek industrialists, headed by the minister of agriculture, visited Britain by invitation and 'nothing was spared to convince them of Britain's industrial power'.[118] By contrast, French commerce in Greece never developed to the extent which the supporters of the Salonika campaign had hoped. Even around Salonika itself, French trading interests remained relatively underdeveloped throughout the inter-war years.

CHAPTER 8
. . . .
Conclusion

The military correspondent of *The Times*, Charles à Court Repington, recorded a conversation with Philippe Berthelot, chef de cabinet at the Quai d'Orsay, in the summer of 1916. 'Monsieur Berthelot, you are jealous of us.' When Berthelot protested, Repington explained: 'The French *must* be jealous, because we thought that we had made the greatest mistake possible at the Dardanelles, and now the French were trying to make a greater one at Salonika.'[1] It would be futile for the historian to try to confirm such an assessment, but plenty of contemporaries did think in these terms. Lord Hardinge, permanent head of the Foreign Office, agreed with Repington that the Salonika expedition was the worst mistake made during the war.[2] Douglas Haig judged that military historians would never forgive the French for bottling up so many troops at Salonika to so little advantage.[3] Certainly, it is hard to escape the conclusion that, as a military initiative, the campaign was doomed from the outset. In the diplomatic and political crisis of late September 1915, Britain became involved in a Balkan campaign almost absent-mindedly. To have wandered into the campaign without due preparation, clear objectives and a precise plan of action was to court disaster, not least because the experience of the Dardanelles expedition should have made Britain's war leaders more wary of the pitfalls of new adventures away from the major front of the war.[4] Prophetically, even Lloyd George, who was to become the most consistent British advocate of a Balkan strategy, warned in January 1915 that 'all this must take time. Expeditions decided upon and organized with insufficient care and preparation generally end disastrously.'[5] Yet, a few months later, when Lloyd George called for an up-to-date map of the Balkans, it was perhaps indicative that the War Office supplied one dating from

1912, with the national boundaries as they had been before the Balkan Wars and with the Romanian army shown on what was by then Bulgarian territory. 'One would think that the War Office are pulling our leg,' commented Miss Stevenson, 'only I do not think they have sufficient sense of humour for that.'⁶

General Philip Howell, chief of staff to the British commander, captured the chaotic situation as British troops began to arrive at Salonika: 'There's an appalling amount to do here with five [British] divisions pouring in, in no sort of order: no plan, no policy: no answer to questions: Nothing known! ... What they are all coming for – heaven knows, or anyhow the British Cabinet certainly does not.'⁷ In practice, the allied force which arrived at Salonika was too small, too ill-prepared and above all too late to fulfil its stated task of assisting the Serbian army. As a result the Serbs decided to retreat over the mountains towards the Adriatic coast, from where they were eventually transported by allied ships to the island of Corfu. 'The original object (the Servian Army's safety) having disappeared,' insisted Henry Wilson, 'we ought to disappear also.'⁸ Instead, Britain bowed before French pressure and remained in the Balkans for the duration of the war, in the face of the consistent and insistent opinion of competent military advisers that little tangible military advantage could be anticipated from the maintenance of the campaign. On balance, indeed, the allied presence in the Balkans almost certainly worked to the benefit of the enemy. Increasingly, the Germans relied upon the Bulgarian forces to hold this new front while withdrawing their own troops for action elsewhere. As a result the expedition succeeded in immobilizing an allied army which reached 600,000 men by 1917. By contrast a smaller Bulgarian force of about 450,000 men – which would in any case have been unlikely to be deployed outside the Balkans – relied on difficulties of terrain to hold down the numerically superior allied army. In practice, that allied army was too strong for defence and not strong enough for attack. Such a situation was bound to damage the allied cause in the war as a whole.

Salonika itself was far from ideal as a base for extended military operations. As Hankey recorded:

> On the quays and in the harbour there is a state of hopeless congestion. The quays are narrow, and most of them unprovided with any facilities for moving goods, except by hand. For want of sidings the railways can

be made little use of. In short, the quays cannot be cleared as quickly as the Navy can land the goods.[9]

In the months that followed it became apparent just how difficult it was to sustain lines of communication with the Greek port. Repington explained:

> We can only just feed our troops on that front as there is only one single and bad line, and one bad road, and if any more men are sent they must remain at the port or be starved. At present we have 69 ships of 420,000 tons (= three tons a man), permanently engaged in supplying our troops at Salonika , besides 8 ships of 33,000 tons lent to the French.[10]

The climate and terrain did little to help matters. 'This is impossible country to fight in,' judged General Milne, 'too cold in winter, too hot in summer, one gets almost two months in spring and two in autumn.'[11]

But it is not really as a military endeavour that the Salonika campaign stands indicted. 'The part played by diplomacy during the present war', concluded General Robertson with uncharacteristic understatement, 'is not as good as it might have been.'[12] Salonika was the price Britain believed it had to pay and indeed did pay for the maintenance of its wartime alliance with France. The nature of that alliance is difficult to encapsulate. On the one hand it must be remembered that as late as the end of July 1914 no alliance had existed at all. The absence of a formal British commitment to intervene on France's behalf in a European crisis had made it impossible to establish the political and military structures necessary to conduct a coalition war.[13] Yet for four years the British and French armies fought side by side against their common enemies and finally, with considerable American assistance, brought the war to a successful conclusion. That said, the path to the armistice of November 1918 was strewn with innumerable crises in the Anglo-French relationship. In the last resort the establishment of the Supreme War Council in November 1917 owed as much to Lloyd George's manoeuvres within the British civil–military conflict as it did to a genuine desire to co-ordinate the war efforts of the two countries. And it needed the strong possibility of a German victory in the spring of 1918 before there was created a central reserve and an allied supreme command. Even thereafter, relations between Britain and France remained tense, with conflict frequently bubbling up from the surface veneer of diplomatic and military alliance. 'Clemenceau is very bitter against the English,' recorded Lord Derby as late as July 1918: 'He says that everything he proposes is turned down and he summed up the situation by saying, "I have always wished to treat the English as friends and Allies. I can now only treat them as Allies."'[14]

'On paper,' judged William Robertson, 'central control seems obviously easy and necessary. In practice it looks rather impracticable because no one country is prepared to hand itself over body and soul to the dictation of another, and quite rightly so.'[15] But even Robertson, accepting that 'the French are difficult people to do business with', recognized that close co-operation was essential to the successful prosecution of the war – 'No Agreement, no Conference, no anything is of the slightest use without some approach to mutual confidence' – and he refused to accept the conclusion that the only way to achieve this goal lay in allowing the French to have their own way.[16] Yet it could be argued, without too much exaggeration, that this is essentially what Britain did. After all, 'provided that they get absolutely their own way, Frenchmen are the easiest people in the world to get on with'.[17] In the closing weeks of the war, as the French objected to Britain determining the outcome of armistice negotiations with Turkey, Lloyd George described the way in which allied co-operation had so far evolved:

> The British Government have agreed to a French Commander-in-Chief on the Western Front; they have agreed to a French Commander-in-Chief in the Balkans; they have agreed to a French Commander-in-Chief in the Mediterranean. Unless it is to be contended that unity of command means that one nation alone among the Allies is to have not only the supreme but the subordinate command wherever Allied forces are employed on a common enterprise together, I do not understand why it is that you wish to deprive the British of a naval command which they have exercised ever since 1915 in order that a French Admiral may be placed in control of an expedition, three-quarters of which is British in material and personnel.[18]

Such a situation was understandable enough in the early stages of the conflict when Britain's contribution to the common cause was easily outweighed by that of France, but its duration for the entire course of the war demands further explanation. 'We must take charge of the thing in politics in the same way as we are gradually beginning to do in military affairs,' wrote Robertson as the British armed forces gathered strength in 1916.[19] But in practice Robertson's wish was never fulfilled. The key lay in the possibility of a separate German peace with France, and for that matter with Russia. As Foreign Secretary Edward Grey explained for the benefit of the War Committee:

> Germany has taken care to make it known to our Allies that each one of them individually, or at any rate France and Russia, could have peace tomorrow on comparatively favourable terms, if they would separate themselves from us. Our Allies have, therefore, an alternative to continuing the war which is not open to us.[20]

This made the British government peculiarly sensitive to the stability of its French counterpart. This crucial factor in the Anglo-French relationship did not really exist in reverse. Paul Cambon might warn Briand of the dire consequences of the French 'tendency to behave as if we were alone, when we are two', but in practice Britain would put up with whatever France threw at it.[21] Neither under Asquith nor Lloyd George did the possibility for Britain of a compromise peace with Germany enter the bounds of practical politics. Those like Lord Lansdowne who came to embrace such an option immediately cast themselves to the periphery of British politics and never came near to attracting majority support inside the House of Commons. In all probability a pro-war majority also existed in France throughout the war, but the British perception was that an alternative strategy leading to a separate Franco-German peace did exist and that it was a constant threat. Lord Bertie reported in August 1914 that, had Caillaux been in power, he would have secured peace by granting Germany an indemnity to leave French soil.[22] Thereafter, the possibility of his return to office remained an on-going source of anxiety. In May 1916 Lord Esher reported that 'the Caillaux and peace crowds are quietly strengthening their positions, and that the danger of France losing heart about the war and being ready to snatch at any tolerable sort of peace may be great in the autumn'.[23] As late as June 1918 Lord Derby reflected on what he considered a still present threat:

> Had a walk and talk with Lloyd George who seems to me not to realize in the very least what the great danger here is, namely that favourable terms will be offered to France and she will accept them and it will be we who will have to be called upon to pay the price. As long as Clemenceau is in power I do not think there is any fear of a separate peace but still at

the same time if Germany does make a favourable offer to France I do not believe we could afterwards get the French soldiers to fight or the French nation to continue the War as they would say it would be simply and solely to fight for our interests. What will happen then Heaven only knows.[24]

It was not that the British held the governments which presided over France's wartime destiny in particularly high regard – far from it. Of Viviani's Sacred Union administration Asquith wrote:

It is a kind of coalition Government of 'all the talents'; its members hating and distrusting one another; afraid of the Chamber; afraid of the Press; afraid (from the President of the Republic downwards) of their own shadows ... Isn't it extraordinary that a country so rich in resources, human and others, as France, should not have been able at a supreme moment in her history to throw up into the highest places what the French themselves call *hommes de gouvernement*?[25]

Two years later we find Haig sympathizing with General Lyautey's position as war minister within 'a government of political jugglers with a chamber of semilunatics'.[26] The British, in fact, had extreme difficulty in understanding how the French political system managed to work at all. Lord Derby commented:

Of course it is somewhat difficult for anybody who is accustomed to the decorum of the House of Commons to understand the attitude of the corresponding French Chamber. Everybody talks at once, Deputies get up and run about the House shouting, and one Deputy just under me hit another in the stomach but apparently that is thought nothing of and it was looked upon as a comparatively quiet Session.[27]

For all that, each French cabinet from Viviani to Clemenceau was committed to fighting the war to the end. If the survival of these governments depended upon committing British troops to the Balkans to no obvious military purpose and, as became increasingly clear, to the furtherance of specifically French war aims, so be it. On balance it seemed a price worth paying.

The whole thing was none the less galling. As General Smuts reflected in April 1917:

While our Army is defending the soil of France as if it were part of the French Forces, the French have taken the military and diplomatic lead in the Balkans and Greece and are either making mistakes which are seriously embarrassing the success of the War in those parts, or, if success is achieved, are after the War going to enjoy all the prestige in the Balkans which should legitimately have gone to the most powerful and disinterested member of the Entente.[28]

At the back of many minds, moreover, was a strong feeling that the existing alignment of great powers was not necessarily permanent and indeed that it might not long survive the end of the present conflict. 'What worries me', confessed Robertson, 'is the making of peace ... I am not thinking so much of the enemy as of the Allies.'[29] Yet in the last resort and whatever the future held, Britain doubted whether it could win the war without French support. As a result, and contrary to what was sometimes claimed, not least by Foreign Secretary Grey, diplomacy lay at the heart of the British war effort. Keeping the alliance in being was a primary task of British policy-makers. In claiming that this goal was 'completely and successfully achieved', Grey did scant justice to the complexities thrown up by the Balkan campaign.[30]

The Salonika expedition thus came to occupy a central position in the Anglo-French wartime relationship, often appearing as the litmus test of the alliance itself. But that relationship was distorted and given extra dimensions by deep divisions inside the two countries and in particular between their political and military hierarchies. This led to a complex pattern of alignments which often cut across the national boundaries of Britain and France. Though Joffre sometimes found it politically expedient to support the campaign, the British General Staff believed that he was at heart an ally in their opposition to the whole Balkan enterprise. To Colonel Repington the French commander admitted that the campaign was a political and diplomatic question. 'He did not attempt to suggest, and in fact contemptuously denied, that there were any military grounds for the operation.'[31] Similarly, Lloyd George often found himself calling upon the support of French politicians such as Briand and Thomas in his efforts to thwart the opposition of the British military establishment to the whole idea of an 'eastern' strategy.[32] It was said that William Robertson's habitual retort to those with whom he disagreed was, 'I've 'eard different'. If so, this phrase must have been used in the context of Salonika to British and French politicians alike.

In the British setting the Balkan campaign reveals the limits of the authority enjoyed by the military in the direction of the war effort.

Throughout his tenure of office as CIGS Robertson was the most consistent critic of the Salonika expedition. 'My personal opinion on the matter', he stressed,

> is that we shall never win this war in the Balkans. We can only win it by defeating the German Army. We shall never find any great number of German troops in the Balkans, and therefore nothing can please the Germans better than to see us being killed by the Bulgars and our killing the Bulgars.[33]

Militarily, the campaign did seem to be a nonsense. Colonel Repington, who found himself close to Robertson on this issue, put it very clearly. 'Why any sane man can continue to advocate this folly, when the Germans are known to have 118 divisions on the West front and maybe more, while we have only 140 and weaker, is one of those mysteries which no one can fathom.'[34] But there was also a political dimension to the question and it was understandably Britain's politicians who were most conscious of this. Robertson believed that politicians and soldiers should each keep 'within their respective sphere'. In practice this meant excluding politicians from the higher direction of war strategy. 'Where the politician goes wrong is in wanting to know the why and the wherefore of the soldier's proposals and of making the latter the subject of debate and argument across a table.'[35] But even at the height of his power in 1916 Robertson was never able, in the Balkan context at least, to impose his will upon the civilian government. That government repeatedly overruled the military authorities in the interests of the Anglo-French alliance. Only in 1917, when Lloyd George's own enthusiasm for a Balkan strategy began to wane, did Robertson make any real progress in terms of reducing Britain's commitment to this theatre.

In France the position was more complex still, since to the struggle between government and high command was added the additional dimension of the Chamber of Deputies, a far less predictable factor than the British House of Commons. The Balkan campaign represented a key element in the attempts of the French government and parliament to re-establish their control over the war effort after the early months of Joffre's ascendancy. The politics and personality of General Sarrail himself only exacerbated matters. His position within the French army was unique and had no parallel in the British situation. 'You are the only general whom the war has shown to be on our side,' suggested one republican enthusiast.[36] Sarrail's abrupt dismissal in the summer of 1915 extended the scope of France's politico-military struggle by pitting a substantial part of the Chamber and even some ministers against the high command and its allies in the Ministry of War. This extension of friction foreshadowed the government's ultimate renunciation of its determination to defend the high command, come what may. Sarrail's removal from the Western Front worked to the advantage of his political supporters and it was only the launching of a new campaign in the east which prevented an open rupture of the Sacred Union. But Joffre's victory over his rival in the summer of 1915 was a Pyrrhic one. For *L'Affaire Sarrail* reopened those internal political conflicts which still lay just beneath the surface of the Sacred Union, making it impossible for parliament and government any longer to accept the existing military dictatorship. Thereafter, the fortunes of the Salonika expedition became inextricably entwined with the wider struggle for control of France's war policy; military considerations became increasingly secondary, passions and animosities ever more bitter.

Not surprisingly, all of this made effective co-operation with Britain more and more improbable. Except in the sense that Britain had no real alternative to going along with French wishes, the Salonika campaign illustrated the Allies' conduct of the war at its worst. It is this factor alone which renders the campaign capable of rational explanation. There is perhaps something to be said for the sentiment variously attributed to Foch, Pétain and Sarrail: 'I lost some of my respect for Napoleon when I learned what it was to fight a coalition war.'[37]

APPENDIX

· ·

Chronology of the Balkan Campaign

1915

6 Sept	Military convention signed by Austria, Germany and Bulgaria to overthrow Serbia.
22 Sept	Bulgaria declares general mobilization.
5 Oct	First British and French troops land at Salonika; Venizelos resigns as Greek prime minister.
7 Oct	Austro-German offensive begins.
11 Oct	Bulgaria joins the attack on Serbia.
12 Oct	Delcassé resigns as French foreign minister.
29 Oct	Briand succeeds Viviani as French prime minister; Galliéni replaces Millerand as war minister.
2 Dec	Joffre's authority extended by decree to Salonika front.
4 Dec	Britain and France agree at Calais to end campaign.
6 Dec	Decision reversed by military conference at Chantilly.
23 Dec	Robertson becomes CIGS.

1916

17 Mar	Galliéni resigns; replaced by Roques.
9 May	Milne replaces Mahon as British commander at Salonika.
26 May	Bulgarians occupy Fort Rupel.
16 June	First Secret Session of the French Chamber.
6 July	Lloyd George succeeds Kitchener as British war minister.
17 Aug	Treaty of Bucharest paves way for Romanian entry into war.
12 Sept	Sarrail launches offensive.
mid-Sept	Romanian advance halted.
9 Oct	Venizelos establishes provisional government at Salonika.

19 Nov	French and Serbian cavalry enter Monastir.
mid-Nov	Roques's report exonerates Sarrail.
28 Nov	Second Secret Session of French Chamber.
1 Dec	Athens ambush.
5 Dec	Asquith resigns as British prime minister; succeeded by Lloyd George.
6 Dec	Central powers enter Bucharest.
12 Dec	Briand reorganizes French cabinet; Lyautey replaces Roques.
26 Dec	Joffre resigns.

1917

5 Jan	Rome Conference opens.
18 Mar	Briand resigns; Ribot becomes prime minister with Painlevé at the War Ministry.
24 April	Milne attacks west of Lake Dojran.
9 May	Sarrail launches offensive.
14 June	King Constantine of Greece deposed.
13 Sept	Painlevé succeeds Ribot as French prime minister.
13 Nov	Painlevé government falls; succeeded by Clemenceau.
10 Dec	Sarrail recalled; replaced by Guillaumat.

1918

18 Feb	Wilson replaces Robertson as CIGS.
30 May	Guillaumat launches operation west of the Vardar.
8 June	Guillaumat recalled to France; replaced by Franchet d'Espérey.
15 Sept	Franchet d'Espérey launches major offensive.
30 Sept	Franchet d'Espérey grants armistice to Bulgaria.

Notes

1. The Uncertain Alliance

1. It was at the time of Fashoda that a French politician and editor wrote that a Franco-German invasion of Britain would be 'the greatest joy of my life as an ardent patriot'. Paul de Cassagnac, cited in E. M. Carroll, *French Public Opinion and Foreign Affairs 1870–1914* (New York,1931), p. 176.

2. D. French, *The Strategy of the Lloyd George Coalition 1916–1918* (Oxford, 1995), pp. 3–4.

3. P. M. H. Bell, *France and Britain 1900–1940: Entente and Estrangement* (London, 1996), p. 7.

4. K. Wilson, 'The Channel Tunnel Question at the Committee of Imperial Defence, 1906–1914', *Journal of Strategic Studies* 13, 2 (1990), p. 119.

5. D. Stevenson, *The First World War and International Politics* (Oxford, 1988), p. 20.

6. T. Wilson, 'Britain's Moral Commitment to France in August 1914', *History* 64 (1979), p. 387.

7. C. M. Andrew and A. S. Kanya-Forstner, *France Overseas: The Great War and the Climax of French Imperial Expansion* (London, 1981), p. 12.

8. D. Porch, 'The French Army in the First World War', in A. R. Millett and W. Murray (eds), *Military Effectiveness: The First World War*, Vol. I (Boston, 1988), pp. 200–1; S. R. Williamson, *The Politics of Grand Strategy: Britain and France Prepare for War 1904–1914* (Cambridge, MA, 1969), ch. 8.

9. Nicolson to Buchanan 7 April 1914, cited in Z. Steiner, *The Foreign Office and Foreign Policy* (Cambridge, 1969), p. 130.

10. Stevenson, *First World War*, p. 34.

11. W. J. Philpott, *Anglo-French Relations and Strategy on the Western Front, 1914–18* (London, 1996), p. 13.

12. Stevenson, *First World War*, p. 37.

13. K. Wilson (ed.), *Decisions for War, 1914* (London, 1995), p. 121.

14. W. K. Hancock and J. van der Poel (eds), *Selections from the Smuts Papers*, Vol. 3 (Cambridge, 1966), p. 488.

15. D. Lloyd George, *War Memoirs*, Vol. 2 (London, 1933), p. 709.

16. D. French, *British Economic and Strategic Planning 1905–1915* (London, 1982), p. 51; D. French, *British Strategy and War Aims 1914–1916* (London, 1986), p. 65; J. L. Wallach, *Uneasy Coalition: The Entente Experience in World War One* (Westport, 1993), p. 25.

17. French, *Strategy and War Aims*, p. xi.

18. Lloyd George explained to the American president, 'As compared with the enemy, the fundamental weakness of the Allies is that the direction of their military operations lacks real unity. At a very early stage of the War, Germany established a practically despotic dominion over all her Allies ... The direction of the War on [the Allies'] side has remained in the hands of four separate Governments and four separate General Staffs.' P. Rowland, *Lloyd George* (London, 1975), p. 416. Valentine Chirol concurred: 'At Berlin they make up their minds to do a thing and just press a button. With us there are interminable consultations between four capitals.' Chirol to Nicolson, 23 August 1915, cited in C. J. Lowe, 'The Failure of British Diplomacy in the Balkans, 1914–1916', *Canadian Journal of History* 3 (1968), p. 100.

19. Public Record Office (PRO), CAB 37/124, 'Some further considerations on the conduct of the war', 22 February 1915; French, *Strategy and War Aims*, p. 92.

20. See, for example, D. French in J. Turner (ed.), *Britain and the First World War* (London, 1988), p. 24: 'The factor which dominated British strategy between 1914 and 1918 was that she fought the war as a member of a coalition.' For some interesting observations on the nature of coalition warfare, see P. Kennedy, 'Military Coalitions and Coalition Warfare over the Past Century', in K. Neilson and R. Prete (eds), *Coalition Warfare: An Uneasy Accord* (Waterloo, Ont., 1983), pp. 3–15.

21. As early as December 1914 the German chancellor wrote that 'for us everything depends on shattering the [enemy] coalition, i.e., on [concluding] a separate peace with one of our enemies'. French, *Strategy and War Aims*, p. 57.

22. G. Clemenceau, *Grandeur and Misery of Victory* (London, 1930), p. 113.

23. M. Cornick, 'The Myth of "Perfidious Albion" and French National Identity', in D. Dutton (ed.), *Statecraft and Diplomacy in the Twentieth Century* (Liverpool, 1995), pp. 7–33.

24. French, *Strategy and War Aims*, p. 82.

25. French, *Economic and Strategic Planning*, p. 127; French, *Strategy and War Aims*, p. 244.

26. Lord Derby diary, 28 August 1921, cited in R. S. Churchill, *Lord Derby: 'King of Lancashire'* (London, 1959), p. 192.

27. French, *Strategy and War Aims*, p. 216.

28. P. Morand, *Journal d'un attaché d'ambassade, 1916–1917* (Paris, 1948), p. 28.

29. Millerand to Delcassé, 5 January 1915, cited in Andrew and Kanya-Forstner, *France Overseas*, p. 70.

30. J. Grigg, *Lloyd George: From Peace to War 1912–1916* (London, 1985), pp. 269–70.

31. Philpott, *Anglo-French Relations*, p. 91.

32. Ibid., pp. 69–70.

33. PRO, FO 371/2880, minute by Balfour on a memorandum by H. Nicolson on allied policy in Greece, 27 January 1917.

34. W. Robertson, *Soldiers and Statesmen 1914–1918*, Vol. 1 (London, 1926), p. 211; see also W. Robertson, *From Private to Field Marshal* (London, 1921), p. 292.

35. A. Adamthwaite, *Grandeur and Misery: France's Bid for Power in Europe 1914–1940* (London, 1995), p. 33.

36. R. A. Prete, 'French Strategic Planning and the Deployment of the BEF in France in 1914', *Canadian Journal of History* 26 (1989), p. 42.

37. Ibid., pp. 61–2; Philpott, *Anglo-French Relations*, p. 13.

38. R. A. Prete, 'Joffre and the Question of Allied Supreme Command, 1914–1916', *Proceedings of the Annual Meeting of the Western Society for French History* 16 (1989), p. 329.

39. B. H. Liddell Hart, *Reputations Ten Years After* (London, 1928), p. 31.

40. E. L. Spears, *Prelude to Victory* (London, 1939), p. 61; Roy Prete has argued that Joffre has received insufficient credit for the progress made towards unity of command during his period as French commander-in-chief. 'Joffre and the Question', pp. 334–5.

41. Spears, *Prelude*, p. 63.

42. T. H. Bliss, 'The Evolution of the Unified Command', *Foreign Affairs* 1, 2 (1922), p. 6; French, *Lloyd George Coalition*, p. 164.

43. Cecil to Balfour, 25 August 1917, cited in V. H. Rothwell, *British War Aims and Peace Diplomacy 1914–1918* (Oxford, 1971), p. 102.

44. O. Esher (ed.), *Journals and Letters of Reginald, Viscount Esher. Vol. 3: 1910–1915* (London, 1938), p. 220.

45. Robertson to Haig, 5 January 1916, cited in R. Blake (ed.), *The Private Papers of Douglas Haig 1914–1919* (London, 1952), p. 122.

46. G. Cassar, *The Tragedy of Sir John French* (Newark, 1985), p. 225.

47. Haig to wife, 23 August 1917.

48. Maréchal Fayolle, *Cahiers Secrets de la Grande Guerre* (Paris, 1964), p. 161.

49. Bell, *Entente and Estrangement*, p. 20.

50. General Henry Wilson, diary 18 March 1917, cited in French, *Lloyd George Coalition*, p. 289.

51. B. Pimlott (ed.), *The Second World War Diary of Hugh Dalton 1940–45* (London, 1986), p. 694. According to Lloyd George, 'in order of [Robertson's] distrust came Frenchmen, first and deepest of all ... and last of all – if at all – Germans': Lloyd George, *War Memoirs*, Vol. 2, p. 780.

52. D. Winter, *Haig's Command* (London, 1991), p. 27.

53. Bliss, 'Unified Command', p. 2.

54. K. Halle, *Irrepressible Churchill: A Treasury of Winston Churchill's Wit* (Cleveland, 1966), p. 157.

55. D. Johnson, F. Bédarida and F. Crouzet (eds), *Britain and France: Ten Centuries* (Folkestone, 1980), p. 269; see also Bell, *Entente and Estrangement*, pp. 82, 91.

56. PRO, CAB 42/3/16, Dardanelles Committee, 20 August 1915.

57. Esher (ed.), *Esher Journals*, Vol. 3, p. 200.

58. Bodleian Library, Gwynne MSS, 17, Callwell to H. Gwynne, 14 June 1914.

59. *L'Homme Enchaîné*, 26 December 1915, cited in D. R. Watson, *Georges Clemenceau: A Political Biography* (London, 1974), p. 255.

60. J. M. Bourne, *Britain and the Great War 1914–1918* (London, 1989), p. 149.

61. A. Moorehead, *Gallipoli* (London, 1956), p. 364.

62. T. Higgins, *Winston Churchill and the Dardanelles* (London, 1963), p. 185.

63. E. Delage, *The Tragedy of the Dardanelles* (London, 1932), p. 251.

64. Ministère des Affaires Etrangères (MAE), Jules Cambon MSS, P. Cambon to J. Cambon, 6 December 1915.

65. R. David, *Le Drame Ignoré de l'Armée d'Orient* (Paris, 1927), p. ix. Churchill at least must be numbered among the campaign's British enthusiasts: 'Yet it is true that if you could have had your way last January about Salonika ... the whole face of the war wd. have been changed.' Churchill to Lloyd George, 25 January 1916, cited in M. Gilbert, *Winston S. Churchill*, Vol. 3 (London, 1971), p. 692.

66. A. Pingaud, *Histoire Diplomatique de la France pendant la Grande Guerre*, Vol. I (Paris, 1937), p. 215.

67. C. B. Falls, *Military Operations: Macedonia*, 2 vols, (London, 1933–35) and Ministère de la Guerre, Etat-Major de l'Armée, Service Historique, *Les Armées françaises dans la grande guerre*, tome 8 (Paris, 1924) remain indispensable. See also A. Palmer, *The Gardeners of Salonika: The Macedonian Campaign 1915–1918* (London, 1965), and J. K. Tanenbaum, *General Maurice Sarrail 1856–1929: The French Army and Left-Wing Politics* (Chapel Hill, 1974).

68. Robertson, *Soldiers and Statesmen*, Vol. 2, p. 83.

69. G. Ward Price, *The Story of the Salonika Army* (London, 1918), p. 237.

2. The Origins of the Campaign

1. Archives de Guerre, 5N132, Sarrail to Millerand, 21 September 1915.

2. MAE, A-Guerre 283, Delcassé to Guillemin 23 September 1915.

3. M. G. Fry, *Lloyd George and Foreign Policy*, Vol. 1 (Montreal, 1977), pp. 267–8; B. B. Gilbert, *David Lloyd George: A Political Life. Organizer of Victory 1912–16* (London, 1992), p. 140.

4. M. and E. Brock (eds), *H. H. Asquith: Letters to Venetia Stanley* (Oxford, 1985), p. 324.

5. K. Neilson, *Strategy and Supply: The Anglo-Russian Alliance, 1914–17* (London, 1984), p. 44; Brock (eds), *Asquith*, p. 386; D. Stevenson, *The First World War and International Politics* (Oxford, 1988), p. 61.

6. E. David (ed.), *Inside Asquith's Cabinet: From the Diaries of Charles Hobhouse* (London, 1977), p. 208.

7. K. Robbins, 'British Diplomacy and Bulgaria 1914–1915', *Slavonic and East European Review* 49 (1971), pp. 560–85.

8. E. Grey, *Twenty-Five Years*, Vol. 1 (London, 1925), p. 263.

9. T. P. Conwell-Evans, *Foreign Policy from a Back Bench 1904–1918: A Study Based on the Papers of Lord Noel-Buxton* (London, 1932), pp. 88–115.

10. Brock (eds), *Asquith*, pp. 380–1.

11. Ibid., p. 449.

12. House of Lords Record Office (HLRO), Lloyd George MSS, C/5/7/13, Lloyd George to Kitchener, 29 January 1915.

13. D. French, *British Strategy and War Aims 1914–1916* (London, 1986), pp. x, xii.

14. Cf. D. R. Woodward (ed.), *The Military Correspondence of Field-Marshal Sir William Robertson, Chief Imperial General Staff, December 1915–February 1918* (London, 1989), pp. 312–13.

15. W. J. Philpott, *Anglo-French Relations and Strategy on the Western Front, 1914–18* (London, 1996), p. 69.

16. W. J. Philpott, 'Kitchener and the 29th Division: A Study in Anglo-French Strategic Relations, 1914–1915', *Journal of Strategic Studies* 16, 3 (1993), pp. 375–6.

17. J. Barnes and D. Nicholson (eds), *The Leo Amery Diaries*, Vol. 1 (London, 1980), p. 122.

18. A. Pingaud, 'Les origines de l'expédition de Salonique', *Revue historique* 176 (1935), p. 449.

19. G. H. Cassar, *The French and the Dardanelles* (London, 1971), p. 35.

20. P. Azan, *Franchet d'Espérey* (Paris, 1949), pp. 42–3.

21. M. A. Leblond, *Galliéni parle* Vol. 2 (Paris, 1920), p. 57; M. Hankey, *The Supreme Command, 1914–1918*, Vol. 1 (London, 1961), p. 254; G. Galliéni (ed.), *Les Carnets de Galliéni* (Paris, 1932), passim; P. Gheusi, *Geurre et Théâtre* (Paris, 1919), p. 136.

22. B. H. Liddell Hart, *Reputations Ten Years After* (London, 1928), p. 93.

23. R. Poincaré, *Au Service de la France*, Vol. 7 (Paris, 1931), p. 128.

24. G. Suarez, *Briand: Sa vie, son oeuvre*, Vol. 3 (Paris, 1939), p. 90.

25. Poincaré, *Au Service*, Vol. 6 (Paris, 1930), p. 3.

26. E. Herbillon, *Souvenirs d'un officier de liaison pendant la guerre mondiale: du général en chef au gouvernement*, Vol. 1 (Paris, 1930), p. 90.

27. Brock (eds), *Asquith*, p. 345.

28. PRO, WO 79/63, Kitchener to French, 2 January 1915.

29. HLRO, Lloyd George MSS, C/16/1/3, 'Suggestions as to the Military Position', 1 January 1915; D. Lloyd George, *War Memoirs*, Vol. 1 (London, 1933), pp. 369–80.

30. HLRO, Lloyd George MSS, C/16/1/4, 'War Council January 13th 1915'.

31. Asquith to Lord Stamfordham, 22 January 1915, cited in G. H. Cassar, *Asquith as War Leader* (London, 1994), p. 65.

202 · *Notes to Chapter 2*

32. Brock (eds), *Asquith*, pp. 388–9.

33. PRO, CAB 42/1/27, War Council, 28 January 1915.

34. Brock (eds), *Asquith*, p. 391.

35. Ibid., p. 393; M. M. Farrar, *Principled Pragmatist: The Political Career of Alexandre Millerand* (Oxford, 1991), p. 179; O. Esher (ed.), *Journal and Letters of Reginald, Viscount Esher 1910–1915* (London, 1938), pp. 208–10.

36. PRO, CAB 42/1/26.

37. HLRO, Lloyd George MSS, C/3/16/17, Lloyd George to Churchill 29 January 1915.

38. Ibid., E/2/15/4, Lloyd George to Grey, 7 February 1915; Lloyd George, *War Memoirs*, Vol. 1, pp. 407–13. In conversation with Poincaré, Lloyd George also 'called the President's attention to the advisability of setting up a Council in France, with representatives from the French, Russian and British Commanders-in-Chief, so that the latter may be kept informed of the intentions and operations of their colleagues, there being at present a lack of co-ordination between the Armies of the Allies'. Lady A. G. Lennox (ed.), *The Diary of Lord Bertie of Thame 1914–1918*, Vol. 1 (London, 1924), pp. 107–8.

39. D. Woodward, *Lloyd George and the Generals* (Newark, 1983), p. 37.

40. S. Roskill, *Hankey, Man of Secrets*, Vol. 1 (London, 1970), p. 155.

41. PRO, CAB 42/1/33.

42. MAE, A-Guerre 219, Delcassé to Viviani, 9 February 1915.

43. PRO, CAB 42/1/35.

44. Brock (eds), *Asquith*, p. 433.

45. HLRO, Lloyd George MSS, C/16/1/9, note by Hankey, 'After the Dardanelles: The Next Steps'.

46. Brock (eds), *Asquith*, p. 456.

47. T. Wilson, *The Myriad Faces of War* (Oxford, 1986), p. 105.

48. Emmott diary, 4 January 1915, cited in D. French, *British Economic and Strategic Planning 1905–1915* (London, 1982), p. 176. 'Remote and secretive, [Kitchener] often kept his strategical views to himself and made little effort to carry his civilian colleagues with him': D. R. Woodward, 'Britain in a Continental War: The Civil–Military Debate over the Strategical Direction of the Great War of 1914–1918', *Albion* 12, 1 (1980), p. 37.

49. Kitchener to Esher, 22 February 1915, cited in J. Gooch, *The Plans of War: The General Staff and British Military Strategy c.1900–1916* (London, 1974), p. 304.

50. A. Pingaud, 'Les origines de l'expédition de Salonique', p. 456.

51. Though published nearly half a century ago, J. C. King, *Generals and Politicians: Conflict between France's High Command, Parliament and Government, 1914–1918* (Berkeley, 1951), remains an essential introduction to the subject of politico-military relations in wartime France.

52. P. Renouvin, *The Forms of War Government in France* (New Haven, 1927), p. 81.

53. J. F. V. Keiger, *Raymond Poincaré* (Cambridge, 1997), pp. 209, 219.

54. P. M. de la Gorce, *The French Army* (New York, 1963), pp. 86–7.

55. J. M. Bourget, *Gouvernement et Commandement* (Paris, 1930), p. 239.

56. Lennox (ed.), *Bertie Diary*, Vol. 1, p. 59.

57. J. Joffre, *The Memoirs of Marshal Joffre*, Vol. 2 (London, 1932), p. 550.

58. Liddell Hart, *Reputations*, p. 7.

59. Farrar, *Principled Pragmatist*, p. 167; J. Horne, 'A Parliamentary State at War: France 1914–1918', in A. Cosgrove and J. I. McGuire (eds), *Parliament and Community* (Belfast, 1983), p. 214.

60. Cassar, *French and Dardanelles*, p. 151.

61. King, *Generals and Politicians*, p. 42; 'Mermeix' G. Terrail, *Joffre: La Première Crise du Commandement* (Paris, 1919), pp. 26, 31.

62. Joffre, *Memoirs*, Vol. 2, p. 391.

63. MAE, Edouard de Billy MSS, diary, 8 March 1915: 'Millerand still very much under attack, still holds on.'

64. Poincaré, *Au Service*, Vol. 6, p. 277.

65. A. Horne, *The French Army and Politics 1870–1970* (London, 1984), p. 37.

66. A. Ferry, *Les Carnets Secrets* (Paris, 1957), p. 89.

67. Cassar, *French and Dardanelles*, p. 12. Sarrail's anti-clericalism was the essential counterpart to his republicanism. As Churchill later put it, 'whatever dispute there might be about his military achievements, his irreligious convictions were above suspicion'. W. S. Churchill, *The World Crisis* (2 vol. edn, London, 1938), Vol. 2, p. 888.

68. Cassar, *French and Dardanelles*, p. 152; J.K.Tanenbaum, *General Maurice Sarrail 1856–1929* (Chapel Hill, 1974), pp. 15–24.

69. Suarez, *Briand*, Vol. 3, p. 432. For a recent assessment of the Radical Socialists during the war, see S. Berstein, 'The Radical Socialist Party During the First World War', in P. Fridenson (ed.), *The French Home Front 1914–1918* (Oxford, 1992), pp. 37–56.

70. Foch to Joffre, 3 December 1914, cited in Joffre, *Memoirs*, Vol. 2, p. 373.

71. H. Cambon (ed.), *Paul Cambon: Correspondance 1870–1924*, Vol. 3 (Paris, 1946), p. 158; See also MAE, Jules Cambon MSS, P. Cambon to J. Cambon, 21 October 1916: 'This fellow Sarrail is the man of the Radical Socialist party which wants to retain power come what may and which dreams of an 18 Fructidor.' This is a reference to the *coup d'état* of 1797 by which the Directory and the Councils were purged of royalist sympathizers.

72. de la Gorce, *French Army*, p. 106; 'Mermeix' G. Terrail, *Sarrail et les Armées d'Orient* (Paris, 1920), p. 178.

73. Terrail, *Joffre*, p. 52.

74. Poincaré, *Au Service*, Vol. 6, p. 137.

75. Ibid., p. 254.

76. PRO, WO 159/11/18, Yarde-Buller to Kitchener, 26 July 1915.

77. Cassar, *French and Dardanelles*, pp. 154–5.

78. Joffre, *Memoirs*, Vol. 2, p. 376.

79. Ferry, *Carnets Secrets*, p. 100.

80. Joffre to Dubail 16 July 1915, cited in Joffre, *Memoirs*, Vol. 2, p. 374.

81. Herbillon, *Souvenirs*, Vol. 1, p. 166.

82. Ferry, *Carnets Secrets*, p. 100.

83. AG, Fonds Joffre, 14N1.

84. Cf. Cassar, *French and Dardanelles*, p. 155. Note that the version of Dubail's report given in Joffre's memoirs is considerably more condemnatory than that to be found in the Fonds Joffre, AG, 14N1. This may account for the remark made by Marcel Sembat at the Council of Ministers that there was a gap between Dubail's memoranda and the severe conclusions which Joffre drew from them: Ferry, *Carnets Secrets*, p. 100.

85. Poincaré, *Au Service*, Vol. 6, p. 332.

86. Herbillon, *Souvenirs*, Vol. 1, p. 170.

87. M. E. Schmidt, *Alexandre Ribot: Odyssey of a Liberal in the Third Republic* (The Hague, 1974), p. 142.

88. Poincaré, *Au Service*, Vol. 6, pp. 336–7.

89. Ibid., p. 304.

90. Ferry, *Carnets Secrets*, p. 101.

91. PRO, WO 159/11/12, Yarde-Buller to Kitchener, 24 July 1915.

92. M. Sarrail, *Mon Commandement en Orient 1916–1918* (Paris, 1920), p. vii.

93. AG, 5N364, censored article.

94. Herbillon, *Souvenirs*, Vol. 1, p. 170.

95. PRO, WO 159/11/13, Yarde-Buller to Kitchener, 26 July 1915.

96. Lennox (ed.), *Bertie Diary*, Vol. 1, p. 204.

97. PRO, Grey MSS, FO 800/58, Bertie to Grey, 27 July 1915; PRO, Bertie MSS, FO 800/167/Fr/15/55, Bertie to Grey, 1 August 1915.

98. Poincaré, *Au Service*, Vol. 6, p. 340.

99. Ibid., p. 341.

100. Ibid., p. 342.

101. Sarrail, *Mon Commandement*, p. viii.

102. Poincaré, *Au Service*, Vol. 6, p. 344; Archives Nationales (AN) C7488.

103. Poincaré, *Au Service*, Vol. 6, pp. 347–8.

104. Cassar, *French and Dardanelles*, p. 163.

105. Poincaré, *Au Service*, Vol. 6, pp. 350–1.

106. Sarrail, *Mon Commandement*, p. viii.

107. PRO, WO 159/11/24, Yarde-Buller to Kitchener, 31 July 1915.

108. PRO, Bertie MSS, FO 800/167/Fr/15/56, Bertie to Grey, 3 August 1915; PRO, Grey MSS, FO 800/58, Bertie to Grey, 6 August 1915.

109. MAE, Edouard de Billy MSS, carton 2.

110. Poincaré, *Au Service*, Vol. 7, p. 11; Sarrail, *Mon Commandement*, p. ix.

111. Ferry, *Carnets Secrets*, p. 100.

112. Joffre, *Memoirs*, Vol. 2, p. 371.

113. AG, 5N132, Joffre to Millerand, 3 August 1915.

114. Sarrail, *Mon Commandement*, p. ix.

115. AG, 5N132, 'Note au sujet de la situation militaire en Orient'; Poincaré,

Au Service, Vol. 7, p. 39; P. Coblentz, *The Silence of Sarrail* (London, 1930), pp. 103–4.

116. Ministère de la Guerre, *Les Armées françaises dans la grande guerre*, tome 8, Vol. I (Paris, 1924), annexe 318; Poincaré, *Au Service*, Vol. 7, p. 37.

117. Poincaré, *Au Service*, Vol. 7, pp. 42, 68.

118. AG, 16N1678, Joffre to Millerand, 1 September 1915.

119. AG, 16N1678, 'Note au sujet des Dardanelles'.

120. AG, 16N1678, Joffre to Millerand, 1 September 1915.

121. MAE, A-Guerre 1065, Millerand to Delcassé, 28 August 1915.

122. Poincaré, *Au Service*, Vol. 7, p. 73.

123. MAE, A-Guerre 1065, Millerand to Delcassé 31 August 1915.

124. Poincaré, *Au Service*, Vol. 7, pp. 79, 83.

125. Herbillon, *Souvenirs*, Vol. 1, p. 183; Ministère de la Guerre, *Les armées françaises*, tome 8, Vol. 1, annexes 348, 351.

126. PRO, CAB 28/1, procès-verbal.

127. Cassar, *French and Dardnelles*, p. 191.

128. MAE, A-Guerre 1066, 'Note au sujet des Dardanelles', 15 September 1915.

129. Millerand to Joffre, 14 September 1915, cited in Ministère de la Guerre, *Les Armées françaises*, tome 8, Vol. 1, annexe 358.

130. AG, 5N132, Joffre to Millerand, 20 September 1915.

131. Poincaré, *Au Service*, Vol. 7, p. 111.

132. Cassar, *French and Dardanelles*, p. 193.

133. AN, C7488, Chamber Foreign Affairs Commission, 22 September 1915.

134. AN, Painlevé MSS, 313AP109, undated note by Paul Bouët, Sarrail's son-in-law.

135. MAE, A-Guerre 283, Guillemin to Delcassé, 19 September 1915.

136. Ibid., Guillemin to Delcassé, 21 September 1915.

137. MAE, A-Guerre 283, Delcassé to Guillemin, 23 September 1915.

138. MAE, A-Guerre 1030, military attaché to Millerand, 24 September 1915.

139. MAE, A-Guerre 283, Delcassé to Cambon, 23 September 1915.

140. PRO, CAB 24/1/23, note on the position in the Balkans.

141. PRO, FO 371/2266, Grey to Elliot, 22 September 1915.

142. PRO, CAB 42/3/28, Dardanelles Committee 23 September 1915.

143. PRO, CAB 37/135/1, Asquith to George V, 2 October 1915.

144. PRO, CAB 42/4/21.

145. Recent writing has tended to stress that, at least in the early stages of the war, Constantine was neither pro-German nor pro-entente, but merely pro-Greek and thus reluctant to enter an unpromising conflict. As he wrote to his brother, 'For the present, at any rate, it is imperative that we should remain neutral. But as to joining Germany, such an eventuality is and always will be an impossibility': J. Van der Kiste, *Kings of the Hellenes: The Greek Kings 1863–1974* (Stroud, 1994), p. 90.

146. Cambon (ed.), *Correspondance*, Vol. 3, p. 83.
147. Sarrail, *Mon Commandement*, pp. xiv–xv.
148. AG, 16N3275, Sarrail to Millerand, 2 October 1915.
149. AG, 7N1338, order by Millerand 2 October 1915.
150. Sarrail, *Mon Commandement*, p. xv.
151. M. Sarrail, 'La Grèce Venizeliste', *Revue de Paris*, 15 December 1919.

3. The Pattern Set

1. PRO, CAB 37/135/20, Nicolson to Grey, 11 October 1915.
2. PRO, CAB 42/4/6, summary of Joffre's note of 9 October 1915.
3. MAE, A-Guerre 1030, Viviani to Delcassé, 7 October 1915.
4. MAE, A-Guerre 1030, Viviani to Cambon, 11 October 1915; PRO, CAB 37/136/3, note by Grey.
5. HLRO, Lloyd George MSS, D/23/4/16, memorandum, 9 October 1915.
6. A. J. P. Taylor (ed.), *Lloyd George: A Diary by Frances Stevenson* (London, 1971), p. 66.
7. PRO, CAB 42/4/6.
8. Taylor (ed.), *Lloyd George Diary*, p. 67.
9. J. Turner, *British Politics and the Great War: Coalition and Conflict 1915–1918* (New Haven, 1992), p. 69.
10. S. Roskill, *Hankey, Man of Secrets*, Vol. 1 (London, 1970), p. 225.
11. P. Williamson (ed.), *The Modernisation of Conservative Politics: The Diaries and Letters of William Bridgeman, 1904–1935* (London, 1988), p. 89.
12. Archives Nationales (AN), C7647.
13. G. Suarez, *Briand: Sa vie, son oeuvre*, Vol. 3 (Paris, 1939), p. 146; R. Poincaré, *Au Service de la France*, Vol. 7 (Paris, 1931), p. 158.
14. Poincaré, *Au Service*, Vol. 7, p. 148.
15. Ibid., p. 168.
16. Archives of the Belgian Ministry of Foreign Affairs, note by Belgian ambassador in Paris, Guillaume, 10 October 1915.
17. A. Ribot, *Letters to a Friend* (London, 1926), p. 122.
18. MAE, de Billy MSS, carton 2, diary, 1 November 1915.
19. Archives of the Belgian Ministry of Foreign Affairs, note by Guillaume, 14 October 1915; A. Ferry, *Les Carnets Secrets* (Paris, 1957), p. 117.
20. Poincaré, *Au Service*, Vol. 7, p. 176.
21. MAE, Delcassé MSS, ix, Braibant to Delcassé, 14 October 1915.
22. J. K. Tanenbaum, *General Maurice Sarrail 1856–1929: The French Army and Left-Wing Politics* (Chapel Hill, 1974), p. 71; C. E. Callwell, *Field-Marshal Sir Henry Wilson: His Life and Diaries*, Vol. 1 (London, 1927), p. 254. In fact Kitchener had already notified the French government that two British divisions being withdrawn from the Somme would be sent to Egypt, not Salonika.
23. Tanenbaum, *Sarrail*, p. 71; Lady A. G. Lennox (ed.), *The Diary of Lord Bertie of Thame 1914–1918*, Vol. 1 (London, 1924), p. 245.

24. Archives of the Senate, procès-verbal Foreign Affairs Commision; Institut de France, Pichon MSS, 4398.

25. AN, C7488.

26. MAE, A-Guerre 1031, Viviani to Cambon, 17 October 1915.

27. PRO, CAB 37/136/17, note from the Serbian legation, 16 October 1915.

28. Taylor (ed.), *Lloyd George Diary*, p. 70.

29. MAE, A-Guerre 1031, Cambon to Viviani, 19 October 1915.

30. Liddell Hart Centre for Military Archives (LHCMA), Robertson MSS, I/8/26, Callwell to Robertson, 20 October 1915.

31. LHCMA, Robertson MSS, I/8/28, Callwell to Robertson, 22 October 1915.

32. LHCMA, Robertson MSS, I/8/29, Robertson to Callwell, 23 October 1915.

33. D. French, *British Strategy and War Aims 1914–1916* (London, 1986), p. 142.

34. PRO, FO 371/2270, Bertie to Grey, 23 October 1915.

35. PRO, FO 371/2270, Nicolson to Grey, 24 October 1915.

36. Cf. Sir F. Maurice, *Lessons of Allied Cooperation* (London, 1942), p. 51.

37. PRO, CAB 42/4/17, Dardanelles Committee, 25 October 1915.

38. AG, 16N1679, Joffre to Millerand, 27 October 1915.

39. PRO, FO 371/2270, Grey to Granville, 28 October 1915.

40. PRO, CAB 42/4/20, appendix C, note by M. Hankey; Maurice, *Allied Cooperation*, p. 54.

41. Lennox (ed.), *Bertie Diary*, Vol. 1, p. 262.

42. AG, 16N1678, Joffre to Millerand, 3 October 1915.

43. On Joffre's changing attitude to the campaign, see University of Birmingham Library, Chamberlain MSS, AC14/6/61, F. S. Oliver to A. Chamberlain, 14 December 1915.

44. G. Galliéni (ed.), *Les Carnets de Galliéni* (Paris, 1932), p. 210; A. Conte, *Joffre* (Paris, 1991), p. 314.

45. MAE, A-Guerre 1031, Fleuriau to Martin, 16 October 1915; Poincaré, *Au Service*, Vol. 7, p. 190.

46. H. Cambon (ed.), *Paul Cambon: Correspondance 1870–1924*, Vol. 3 (Paris, 1946), p. 89.

47. AN, Painlevé MSS, 313AP56, note by H. Niche, 26 December 1916.

48. PRO, Bertie MSS, FO 800/167, Bertie to Grey, 25 December 1915.

49. A. Adamthwaite, *Grandeur and Misery: France's Bid for Power in Europe 1914–1940* (London, 1995), p. 112.

50. HLRO, Lloyd George MSS, E/3/14/32, Le Roy Lewis to Lloyd George, 30 November 1916.

51. HLRO, Lloyd George MSS, E/2/15/4, Lloyd George to Grey, 7 February 1915; Lord Riddell, *War Diary 1914–1918* (London, 1933), p. 60.

52. Liverpool Record Office (LRO), Derby MSS, 920 DER(17) 28/1/1,

diary, 30 October 1918; cf. Viscount Cecil of Chelwood, *All the Way* (London, 1949), p. 201: 'Physically [Lloyd George and Briand] were wonderfully alike, obviously of the same race, with the same personal charm and the same conversational attraction.'

53. Lennox (ed.), *Bertie Diary*, Vol. 2, p. 32.

54. Ibid., p. 104

55. PRO, CAB 37/137/39, memorandum by Joffre, 29 October 1915.

56. M. Hankey, *The Supreme Command, 1914–1918*, Vol. 1 (London, 1961), p. 434.

57. PRO, CAB 37/137/39, Kitchener to Joffre, 30 October 1915.

58. PRO, Bertie MSS, FO 800/172/Gr/15/15, record of conversation with Lansdowne, Curzon and Lloyd George, 28 October 1915.

59. PRO, CAB 42/4/20.

60. PRO, WO 106/1335, 'The Military Position of the Allies in the Near-East', n.d.

61. PRO, WO 32/5122, 'Appreciation of the Military Situation', 31 October 1915.

62. PRO, FO 371/2272, Grey to Bertie, 4 November 1915.

63. MAE, A-Guerre 1032, Fleuriau to Briand, 4 November 1915.

64. PRO, CAB 42/5/5, Kitchener to Asquith, 5 November 1915; British Library, Balfour MSS, Add. MS 49726, Kitchener to Balfour, 5 November 1915.

65. Poincaré, *Au Service*, Vol. 7, p. 225.

66. Suarez, *Briand*, Vol. 3, p. 191.

67. AG, 16N3136, Galliéni to Sarrail, 6 November 1915.

68. AG, 16N3142, Galliéni to Sarrail, 11 November 1915.

69. PRO, FO 371/2270, Grey to Bertie, 10 November 1915.

70. Poincaré, *Au Service*, Vol. 7, p. 248.

71. PRO, CAB 42/5/8, War Committee, 12 November 1915.

72. MAE, A-Guerre 1033, Girondon to Galliéni, 11 November 1915.

73. PRO, WO 106/1337, Kitchener to Asquith, 16 November 1915.

74. PRO, FO 371/2278, Kitchener to Asquith, 17 November 1915.

75. PRO, CAB 37/137/34; Suarez, *Briand*, Vol. 3, p. 197.

76. MAE, A-Guerre 981, procès-verbal of Paris Conference.

77. AG, 5N150, Cambon to Briand, 18 November 1915.

78. PRO, FO371/2279, War Committee, 19 November 1915.

79. MAE, A-Guerre 247, Guillemin to Briand, 22 November 1915.

80. PRO, FO 371/2272, Mahon to War Office, 20 November 1915.

81. PRO, WO 158/755, Mahon to War Office, 24 November 1915.

82. MAE, A-Guerre 1034, Sarrail to Galliéni, 27 November 1915.

83. HLRO, Bonar Law MSS, 53/6/50, Bonar Law to Wilson, 22 November 1915.

84. University of Birmingham Library, Chamberlain MSS, AC19/8/11, paper by Murray, 23 November 1915.

85. PRO, FO 371/2278, Grey to Bertie, 25 November 1915.

86. PRO, WO 106/1337, Callwell to Murray, 25 November 1915.

87. MAE, A-Guerre 247, Briand to Guillemin, 28 November 1915.

88. PRO, CAB 42/5/24.

89. PRO, FO 371/2278, minute by G. Clerk on Elliot to Grey, 29 November 1915.

90. PRO, CAB 42/6/1.

91. PRO, FO 371/2278, Grey to Bertie, 1 December 1915.

92. PRO, FO 371/2280, Mahon to Kitchener, 1 December 1915.

93. AG, 16N3014, Joffre to Galliéni, 30 November 1915; 16N3056, Note d'Introduction à la Conférence du 5 décembre, 30 November 1915.

94. AG, 16N3162, note by William Martin, 1 December 1915.

95. Poincaré, *Au Service*, Vol. 7, p. 295.

96. MAE, A-Guerre 285, Briand to Cambon 1 December 1915; A-Guerre 1034, Cambon to Briand, 1 December 1915; Poincaré, *Au Service*, Vol. 7, p. 309.

97. PRO, FO 371/2278, Bertie to Grey 1 December 1915; Lennox (ed.), *Bertie Diary*, Vol. 1, p. 271.

98 MAE, A-Guerre 1034, Briand to Cambon, no. 4109, 2 December 1915.

99. MAE, A-Guerre 1034, Briand to Cambon, no. 4101–7, 2 December 1915.

100. MAE, A-Guerre 1034, Cambon to Briand, 2 December 1915.

101. MAE, A-Guerre 1034, Doumayrou to Galliéni, 2 December 1915.

102. AG, 5N151, Doumayrou to 'mon colonel', 2 December 1915.

103. MAE, A-Guerre 285, Briand to Cambon, 2 December 1915; Poincaré, *Au Service*, Vol. 7, p. 303.

104. AG, 16N3136, Joffre to Sarrail, 3 December 1915.

105. PRO, FO 371/2278, Grey to Bertie, 2 December 1915.

106. PRO, FO 371/2280, Grey to Bertie, 3 December 1915.

107. AG, 5N151, Panouse to Galliéni, 2 December 1915.

108. PRO, CAB 37/139/7, Asquith to George V, 3 December 1915.

109. R. Blake (ed.), *The Private Papers of Douglas Haig 1914–1919* (London, 1952), p. 115.

110. W. S.Churchill, *The World Crisis 1915* (London, 1923), p. 172.

111. P. Magnus, *Kitchener: Portrait of an Imperialist* (London, 1958), p. 288. But for a positive reassessment of Kitchener's contribution to the British war effort, see K. Neilson, 'Kitchener: A Reputation Refurbished?', *Canadian Journal of History* 15, 2, pp. 207–27, and G. Cassar, *Kitchener: Architect of Victory* (London, 1977).

112. PRO, FO 371/2278, Grey to Bertie, 3 December 1915; compare the rather strange statement in D. Lloyd George, *War Memoirs*, Vol. 1 (London, 1933), p. 526: 'As yet the British cabinet had not reached a definite decision upon the issue.'

113. MAE, A-Guerre 1034, Cambon to Briand, 3 December 1915.

114. PRO, Bertie MSS, FO 800/172/Gr/15/26, memorandum by Bertie, 4 December 1915.

115. Taylor (ed.), *Lloyd George Diary*, p. 84.

116. MAE, A-Guerre 981, 'Petite note pour le président du conseil', 4 December 1915. If, argued Jules Cambon, Briand failed to convince Britain to remain at Salonika, a ministerial crisis would develop: R. Marchand (ed.), *Un Livre Noir: Diplomatie d'avant Guerre et de Guerre d'après les documents des Archives Russes 1910–1917*, Vol. 3, part 2 (Paris, 1926), p. 54.

117. PRO, Bertie MSS, FO800/172/Gr/15/29, note by Bertie, 6 December 1915.

118. PRO, CAB 37/139/15, note on the conference.

119. PRO, CAB 28/IC4, procès-verbal of Calais Conference.

120. PRO, FO 371/2280, Elliot to Grey, 4 December 1915.

121. MAE, A-Guerre 1034, note by Berthelot, 4 December 1915; A. Bréal, *Philippe Berthelot* (Paris, 1937), p. 144; J.-L.Barré, *Le Seigneur Chat: Philippe Berthelot 1866–1934* (Paris, 1988), p. 231; G. Cassar, *The French and the Dardanelles* (London, 1971), pp. 231–2. Cassar, however, largely misses the point that the importance of Berthelot's note is in showing that France had indeed agreed to evacuation. His purpose now was to relieve the French government of responsibility for the decision.

122. Suarez, *Briand*, Vol. 3, p. 213: 'In truth there was still complete disagreement. Briand had secured a postponement of the evacuation. Joffre had suggested the creation of an entrenched base, but each party still reserved its position.' For the more accurate assessment of one French delegate see Ribot, *Letters*, p. 300.

123. H. Asquith, *Memories and Reflections*, Vol. 2 (London,1928), p. 111.

124. Poincaré, *Au Service*, Vol. 7, p. 309.

125. Ibid., pp. 311–12; Cassar, *French and Dardanelles*, pp. 232–3; Cambon (ed.), *Correspondance*, Vol. 3, p. 91. For Galliéni's vivid description of the chaos of this meeting, see M. Leblond, *Galliéni Parle*, Vol. 2 (Paris, 1920), p. 195.

126. MAE, Jules Cambon MSS, P. Cambon to J. Cambon, 6 December 1915.

127. Cambon (ed.), *Correspondance*, Vol. 3, p. 91.

128. Ibid., p. 92.

129. MAE, A-Guerre 1034, Briand to Cambon, 5 December 1915.

130. PRO, FO 371/2278, minute on Bertie to Grey, 7 December 1915.

131. MAE, Jules Cambon MSS, P. Cambon to J. Cambon, 6 December 1915.

132. PRO, CAB 42/6/3.

133. Lloyd George, *War Memoirs*, Vol. 1, p. 528.

134. MAE, Jules Cambon MSS, P. Cambon to J. Cambon 6 December 1915.

135. Poincaré, *Au Service*, Vol. 7, p. 312.

136. MAE, Jules Cambon MSS, P. Cambon to J. Cambon, 6 December 1915.

137. MAE, A-Guerre 1034 contains two versions of the procès-verbal, with Briand's handwritten alterations on one or, as de Margerie put it, 'corrected by M. Briand'. Compare the strange statement in A. S. Mitrakos, *France in Greece during World War One: A Study in the Politics of Power* (Boulder, 1982),

p. 202: 'There are no documents whatever at the Archives of the Ministère des Affaires Etrangères on this Conference.'

138. Lennox (ed.), *Bertie Diary*, Vol. 1, p. 274.

139. PRO, FO371/2278, Bertie to Grey, 7 December 1915.

140. MAE, A-Guerre 1035, Briand to Cambon, 6 December 1915.

141. HLRO, Bonar Law MSS, 52/1/15, H.Wilson to Law, 6 December 1915.

142. PRO, CAB42/6/6.

143. LHCMA, Robertson MSS, I/10/10, procès-verbal of Chantilly Conference.

144. G. Cassar, *Asquith as War Leader* (London, 1994), p. 142: Asquith to Sylvia Henley, 7 December 1915.

145. AG, 16N3136, Sarrail to Joffre, 7 December 1915.

146. PRO, CAB 42/6/6, War Committee, 8 December 1915.

147. Cassar, *Asquith*, pp. 142–3: Asquith to Sylvia Henley, 8 December 1915.

148. PRO, Grey MSS, FO 800/58, Grey to Bertie, 8 December 1915.

149. Taylor (ed.), *Lloyd George Diary*, p. 86.

150. L.H.C.M.A., Robertson MSS, I/8/38, Callwell to Robertson, 9 December 1915.

151. PRO, CAB 37/139/24.

152. PRO, FO 371/2278, Bertie to Foreign Office, 9 December 1915.

153. University of Birmingham Library, Chamberlain MSS, AC 13/3/94, Selborne to A. Chamberlain, 10 December 1915.

154. PRO, CAB 37/139/27, Asquith to George V, 14 December 1915.

155. PRO, CAB 42/6/7, War Committee, 13 December 1915.

156. Lennox (ed.), *Bertie Diary*, Vol. 1, p. 276.

157. Roskill, *Hankey*, Vol. 1, p. 237.

158. Cassar, *Asquith*, p. 143: Asquith to S. Henley, 8 December 1915.

159. HLRO, Bonar Law MSS, 52/1/15, Wilson to Law, 6 December 1915.

4. Soldiers and Statesmen; Generals and Politicians

1. V. H. Rothwell, *British War Aims and Peace Diplomacy 1914–1918* (Oxford, 1971), p. 87.

2. M. Hankey, *The Supreme Command*, Vol. 2 (London, 1961), p. 446.

3. D. R. Woodward, *Lloyd George and the Generals* (Newark, 1983), p. 113.

4. D. Dutton, 'The Fall of General Joffre: An Episode in the Politico-Military Struggle in Wartime France', *Journal of Strategic Studies* 1, 3 (1978), pp. 338–51.

5. Liddell Hart Centre for Military Archives (LHCMA), Robertson MSS, I/8/9, Robertson to Callwell, 22 February 1915.

6. W. Robertson, *From Private to Field Marshal* (London, 1921), pp. 147, 149. Robertson's personal experience of the area was evident in his contempt for Lloyd George's simplistic belief in the possibility of offensive operations in the Balkans. 'It would be valuable', he told Lord Curzon, 'if you would

kindly explain to the Prime Minister ... what the nature of the Balkan Country is ... Amongst other things he seems to think that there is a single range of hills between the Salonika Force and Sofia, whereas the whole country is a mass of mountains. The country is ... of a highly defensible nature. No amount of argument and no amount of heavy artillery will alter it.' LHCMA, Robertson MSS, I/36/19, Robertson to Curzon, 4 July 1917.

7. LHCMA, Robertson MSS, I/22/8, Robertson to Haig, 5 January 1916.
8. LHCMA, Robertson MSS, I/12/5, Robertson to Stamfordham, 1 October 1915.
9. PRO, CAB 42/9/3, Note prepared by the CIGS for the War Committee on the assistance that diplomacy might render to naval and military operations, 12 February 1916.
10. W. Robertson, *Soldiers and Statesmen 1914–1918*, Vol. 1 (London, 1926), p. 277.
11. HLRO, Lloyd George MSS, D/23/5/7, Views of the General Staff on the present situation at Salonika and in the Balkans with deductions as to our wisest course of action there, 23 November 1915.
12. C. B. Falls, *Military Operations: Macedonia*, Vol. 1 (London, 1933), p. 50.
13. AG, 16N3136, Doumayrou to Joffre, 28 and 30 December 1915; MAE, A-Guerre 1035, Briand to Cambon, 30 December 1915.
14. Falls, *Military Operations*, Vol. 1, p. 97.
15. PRO, CAB 42/6/14, Examination by the General Staff into the factors affecting the choice of a plan of campaign, 16 December 1915.
16. LHCMA, Robertson MSS, I/6/73, note for War Committee, 23 December 1915.
17. PRO, CAB 42/6/14.
18. J. Grigg, *Lloyd George: From Peace to War 1912–1916* (London, 1985), p. 370.
19. PRO, WO 106/1355, Robertson to Joffre, 18 January 1916.
20. PRO, CAB 37/141/12, Conference Conclusions.
21. PRO, CAB 42/11/9, note by Robertson, 22 March 1916.
22. AG, 14N10, note of conversation with Robertson 14 February 1916; PRO, WO 106/396, note of conversation; K. Neilson, *Strategy and Supply: The Anglo-Russian Alliance, 1914–17* (London, 1984), p. 146.
23. LHCMA, Robertson MSS, I/35/57, Robertson to Hanbury Williams, 16 February 1916.
24. LHCMA, Robertson MSS, I/22/22, Robertson to Haig, 17 February 1916.
25. PRO, FO 371/2605, Robertson to Mahon, 21 February 1916.
26. LHCMA, Robertson MSS, I/35/72, Robertson to Mahon, 21 February 1916.
27. LHCMA, Robertson MSS, I/22/27, Robertson to Haig, 21 February 1916.
28. PRO, CAB 42/9/3.
29. Falls, *Military Operations*, Vol. 1, p. 109.

30. LHCMA, Robertson MSS, I/32/9, Robertson to Murray, 6 March 1916.

31. PRO, WO 106/1339, Robertson to Mahon, 4 March 1916.

32. R. Poincaré, *Au Service de la France*, Vol. 6 (Paris, 1930), p. 283.

33. Lady A. G. Lennox (ed.), *The Diary of Lord Bertie of Thame 1914–1918*, Vol. I (London, 1924), pp. 298–9.

34. J. C. King, *Generals and Politicians: Conflict Between France's High Command, Parliament and Government, 1914–1918* (Berkeley, 1951), p. 108; G. Bonnefous, *Histoire Politique de la Troisième République*, Vol. 2 (Paris, 1957), p. 122.

35. King, *Generals and Politicians*, pp. 103–6; G. Terrail, *Sarrail et les Armées d'Orient* (Paris, 1920) pp. 231–46.

36. Galliéni was certainly a sick man, in need of surgery, but his resignation was politically motivated. HLRO, Lloyd George MSS, D/19/7/11, Bertie to Grey, 18 March 1916.

37. Lennox (ed.), *Bertie Diary*, Vol. 1, p. 316.

38. Ibid., pp. 324–5.

39. LHCMA, Robertson MSS, I/35/74, Robertson to Mahon, 6 March 1916.

40. Falls, *Military Operations*, Vol. 1, p. 110.

41. Robertson to Murray, 15 March 1916, cited in D. R. Woodward (ed.), *The Military Correspondence of Field-Marshal Sir William Robertson, Chief Imperial General Staff, December 1915–February 1918* (London, 1989), pp. 41–2.

42. PRO, CAB 42/11/9, note on the situation at Salonika, 22 March 1916.

43. PRO, CAB 42/11/9, War Committee, 23 March 1916.

44. Lennox (ed.), *Bertie Diary*, Vol. 1, p. 327. See also Robertson, *Private to Field Marshal*, p. 287: '[Kitchener] was easily the most outstanding personality at the Allied conferences, and was listened to with more deference than was vouchsafed to any one else during the two and a half years that I attended these meetings.'

45. Clive diary, 27 March 1916, cited in D. French, *British Strategy and War Aims 1914–1916* (London, 1986), p. 207.

46. S. Roskill, *Hankey, Man of Secrets*, Vol. 1 (London, 1970), p. 259.

47 LHCMA, Robertson MSS, I/32/19, Robertson to Murray, 5 April 1916.

48. Robertson, *Soldiers and Statesmen*, Vol. 2 (London,1926), p. 105. It is only fair to point out that French observers were capable of reaching exactly opposite conclusions. Prior to the Boulogne Conference in October 1916, Paul Cambon noted: 'The English have set off well briefed on all points; papers, statistics, state of their forces and transport resources. They have all that is needed for a serious discussion and will find themselves, as last time, in the presence of people without precise ideas on anything. At the last conference in London Briand and Joffre came to ask as always for men for Salonika. They were told with chapter and verse of the transport difficulties. Our representatives had nothing to counter these figures. It was deplorable.' A. Adamthwaite, *Grandeur and Misery: France's Bid for Power in Europe 1914–1940* (London, 1995), p. 32.

49. Lord Riddell, *War Diary 1914–1918* (London, 1933), p. 168.

50. PRO, CAB 42/12/5, War Committee, 7 April 1916.

51. PRO, WO 106/1340, Robertson to Mahon, 26 April 1916.

52. PRO, CAB 42/12/12, War Committee, 28 April 1916.

53. PRO, CAB 42/13/2, War Committee, 3 May 1916; French, *Strategy and War Aims*, pp. 207–8; Woodward, *Lloyd George and Generals*, p. 89.

54. PRO, CAB 42/13/2, Offensive Operations in the Balkans, 29 April 1916.

55. PRO, CAB 42/13/2, War Committee, 3 May 1916.

56. LHCMA, Robertson MSS, I/32/24, Robertson to Murray, 3 May 1916.

57. Falls, *Military Operations*, Vol. 1, p. 97.

58. R. Marchand (ed.), *Un Livre Noir: Diplomatie d'avant Guerre et de Guerre d'après les documents des Archives Russes 1910–1917*, Vol. 3, part 4 (Paris, 1931), p. 22.

59. PRO, FO 371/2282, Mahon to Robertson, 30 December 1915.

60. PRO, FO 371/2615, Grey to Bertie, 28 January 1916; Falls, *Military Operations*, Vol. 1, p. 100.

61. PRO, CAB 42/14/12, Fairholme to Robertson, 12 May 1916. Sarrail had found Mahon 'a man he could twist round his little finger': G. Nicol, *Uncle George: Field-Marshal Lord Milne of Salonika and Rublislaw* (London, 1976), p. 89.

62. Nicol, *Uncle George*, p. 88.

63. LHCMA, Robertson MSS, I/14/16, Robertson to Milne, 8 May 1916.

64. LHCMA, Robertson MSS, I/14/17, Robertson to Milne, 12 May 1916.

65. LHCMA, Robertson MSS, I/14/18, Milne to Robertson, 12 May 1916.

66. Poincaré, *Au Service*, Vol. 8, p. 214.

67. Presumably a reference to the crisis of December 1915.

68. MAE, A-Guerre 1036, Briand to Cambon, 12 May 1916.

69. PRO, CAB 42/14/1, Offensive Operations in the Balkans, 16 May 1916.

70. PRO, CAB 42/14/1, War Committee, 17 May 1916.

71. Falls, *Military Operations*, Vol. 1, p. 117.

72. LHCMA, Robertson MSS, I/22/36, Robertson to Haig, 18 May 1916.

73. PRO, CAB 42/14/11.

74. MAE, A-Guerre 1037, Briand to Cambon, 23 May 1916.

75. PRO, CAB 42/14/12.

76. MAE, A-Guerre 1037, Joffre to Briand, 2 June 1916.

77. A.N., C7490, Chamber Foreign Affairs Commission.

78. Lloyd George even insisted that the War Committee minutes should be amended so as to avoid giving the impression that the British government was opposed to the idea of an offensive as a matter of principle: HLRO, Lloyd George MSS, D/17/3/37, Lloyd George to Hankey 8 June 1916.

79. PRO, CAB 42/15/6, War Committee, 7 June 1916.

80. MAE, Jules Cambon MSS, P. Cambon to J. Cambon, 15 May 1916. Berthelot's position as head of the Maison de la Presse gave Briand a firm grip over what was published.

81. H. Cambon (ed.), *Paul Cambon: Correspondance 1870–1924*, Vol. 3 (Paris, 1946), p. 115.

82. Lennox (ed.), *Bertie Diary*, Vol. 1, pp. 363–4; P. Allard, *Les Dessous de la Guerre révélés par les Comités Secrets* (Paris, 1932), pp. 31–2.

83. J. Joffre, *The Memoirs of Marshal Joffre*, Vol. 2 (London, 1932), p. 522.

84. A. Horne, *The Price of Glory: Verdun 1916* (London, 1962), p. 275.

85. See, in particular, G. Rousseau, 'Le Conseil des Ministres en 1916, d'après les notes d'Etienne Clémentel', *Guerres mondiales et conflits contemporains*, 171 (1993), pp. 139–160.

86. Cambon (ed.), *Correspondance*, Vol. 3, p. 153.

87. Joffre, *Memoirs*, Vol. 2, p. 373.

88. AG, 16N3136, Joffre to Sarrail, 17 January 1916.

89. AN, Painlevé MSS, 313AP110, Painlevé to Sarrail, 18 February 1916.

90. AN, 313AP109, Fleurot to Painlevé, 8 October 1916.

91. AN, 313AP110, Sarrail to Painlevé, 12 November 1915.

92. AN, 313AP110, Sarrail to Painlevé, 21 November 1915.

93. MAE, A-Guerre 982, Pellé to 'M. le Ministre', 6 February 1916.

94. PRO, CAB 28/IC8, procès-verbal; HLRO, Lloyd George MSS, D/22/5/8, Proceedings of Conference at 10, Downing Street, 9 June 1916.

95. HLRO, Lloyd George MSS, D/19/7/16, Bertie to Grey, 9 June 1916.

96. LHCMA, Robertson MSS, I/22/48, Haig to Robertson, 16 June 1916.

97. MAE, A-Guerre 1037, summary of British views, 9 June 1916; PRO, CAB 37/149/27, note by Grey, 10 June 1916; Falls, *Military Operations*, Vol. 1, p. 136.

98. Robertson, *Soldiers and Statesmen*, Vol. 2, p. 116.

99. LHCMA, Robertson MSS, I/22/49, Robertson to Haig, 22 June 1916.

100. PRO, CAB 42/15/8, Policy regarding operations in the Balkans, 14 June 1916.

101. PRO, CAB 42/15/8, War Committee, 16 June 1916.

102. LHCMA, Robertson MSS, I/22/49, Robertson to Haig, 22 June 1916.

103. MAE, A-Guerre 1037, Cambon to Briand, 29 June 1916.

104. Falls, *Military Operations*, Vol. 1, p. 136.

105. PRO, CAB 42/16/1, note for War Committee, 5 July 1916.

106. Neilson, *Strategy and Supply*, p. 152.

107. PRO, CAB 42/16/1, War Committee, 6 July 1916.

108. PRO, CAB 42/16/10, War Committee, 20 July 1916.

109. MAE, A-Guerre 1038, note for de Margerie, 11 August 1916.

110. PRO, FO 371/2607, Robertson to Hardinge, 15 August 1916.

111. PRO, FO 371/2607, Robertson to Milne, 19 August 1916.

112. PRO, CAB 42/18/16, Robertson to Hankey, 23 August 1916.

113. LHCMA, Robertson MSS, I/22/70, Robertson to Haig, 25 August 1916.

114. Robertson to Haig, 7 September 1916, cited in Woodward (ed.), *Robertson Correspondence*, p. 85.

115. Liverpool Record Office (LRO), Derby MSS, 920DER(17) 27/5, Lloyd George to Director of Military Operations, 4 September 1916; PRO, CAB 42/19/3, War Committee, 5 September 1916.

116. PRO, CAB 42/19/6.

117. PRO, CAB 42/21/3; Woodward, *Lloyd George and the Generals*, p. 110.

118. LHCMA, Robertson MSS, I/19/6–7, Robertson to Lloyd George and Lloyd George to Robertson, 11 October 1916.

119. PRO, FO371/2624, Robertson to Joffre, 12 October 1916.

120. A. J. P. Taylor (ed.), *Lloyd George: A Diary by Frances Stevenson* (London, 1971), pp. 115–16.

121. LHCMA, Robertson MSS, I/32/48, Robertson to Murray, 16 October 1916; Robertson MSS, I/22/83, Robertson to Haig, 16 October 1916.

122. Woodward, *Lloyd George and the Generals*, p. 112; Hankey, *Supreme Command*, Vol. 2, p. 536.

123. Haig diary (microfilm), 20 October 1916.

124. Roskill, *Hankey*, Vol. 1, p. 309; Taylor (ed.), *Lloyd George Diary*, p. 118.

125. Taylor (ed.), *Lloyd George Diary*, p. 119.

126. Ibid.

127. PRO, CAB 42/22/5, War Committee, 24 October 1916.

128. PRO, FO 371/2624, Grey to Granville, 24 October 1916.

129. LHCMA, Robertson MSS, I/14/47, Robertson to Milne, 25 October 1916.

130. LHCMA, Robertson MSS, I/22/84, Robertson to Haig, 25 October 1916.

131. PRO, CAB 24/2/85, General Review of the Situation October 1916.

132. PRO, CAB 42/22/5, War Committee, 24 October 1916.

133. HLRO, Lloyd George MSS, E/3/14/21, Le Roy Lewis to Lloyd George, 23 Octobr 1916.

134. PRO, Bertie MSS, FO 800/172/Gr/16/24, Bertie to Hardinge, 7 September 1916; Painlevé's misgivings about de Castelnau were perhaps justified. This 'monk in uniform' represented everything which Sarrail and the Radicals detested. D. W. Brogan, *The Development of Modern France 1870–1939* (London, 1940), p. 483.

135. AN, Painlevé MSS, 313AP109, Bourguignon to Fleurot, 28 October 1916; 313AP109, Painlevé to Sarrail 28 October 1916; G. Suarez, *Briand: Sa vie, son oeuvre*, Vol. 3 (Paris, 1939), p. 463; Marchand (ed.), *Livre Noir*, Vol. 3, part 4, p. 33.

136. E. Herbillon, *Souvenirs d'un officier de liaison pendant la guerre mondiale: du général en chef au gouvernement*, Vol. 1 (Paris, 1930), p. 354. Compare Suarez, *Briand*, Vol. 4 (Paris, 1940), pp. 14–15.

137. Herbillon, *Souvenirs*, Vol. 1, p. 355.

138. AN, Painlevé MSS, 313AP110, note by Painlevé of conversation with Lloyd George, 6 November 1916.

139. AG, 16N3144, Requin to 'mon colonel', 31 October 1916; Institut de France, Pellé MSS, 4429, report on the Armée d'Orient, 2 November 1916.

140. PRO, CAB 42/23/9, War Committee, 7 November 1916.

141. PRO, CAB 28/IC12e, procès-verbal.

142. PRO, CAB 28/IC12e, decisions taken at Chantilly, 15–16 November 1916.

143. Taylor (ed.), *Lloyd George Diary*, p. 124.

144. PRO, WO 106/1355, Robertson to Lloyd George, 3 December 1916.

145. Falls, *Military Operations*, Vol. 1, p. 252.

146. AG, 5N145, Roques to Joffre, 5 December 1916.

147. A. Pingaud, 'Le second ministère Venizelos (24 août–5 octobre 1915) et les origines de l'expédition de Salonique', *Revue d'histoire de la guerre mondiale* 12 (1934), p. 147. Even the far from intellectual King George V recognized the problem. 'Are we justified', he asked Asquith in September 1916, 'in interfering to this extent in the internal Government of a neutral and friendly country, even though we be one of the guarantors of its Constitution? Are we acting up to our boasted position as the protector of smaller Powers?' H. Nicolson, *King George V: His Life and Reign* (London, 1952), p. 282.

148. MAE, Delcassé MSS, 6, Cochin to Ribot, 27 July 1916.

149. Suarez, *Briand*, Vol. 3, p. 284.

150. Poincaré, *Au Service*, Vol. 8, pp. 166, 180, 267.

151. AN, C7490, Chamber Foreign Affairs Commission, 26 October 1916.

152. A. Ferry, *Les Carnets Secrets* (Paris, 1957), p. 152.

153. AN, Painlevé MSS, 313AP118, Mathieu to Paix-Séailles, 14 June 1916.

154. C. Bertin, *Marie Bonaparte: A Life* (New Haven, 1987), p. 121.

155. PRO, Bertie MSS, FO 800/172/Gr/16/7, Bertie to Grey, 15 June 1916.

156. MAE, A-Guerre 258, Lacaze to Briand, 15 August 1916; A-Guerre 259, Briand to Guillemin, 22 August 1916.

157. Poincaré, *Au Service*, Vol. 8, p. 322.

158. MAE, A-Guerre 259, Briand to Guillemin, 26 August 1916.

159. Cambon (ed.), *Correspondance*, Vol. 3, p. 121.

160. PRO, FO 371/2621, Grey to Bertie, 26 August 1916.

161. PRO, FO 371/2621, Bertie to Grey, 27 August 1916; Poincaré, *Au Service*, Vol. 8, p. 324.

162. MAE, Jules Cambon MSS, P. Cambon to J. Cambon, 31 August 1916.

163. Cambon (ed.),*Cambon Correspondance*,Vol. 3, p. 126; HLRO, Lloyd George MSS, E/3/15/3, Elliot to Hardinge, 21 October 1916.

164. Poincaré, *Au Service*, Vol. 8, p. 338.

165. HLRO, Lloyd George MSS, E/1/2/1, Lee to Lloyd George, 22 September 1916.

166. MAE, Jules Cambon MSS, P. Cambon to J. Cambon, 14 October 1916. For Cambon's reluctance to play the role of puppet of the Quai d'Orsay, see W. K. Eubank, *Paul Cambon, Master Diplomatist* (Oklahoma, 1960), pp. 202–3.

167. PRO, CAB 42/21/6, War Committee, 12 October 1916.

168. MAE, Jules Cambon MSS, P. Cambon to J. Cambon, 15 October 1916.

169. MAE, A-Guerre 267, Briand to Guillemin, 3 January 1917.

170. Institut de France 4542, undated note by Charles Benoist.

171. HLRO, Lloyd George MSS, E/3/14/28, Bertie to Hardinge, 19 November 1916.

172. MAE, A-Guerre 262, Guillemin to Briand, 22 October 1916.

173. MAE, Bourgeois MSS, 9, Lecoq to Bourgeois, 23 October 1916.

174. MAE, A-Guerre 263, Bertie to Briand, 5 November 1916.

175. PRO, CAB 42/23/9, War Committee, 7 November 1916.

176. PRO, FO 371/2627, Bertie to Grey, 12 November 1916.

177. AG, 5N149, du Fournet to Lacaze, 28 November 1916; E. Helsey, 'Le Guet-apens d'Athènes (ler décembre 1916)', *Revue des deux mondes* (1955) part 2, pp. 487–500.

178. PRO, Bertie MSS, FO 800/172/Gr/56, Bertie to Hardinge, 4 December 1916.

179. A.N., C7648–9; Tanenbaum, *Sarrail*, pp. 134–40; Joffre, *Memoirs*, Vol. 2, p. 536; A. Conte, *Joffre* (Paris, 1991), p. 382. Briand's intention in giving Joffre overall command over the two fronts by the decree of 2 December 1915 may have been to deprive him of day-to-day control of both theatres: AN, Painlevé MSS, 313AP110, note by Painlevé on the application of the decree, November 1916.

180. Lennox (ed.), *Bertie Diary*, Vol. 2, pp. 67–8; Marchand (ed.), *Livre Noir*, Vol. 3, part 4, pp. 77–8.

181. As Joffre later recalled: 'that evening the general impression was optimistic and it was supposed that the debate would quickly close.' Joffre, *Memoirs*, Vol. 2, p. 535.

182. Joffre, *Memoirs*, Vol. 2, pp. 536–7; L. Loucheur, *Carnets Secrets 1908–1932* (Brussels, 1962), p. 23; this scheme bears some resemblance to that which Asquith forced on Kitchener in the autumn of 1915, under which the real direction of the British war effort passed into the hands of the chief of the Imperial General Staff, while Kitchener retained his title as secretary of state for war.

183. Lennox (ed.), *Bertie Diary*, Vol. 2, p. 72.

184. AG, 16N3275, Joffre to Briand, 5 December 1916.

185. Lennox (ed.), *Bertie Diary*, Vol. 2, p. 73.

186. Bonnefous, *Histoire Politique*, Vol. 2, pp. 200–1.

187. Lennox (ed.), *Bertie Diary*, Vol. 2, p. 75.

188. AN, Painlevé MSS, 313AP56, note by Henri Niche, 26 December 1916.

189. Bonnefous, *Histoire Politique*, Vol. 2, pp. 203–4.

190. Ibid., p. 206; Marchand (ed.), *Livre Noir*, Vol. 3, part 4, pp. 94–5.

191. Suarez, *Briand*, Vol. 4, p. 61.

192. AN, Painlevé MSS, 313AP56, Painlevé to Briand, 11 December 1916; Tanenbaum, *Sarrail*, p. 139; Loucheur, *Carnets Secrets*, p. 26.

193. Dutton, 'Fall of General Joffre', pp. 347–8; R. M. Watt, *Dare Call it Treason* (London, 1964), p. 129.

194. Unlike that in France, the crisis of December 1916 in British politics is not directly linked with the Salonika expedition, though the fall of Romania did form a significant backdrop to the development of events: G. E. Torrey, 'The Rumanian Campaign of 1916: Its Impact on the Belligerents', *Slavic*

Review 39 (1980), pp. 40–1. The details of the crisis may be traced in J. Turner, *British Politics and the Great War: Coalition and Conflict 1915–1918* (New Haven, 1992).

195. LHCMA, Robertson MSS, I/22/94, Robertson to Haig, 7 December 1916.

196. PRO, CAB 23/1/1, War Cabinet, 9 December 1916.

197. MAE, Paul Cambon MSS, Cambon to Briand, 9 December 1916.

198. LHCMA, Robertson MSS, I/22/84, Robertson to Haig, 25 October 1916.

199. Robertson, *Soldiers and Statesmen*, Vol. 1, p. 288.

200. Roskill, *Hankey*, Vol. 1, p. 348.

5. The Troubled Year

1. D. French, *The Strategy of the Lloyd George Coalition 1916–1918* (Oxford, 1995), p. 94; W. J. Philpott, *Anglo-French Relations and Strategy on the Western Front, 1914–1918* (London, 1996), p. 86. As General Henry Wilson put it: 'We are now [January 1917] the most important of the Allies, in money, in fleets, in shipping, in coal and (almost) in armies, and yet we allow our Allies to do things of which we entirely disapprove, and, although it is quite true that we cannot dictate, still we can get our own way to a great extent by bargaining.' C. E. Callwell, *Field-Marshal Sir Henry Wilson: His Life and Diaries*, Vol. 1 (London, 1927), p. 307.

2. PRO, Bertie MSS, FO 800/169/Fr/17/4, Bertie to Hardinge, 11 January 1917.

3. MAE, A-Guerre 994, procès-verbal, Paris Conference, 4 May 1917.

4. D. R. Woodward, *Lloyd George and the Generals* (Newark, 1983), p. 129. In his first letter to the new War Minister, Lord Derby, Haig wrote: 'I do sincerely trust there is no idea of sending more troops to Salonika. Sound strategy really indicates that that theatre should be reduced to a minimum and every division and gun be brought to France for the coming summer.' R. S. Churchill, *Lord Derby: 'King of Lancashire'* (London, 1959), p. 245.

5. W. Robertson, *Soldiers and Statesmen 1914–1918*, Vol. 2 (London, 1926), p. 300.

6. MAE, Barrère MSS, P. Cambon to Barrère, 22 December 1916.

7. Robertson, *Soldiers and Statesmen*, Vol. 1, p. 277.

8. PRO, CAB 28/IC15a, memorandum by Lloyd George.

9. MAE, A-Guerre 991, procès-verbal of Rome Conference.

10. D. Lloyd George, *War Memoirs*, Vol. 3 (London, 1934), p. 1429.

11. HLRO, Lloyd George MSS, F/44/3/6, Robertson to Lloyd George 6 January 1917; D. R. Woodward (ed.), *The Military Correspondence of Field-Marshal Sir William Robertson, Chief Imperial General Staff, December 1915–February 1918* (London, 1989), p. 125.

12. LHCMA, Robertson MSS, I/12/31, Robertson to C. Wigram, 12 January 1917.

13. G. Suarez, *Briand: Sa vie, son oeuvre*, Vol. 4 (Paris, 1940), p. 109.

14. Woodward (ed.), *Robertson Correspondence*, p. 137: Robertson to Murray, 10 January 1917.

15. By contrast, Milne, who also attended the conference, seems to have formed a fairly low opinion of Lloyd George who 'is so accustomed to drowning other people's voices that he never listens to arguments and merely listens to the sound of his own voice': G. Nicol, *Uncle George: Field-Marshal Lord Milne of Salonika and Rubislaw* (London, 1976), p. 150.

16. A. J. P. Taylor (ed.), *Lloyd George: A Diary by Frances Stevenson* (London, 1971), pp. 136–7. Yet privately Sarrail was 'disgusted' by the Rome Conference and its lack of clear decisions: AN, Painlevé MSS, 313AP26, Sarrail to Painlevé, 21 January 1917.

17. LHCMA, Robertson MSS, I/12/31, Robertson to C. Wigram, 12 January 1917.

18. B. Oudin, *Aristide Briand: La Paix, une idée neuve en Europe* (Paris, 1987), p. 351; M. Sarrail, *Mon Commandement en Orient 1916–1918* (Paris,1920), p. 213.

19. PRO, CAB 28/IC15.

20. HLRO, Lloyd George MSS, F55/3/1, Granville to Lloyd George, 6 February 1917.

21. Robertson, *Soldiers and Statesmen*, Vol. 2, p. 143. Less than a week after Lloyd George became Prime Minister, Robertson had commented: 'He is at last convinced Salonika is crazy and is going to tell Briand so next week ... Though he is off Salonika he is *on* Egypt, and wants to get to Jerusalem!' Woodward (ed.), *Robertson Correspondence*, p. 129.

22. PRO, CAB 28/IC17; MAE, A-Guerre 993, procès-verbal.

23. AG, 16N3139, Lyautey to Sarrail, 9 March 1917; PRO, CAB 28/2, note by Hankey.

24. MAE, Barrère MSS, de Margerie to Barrère, 20 March 1917; Jules Cambon MSS, P. Cambon to J. Cambon, 22 March 1917. R. Marchand (ed.), *Un Livre Noir: Diplomatie d'avant Guerre et de Guerre d'après les documents des Archives Russes 1910–1917*, Vol. 3, part 4 (Paris, 1931), pp. 192–4. By June Cambon was commenting that Ribot was frightened of Painlevé: P. Cambon to J. Cambon, 10 June 1917. Earlier in the war Frances Stevenson had noted that Ribot was 'a dear old man, Sir J[ohn] Simon calls him the "only honest politician in France"': Taylor (ed.), *Lloyd George Diary*, p. 48.

25. H. Cambon (ed.), *Paul Cambon: Correspondance 1870–1924*, vol 3 (Paris, 1946), p. 153.

26. AG, Fonds Clemenceau, 6N200, Decrais to Sarrail, 22 April 1917.

27. C. à C. Repington, *The First World War 1914–1918*, Vol. 1 (London, 1920), p. 419.

28. PRO, CAB 23/2/109, War Cabinet, 30 March 1917.

29. PRO, CAB 24/9/347, 'The Situation at Salonika', 2 April 1917.

30. PRO, CAB 23/2/113, War Cabinet, 4 April 1917.

31. PRO, Bertie MSS, FO 800/173/It/17/6, Bertie to Hardinge, 8 April 1917; Repington, *First World War*, Vol. 1, pp. 514–15.

32. LHCMA, Robertson MSS, I/33/45, Robertson to Smuts, 12 April 1917. Robertson's initiative was not without effect. In a paper on 'the General Strategic and Military Situation and in Particular that on the Western Front' dated 29 April, the South African described the Salonika campaign as 'the least promising to the attainment of our ends'. It had 'failed in its original intention, and will more and more become not only a military and naval but possibly also a political embarrassment': Liverpool Record Office, Derby MSS, 920 DER(17) 27/6.

33. LHCMA, Robertson MSS, I/23/18, Robertson to Haig, 14 April 1917.

34. LHCMA, Robertson MSS, I/32/57, Robertson to Monro, 19 April 1917.

35. P. G. Halpern, *A Naval History of World War One* (Annapolis, 1994), p. 391.

36. PRO, CAB 23/2/122, War Cabinet, 18 April 1917.

37. PRO, CAB 28/IC20.

38. M. E. Schmidt, *Alexandre Ribot: Odyssey of a Liberal in the Third Republic* (The Hague, 1974), p. 149; MAE, A-Guerre 272, note by Ribot, 20 April 1917.

39. PRO, CAB 23/2/124, War Cabinet, 23 April 1917.

40. LHCMA,Robertson MSS, I/23/24, Robertson to Haig, 28 April 1917.

41. PRO, CAB 23/2/128, War Cabinet, 1 May 1917; CAB 24/12/606, 'Withdrawal of the British from Salonika', 1 May 1917.

42. PRO, CAB 23/40/IWC14, Imperial War Cabinet, 2 May 1917.

43. MAE, Bourgeois MSS, de Fontenay to Bourgeois, 23 March 1917.

44. PRO, FO 371/2865, Bertie to Balfour, 30 March 1917.

45. Lady A. G. Lennox (ed), *The Diary of Lord Bertie of Thame 1914–1918*, Vol. 2 (London, 1924), p. 117.

46. PRO, CAB 23/40/IWC9, Imperial War Cabinet, 12 April 1917.

47. Cambon (ed.), *Correspondance*, Vol. 3, pp. 165–6.

48. PRO, FO371/2878, Bertie to Cecil, 4 May 1917.

49. MAE, A-Guerre 994, procès-verbal of the Paris Conference, 4–5 May 1917; PRO, CAB 24/2/657, resolutions proposed by Lloyd George, 5 May 1917.

50. AG, 16N3161, note on the Paris Conference, 6 May 1917.

51. LHCMA, Robertson MSS, I/33/70, Robertson to Stamfordham, 7 May 1917.

52. G. Ward Price, *The Story of the Salonika Army* (London, 1918), p. 205.

53. AG, 16N2991, Painlevé to Sarrail, 21 May 1917; R. Poincaré, *Au Service de la France*, vol 9 (Paris 1932), p. 143.

54. PRO, CAB 23/2/WC144, War Cabinet, 23 May 1917.

55. PRO, CAB 24/14/840, memorandum by Robertson on the French proposal to occupy Greece, 25 May 1917.

56. M. Hankey, *The Supreme Command 1914–1918*, Vol. 2 (London, 1961), p. 636.

57. A. Ribot (ed.), *Journal d'Alexandre Ribot et Correspondances Inédites 1914–22* (Paris, 1936), p. 134.

58. PRO, CAB 28/IC22-3, procès-verbal, London Conference, 28–9 May 1917; CAB 23/2/WC148–9, War Cabinet, 28 and 29 May 1917.

59. Taylor (ed.), *Lloyd George Diary*, p. 161.

60. PRO, FO 371/2886, 'Recent criticisms of General Sarrail', 5 June 1917. It was at this early stage of his varied career that Harold Nicolson developed a reputation for his skill in drawing up memoranda and reports for his seniors in the Foreign Office. Those on the Balkan situation are particularly lucid – and valuable for the historian. J. Lees-Milne, *Harold Nicolson: A Biography*, Vol. 1 (London, 1980), p. 100.

61. PRO, CAB 23/3/155, War Cabinet, 5 June 1917.

62. MAE, A-Guerre 1042, Lloyd George to Ribot, 6 June 1917.

63. Poincaré, *Au Service*, Vol. 9, p. 158.

64. Ibid., p. 159.

65. MAE, A-Guerre 1042, Ribot to Lloyd George, 7 June 1917.

66. HLRO, Lloyd George, MSS, F/41/6/2, H. Norman to Lloyd George, 7 June 1917.

67. PRO, CAB 23/3/160, War Cabinet, 11 June 1917.

68. HLRO, Lloyd George MSS, F/51/4/25, Bertie to Balfour, 24 June 1917.

69. MAE, A-Guerre 293, Ribot to Guillemin, 5 June 1917; Cecil to Grahame, 8 June 1917.

70. MAE, A-Guerre 293, Cecil to Grahame, 9 June 1917.

71. MAE, Jules Cambon MSS, P. Cambon to J. Cambon, 10 June 1917; Cambon (ed.), *Correspondance*, Vol. 3, p. 173.

72. PRO, CAB23/3/160, War Cabinet, 11 June 1917.

73. D. Dutton, 'The Deposition of King Constantine of Greece, June 1917: an Episode in Anglo-French Diplomacy', *Canadian Journal of History* 12, 3 (1978), pp. 325–45; Y. Mourelos, 'British Policy towards King Constantine's Dethronement and Greece's Entry into the War', in P. Calvocoressi et al., *Greece and Great Britain during World War One* (Thessaloniki,1985), pp. 131–8.

74. PRO, CAB 23/3/169, War Cabinet, 26 June 1917.

75. PRO, FO 371/2889, memorandum by Malkin, 25 June 1917. It is clear that Lloyd George and the Foreign Office had been at odds over policy towards Greece for much of 1917: Lloyd George MSS, F/41/6/4, H. Norman to Lloyd George, 12 June 1917. Cf. V. H. Rothwell, *British War Aims and Peace Diplomacy 1914–1918* (Oxford, 1971), p. 9: 'It must be understood that after Lloyd George's advent to power, Britain had two foreign policies, those of the Prime Minister and of the Foreign Office.'

76. Hankey, *Supreme Command*, Vol. 2, p. 684.

77. LHCMA,Robertson MSS, I/36/19, Robertson to Curzon, 4 July 1917.

78. PRO, CAB 27/7/WP31, Milner to Hankey, 3 July 1917.

79. Nicol, *Uncle George*, p. 145.

80. PRO, CAB 27/7/WP42, draft report, 19 July 1917.

81. PRO, CAB 23/13/191a, War Cabinet, 20 July 1917.

82. MAE, A-Guerre 996, procès-verbal; Robertson called it 'the worst

conference I ever attended': Robertson to Kiggell, 27 July 1917, cited in K. Neilson, *Strategy and Supply: The Anglo-Russian Alliance, 1914–17* (London, 1984), p. 278.

83. AG, Fonds Clemenceau, 6N200, Decrais to Sarrail, 27 July 1917.

84. LHCMA, Robertson MSS, I/17/3, 'The Present Military Situation in Russia and its effect on our Future Plans', 29 July 1917.

85. LHCMA, Robertson MSS, I/32/65, Robertson to Monro, 1 August 1917.

86. PRO, CAB 23/3/205, War Cabinet, 7 August 1917.

87. MAE, A-Guerre 997, procès-verbal; Schmidt, *Ribot*, p. 151.

88. PRO, CAB 23/3/219, War Cabinet, 20 August 1917.

89. R. Blake (ed.), *The Private Papers of Douglas Haig 1914–1919* (London, 1952), pp. 251–2: Robertson to Haig, 9 August 1917.

90. Robertson, *Soldiers and Statesmen*, Vol. 2, p. 144.

91. A. Palmer, *The Gardeners of Salonika: The Macedonian Campaign 1915–1918* (London, 1965), p. 154.

92. PRO, CAB 23/4/230, War Cabinet, 10 September 1917.

93. HLRO, Lloyd George MSS, F/14/4/68, Derby to Lloyd George, 8 September 1917.

94. AG, Fonds Clemenceau, 6N200, Decrais to Sarrail, 27 September 1917.

95. J. K. Tanenbaum, *General Maurice Sarrail 1856–1929: The French Army and Left-Wing Politics* (Chapel Hill, 1974), pp. 174–5.

96. PRO, CAB 27/6, Cabinet Committee on War Policy, 11 June 1917.

97. PRO, Bertie MSS, FO 800/169, Bertie to Balfour, 25 August 1917 and 29 October 1917; K. Hamilton, *Bertie of Thame: Edwardian Ambassador* (London, 1990), p. 373

98. LRO, Derby MSS, 920 DER(17) 27/6, E. Spears to Derby, 17 October 1917.

99. S. Roskill, *Hankey: Man of Secrets*, Vol. 1 (London, 1970), p. 456.

100. J. F. V. Keiger, *Raymond Poincaré* (Cambridge, 1997), pp. 232–4.

101. AG, 16N2991, Painlevé to Sarrail, 20 October 1917.

102. PRO, CAB 24/32/2615, 'The Situation in Macedonia', 14 November 1917.

103. MAE, Jules Cambon MSS, P. Cambon to J. Cambon, 24 October 1917. Bertie noted of Painlevé: 'He is charming, intelligent and speaks well, but he has not sufficient grit': Lennox (ed.), *Bertie Diary*, Vol. 2, p. 149.

104. Keiger, *Poincaré*, pp. 231–2.

105. D. Dutton, 'The Ministerial Career of Paul Painlevé and the End of the Sacred Union in Wartime France', *Journal of Strategic Studies* 4, 1 (1981), pp. 46–59.

106. PRO, CAB 23/4/275, War Cabinet, 16 November 1917.

107. PRO, CAB 23/4/277, War Cabinet, 19 November 1917.

108. AG, Fonds Clemenceau, 6N209, Lloyd George to Clemenceau, 21 November 1917.

109. Poincaré, *Au Service*, Vol. 9, pp. 388–90.

110. MAE, A-Guerre 1043, Viviani to Ribot, 6 August 1917.

111. Poincaré, *Au Service*, Vol. 9, p. 231.

112. AN, Painlevé MSS, 313AP56, Mathieu to Paix-Séailles, 10 May 1916.

113. AG, Fonds Clemenceau, 6N200, Decrais to Sarrail, 28 August 1917 and 8 October 1917.

114. Poincaré, *Au Service*, Vol. 9, p. 257; Tanenbaum, *Sarrail*, p. 178.

115. AG, Fonds Clemenceau, 6N200, Decrais to Sarrail, 9 October 1917.

116. AN, Painlevé MSS, 313AP105, Sarrail to Decrais, 13 October 1917.

117. AG, Fonds Clemenceau, 6N200, Sarrail to Decrais, 9 October 1917.

118. AG, Fonds Clemenceau, 6N200, Decrais to Sarrail, 7 November 1917.

119. PRO, CAB 28/3/IC36.

120. Hankey, *Supreme Command*, Vol. 2, pp. 732–3.

121. Cambon (ed.), *Correspondance*, Vol. 3, p. 187.

122. PRO, CAB 23/13/259a, War Cabinet, 30 October 1917. Compare Lloyd George's speech in Paris on 12 November 1917: 'Stitching is not strategy. So it came to pass that when these plans were worked out in the terrible realities of war, the stitches came out and disintegration was complete.'

6. Underlying Motives

1. LHCMA, Robertson MSS, I/32/9, Robertson to Murray, 6 March 1916.

2. PRO, CAB 42/4/17, Dardanelles Committee, 25 October 1915.

3. LHCMA, Robertson MSS, I/35/5, Robertson to Balfour, 26 August 1916.

4. PRO, CAB 42/11/6, War Committee, 21 March 1916.

5. R. Blake (ed.), *The Private Papers of Douglas Haig 1914–1919* (London, 1952), p. 137. The editor of Haig's papers, analysing this 'remarkable conversation', judged that 'Kitchener was wrong'. The French refusal to withdraw their army from Salonika was based 'neither on strategy nor a subtle foreign policy; it was based on the character of General Sarrail'. Much of what follows throws this conclusion into question.

6. LHCMA, Robertson MSS, I/32/19, Robertson to Murray, 5 April 1916.

7. LHCMA, Robertson, MSS I/32/65, Robertson to Monro, 1 August 1917.

8. PRO, Bertie MSS, FO 800/172/Gr/16/38, Hardinge to Bertie, 10 October 1916.

9. PRO, CAB 23/40/IWC14, Imperial War Cabinet, 2 May 1917.

10. PRO, CAB 27/7/WP35, memorandum by Lord Milner, 8 July 1917.

11. PRO, CAB 24/6/GT84, note by Balfour, 27 February 1917, concerning a letter to Lord Stamfordham.

12. M. Hankey, *The Supreme Command, 1914–1918*, Vol. 2 (London, 1961), p. 821.

13. LHCMA, Robertson MSS, I/14/48, Milne to Robertson, 27 October 1916.

14. PRO, Balfour MSS, FO 800/202, Milne to Robertson, 28 January 1917.

15. PRO, FO 371/2865, memorandum by Compton Mackenzie, 5 March 1917; C. Mackenzie, *Aegean Memories* (London, 1940), pp. 114–21.

16. Cf. C. Mackenzie, *Greek Memories* (London, 1939), p. 75.

17. Ibid., pp. 74–5.

18. Ibid., p. 336.

19. Ibid., p. 66.

20. PRO, FO 371/2632, Elliot to Grey, 18 November 1916.

21. PRO, FO 371/2876, Elliot to Balfour, 9 March 1917.

22. HLRO, Lloyd George MSS F/55/3/2, Elliot to Hardinge, 9 April 1917; Mackenzie, *Aegean Memories*, p. 173.

23. PRO, FO 371/2865, minutes on Bertie to Balfour, 30 March 1917.

24. PRO, FO 371/2878, draft of Cecil to Bertie, April 1917.

25. P. Renouvin, 'Les buts de guerre du gouvernement français, 1914–1918', *Revue historique* 225 (1966), pp. 1–38.

26. See, in particular, D. Stevenson, *French War Aims against Germany 1914–1919* (Oxford, 1982); C. M. Andrew and A. Kanya-Forstner, *France Overseas: The Great War and the Climax of French Imperial Expansion* (London, 1981); R. A. Prete, 'French Military War Aims 1914–1916', *Historical Journal* 28, 4 (1985), pp. 887–99; G. Soutou, 'La France et les marches de l'est, 1914–1919', *Revue historique* 528 (1978), pp. 341–88.

27. French Foreign Ministry documents for the Great War were divided from the outset into two basic categories, those concerned with the prosecution of the war itself and those appertaining to war aims and the future peace. Approximately 80 per cent of the second category (Série A-Paix) seem to have been destroyed during the Second World War. But German copies of some of these lost documents have since been discovered. See Soutou, 'Les marches de l'est', p. 342.

28. Stevenson, *French War Aims*, p. 30.

29. A. Adamthwaite, *Grandeur and Misery: France's Bid for Power in Europe 1914–1940* (London, 1995), p. 10.

30. Stevenson, *French War Aims*, p. 206.

31. Andrew and Kanya-Forstner, *France Overseas*, passim.

32. Prete, 'French Military War Aims', p. 899.

33. D. Johnson, 'French War Aims and the Crisis of the Third Republic', in B. Hunt and A. Preston (eds), *War Aims and Strategic Policy in the Great War* (London, 1977), p. 41.

34. HLRO, Lloyd George MSS, E/2/15/4, Lloyd George to Grey, 7 February 1915; D. Lloyd George, *War Memoirs*, Vol. 1 (London, 1933), p. 409.

35. PRO, Bertie MSS, FO 800/172/Gr/15/5, note by Bertie of talk between Lloyd George and Briand, 5 February 1915.

36. AN, C7488, meeting of the Chamber Foreign Affairs Commission, 26 April 1915.

37. AN, C7488, 'ordre du jour', Chamber Foreign Affairs Commission, 20 July 1915.

38. AN, C7647, secret session of the Chamber, 20 June 1916.

39. AN, C7490, meeting of the Chamber Foreign Affairs Commission, 26 October 1916.

40. The economic sphere was one of the first areas in which France consciously formulated war aims. From the very beginning of the war enquiries were made to determine how French industrial products could replace German competition in foreign markets. Renouvin, 'Les buts de guerre', p. 8; MAE, A-Guerre 1499, Briand to Diplomatic, Consular and Commercial Agents, 1 January 1916.

41. MAE, Berthelot MSS, carton 6, Tavernier to Perroy, 11 July 1916.

42. MAE, Berthelot MSS, carton 6, report by Tavernier, 3 October 1916.

43. MAE, Berthelot MSS, carton 6, Doumergue to Ministry of Commerce, 18 July 1916.

44. MAE, Berthelot MSS, carton 6, undated note of visit by M. Perroy to de Margerie.

45. G. H. Cassar, *The French and the Dardanelles* (London, 1971), pp. 34–5.

46. W. W. Gottlieb, *Studies in Secret Diplomacy during the First World War* (London, 1957), p. 98. A common image of early twentieth-century colonialist literature was of a Greater France reviving the Mediterranean Empire of the Romans. Andrew and Kanya-Forstner, *France Overseas*, p. 35.

47. MAE, Nouvelle Série 53, report by Lefeuvre-Méaulle, Attaché Commercial de la France en Orient, 1916.

48. A. S. Mitrakos, *France in Greece during World War One: A Study in the Politics of Power* (Boulder, 1982), p. 181.

49. F. H. Hinsley (ed.), *British Foreign Policy under Sir Edward Grey* (Cambridge, 1977), p. 429; C. J. Smith Jr, 'Great Britain and the 1914–1915 Straits Agreement with Russia: The British Promise of November 1914', *American Historical Review* 70 (1965), pp. 1031–2.

50. Gottlieb, *Studies in Secret Diplomacy*, p. 65.

51. Cassar, *French and Dardanelles*, p. 60.

52. AG, 7N1344, Delcassé to Millerand, 28 April 1915.

53. Andrew and Kanya-Forstner, *France Overseas*, p. 89.

54. Lady A. G. Lennox (ed.), *The Diary of Lord Bertie of Thame 1914–1918*, Vol. 1 (London, 1924), pp. 132, 134–5, 141.

55. Lennox (ed.), *Bertie Diary*, Vol. 1, p. 132.

56. A. Ribot (ed.), *Journal d'Alexandre Ribot et Correspondances Inédites 1914–1922* (Paris, 1936), p. 131.

57. Institut de France, Pichon MSS 4397, Poincaré to Paléologue, 9 March 1915; R. Poincaré, *Au Service de la France*, Vol. 6 (Paris, 1930), p. 94; Soutou, 'Les marches de l'est', p. 350.

58. Mitrakos, *France in Greece*, p. xvi.

59. MAE, A-Paix 130, Berthelot to Barrère, 21 September 1916; A. Ribot, *Letters to a Friend* (London, 1926), p. 130; M. S. Anderson, *The Eastern Question 1774–1923* (London, 1966), p. 325.

60. AG, 16N3057, note on French policy towards Greece, 31 August 1916.

61. Berthelot MSS, Berthelot to Cambon, 12 January 1917.

62. Gottlieb, *Studies in Secret Diplomacy*, p. 103.

63. Institut de France, Pichon MSS 4398, transcript of speech by de Frey-cinet, 22 February 1915.

64. Institut de France, Pichon MSS 4398, transcript of speech by Clemen-ceau, 30 April 1915.

65. AG, 16N1678, erased extract from Joffre to Millerand, 3 October 1915.

66. Gottlieb, *Studies in Secret Diplomacy*, p. 103.

67. MAE, A-Guerre 1030, War Ministry note, 7 October 1915.

68. MAE, A-Guerre 1038, Barrère to Briand, 9 August 1916.

69. MAE, Bourgeois MSS, Vol. 9, Lecoq to Bourgeois, 7 September 1916.

70. MAE, Bourgeois MSS, Vol. 8, de Fontenay to Bourgeois 28 November 1916.

71. MAE, Bourgeois MSS, Vol. 8, de Fontenay to Bourgeois, 22 December 1916.

72. HLRO, Lloyd George MSS, F/55/3/2, Elliot to Hardinge, 9 April 1917.

73. AG, 16N2944, 'L'Avenir Balkanique', 12 June 1916, by René Pinon, influential political commentator and assistant to Poincaré.

74. MAE, A-Guerre 1040, note on the situation on the Eastern Front, 2 November 1916.

75. MAE, Bourgeois MSS, Vol. 8, de Fontenay to Bourgeois, 14 August 1917.

76. M. Sarrail, *Mon Commandement en Orient 1916–1918* (Paris, 1920), p. 271.

77. MAE, A-Guerre 1030, Delcassé to Millerand, 1 October 1915.

78. MAE, A-Guerre 252, Graillet to Briand, 19 February 1916.

79. MAE, A-Guerre 302, Sarrail to Briand, 3 August 1916.

80. MAE, Bourgeois MSS, Vol. 9, Lecoq to Bourgeois, 26 July 1916.

81. MAE, A-Guerre 302, Sarrail to Briand, 3 August 1916.

82. MAE, Nouvelle Série 53, Sarrail to Presidents of French Chambers of Commerce, 1 August 1916.

83. Note by Berthelot on above.

84. MAE, Bourgeois MSS, Vol. 9, Lecoq to Bourgeois, 20 August 1916.

85. AN, Painlevé MSS, 313AP109, report by the deputy, Meunier-Surcouf, 25 October 1916.

86. MAE, A-Guerre 302, Bonnier to Péan, 7 September 1916.

87. MAE, A-Guerre 304, Bonnier to Péan, 30 January 1917.

88. MAE, Nouvelle Série 53, note by Bonnier on circular of National Association of Economic Expansion, 25 January 1917.

89. AG, 5N287, note on the Commercial Bureau, 24 October 1917.

90. MAE, A-Guerre 302, Bulletin Commercial de Macédoine, no. 1, 1 September 1916.

91. AN, Painlevé MSS, 313AP110, Bulletin Commercial de Macédoine, no. 3, 1 November 1916.

92. AN, Painlevé MSS, 313AP110, Bulletin Commercial de Macédoine, no. 4, 1 December 1916.

93. AN, Painlevé MSS, 313AP95, Bulletin Commercial de Macédoine, no. 2, 1 October 1916.

94. AN, Painlevé MSS, 313AP95, Bulletin Commercial de Macédoine, no. 10, 1 June 1917.

95. PRO, CAB 24/8/249, Stead to Lloyd George, 12 March 1917.

96. HLRO, Lloyd George MSS, F/55/3/1, Granville to Lloyd George, 6 February 1917.

97. L. Villari, *The Macedonian Campaign* (London, 1922), p. 59.

98. AG, 5N153, Sarrail to Painlevé, 2 April 1917.

99. AN, Painlevé MSS, 313AP96, Bonnier to Presidents of French Chambers of Commerce, 1 July 1917.

100. AG, 16N3145, Sarrail to Painlevé, 5 September 1917.

101. AN, Painlevé MSS, 313AP109, Lecoq to Painlevé, 26 January 1918.

102. Compare the strange assessment in J. K. Tanenbaum's generally excellent study of Sarrail's career: 'the overwhelming collection of evidence strongly suggests that if Sarrail or Briand were motivated by other than military concerns, it was an extremely well-kept secret.' *General Maurice Sarrail 1856–1929: The French Army and Left-Wing Politics* (Chapel Hill, 1974), p. 156.

103. MAE, A-Guerre 1042, parliamentary report on the Armeé d'Orient by de Chappedelaine and others, 1 June 1917.

104. MAE, A-Paix 130, note by Berthelot, 27 August 1917.

105. AG, 5N287, note on commercial relations between France and Macedonia, 3 December 1917.

106. MAE, A-Guerre 1042, report by de Chappedelaine, 1 June 1917.

107. C. M. Andrew and A. S. Kanya-Forstner, 'The French Colonial Party and French Colonial War Aims, 1914–18', *Historical Journal* 17 (1974), p. 106.

7. The End of the Campaign

1. MAE, A-Guerre 281, note sur les affaires de Grèce, 15 February 1918.

2. MAE, A-Guerre 1043, Pichon's instructions for Guillaumat, 17 December 1917; see also MAE, A-Guerre 1044, note for Pichon, 24 March 1918: 'The question of Salonika which had, on many occasions, been the subject of quite agitated debate between the Allies ... no longer gives rise to serious discussion ... The personality of the commanding general has been a factor in this ... His past and the reputation he has for only considering things from a military point of view assure him an uncontested moral ascendancy.'

3. PRO, CAB 23/4/296, War Cabinet, 12 December 1917.

4. PRO, CAB 25/27/9A, Milne to Robertson, 30 December 1917.

5. PRO, CAB 25/27/9A, Milne to Robertson, 17 January 1918.

6. PRO, WO 106/1347, report on seventh visit to Salonika, 22 January 1918.

7. Liverpool Record Office, 920 DER(17) 28/1/1, Derby diary, 18 August 1918; Clemenceau replied to Painlevé's suggestion that some of his colleagues should retain their posts in the new government: 'I'm burning everything, even the furniture.' P. Bernard, *La fin d'un monde 1914–1929* (Paris, 1975), pp. 84–5.

8. A. Ferry, *Les Carnets Secrets* (Paris, 1957), p. 209.

9. Bertie to Lloyd George, 9 December 1917, cited in D. R. Watson, *Georges Clemenceau: A Political Biography* (London, 1974), p. 279.

10. E. Herbillon, *Souvenirs d'un officier de liaison pendant la guerre mondiale: du général en chef au gouvernement*, Vol. 2 (Paris, 1930), p. 186. It was also important that the Radical Socialists' political effectiveness was greatly compromised by Clemenceau's determination to act against Caillaux and Malvy. On 11 December 1917 the government asked the Chamber to remove Caillaux's parliamentary immunity so that he could stand trial. The nomination of Sarrail as generalissimo in Caillaux's celebrated 'Rubicon' document left the general particularly vulnerable. J. K. Tanenbaum, *General Maurice Sarrail 1856–1929: The French Army and Left-Wing Politics* (Chapel Hill, 1974), pp. 181–2. Clemenceau skilfully equated a less than whole-hearted commitment to total victory on the part of Caillaux and Malvy with outright treason. S. Berstein, 'The Radical Socialist Party During the First World War', in P. Fridenson (ed.), *The French Home Front 1914–1918* (Oxford, 1992), p. 50.

11. LRO, 920 DER(17)28/2/1, Derby to Balfour, 24 May 1918.

12. *L'homme Enchaîné*, 6 May 1917.

13. P. Coblentz, *The Silence of Sarrail* (London, 1930), p. 111.

14. AN, C7491, meeting of 3 May 1918. See also H. Cambon (ed.), *Paul Cambon: Correspondance 1870–1924*, Vol. 3 (Paris, 1946), p. 275: 'Clemenceau is not at all interested in the East.'

15. MAE, de Freycinet MSS, Vol. 1, d'Espérey to de Freycinet, 4 February 1919.

16. AG, 16N3146, Guillaumat to Foch, 13 February 1918.

17. PRO, CAB 23/6/394, War Cabinet, 18 April 1918.

18. J. C. King, *Generals and Politicians* (Berkeley, 1951), pp. 165, 170.

19. J. M. Bourget, *Gouvernement et Commandement* (Paris, 1930), p. 109.

20. P. Painlevé, *Comment j'ai nommé Foch et Pétain* (Paris, 1923), p. ix.

21. Ibid., p. 241.

22. T. H. Bliss, 'The Evolution of the Unified Command', *Foreign Affairs* 1, 2 (1922), p. 6.

23. D. R. Woodward, *Lloyd George and the Generals* (Newark, 1983), pp. 133–56.

24. C. E. Callwell, *Field-Marshal Sir Henry Wilson: His Life and Diaries*, Vol. 1 (London, 1927), p. 253.

25. AG, 16N2991, Directives pour le Général Commandant en Chef des Armées Alliées d'Orient, 16 December 1917; PRO, FO 371/2895, note from Supreme War Council, 19 December 1917.

26. C. B. Falls, *Military Operations: Macedonia*, Vol. 2 (London, 1935), p. 49. The term 'Old Greece' refers to the country's territory before the Balkan Wars.

27. F. Maurice, *Lessons of Allied Cooperation* (London, 1942), p. 112.

28. PRO, CAB 23/4/307, War Cabinet, 27 December 1917.

29. AG, 16N3060, GQG note on the General Situation, 19 December 1917.

30. A. Palmer, *The Gardeners of Salonika: The Macedonian Campaign 1915–1918* (London, 1965), p. 169.

31. PRO, CAB 23/6/395, note by Smuts on the mobilization of Greece, 17 April 1918.

32. PRO, CAB 25/25/8A, note by General Studd, 15 January 1918.

33. PRO, CAB 23/5/331, War Cabinet, 25 January 1918.

34. PRO, CAB 23/5/350, War Cabinet, 20 February 1918.

35. PRO, CAB 25/25/21H, notes on the situation in the Balkans, 21 February 1918.

36. PRO, CAB 23/5/371, War Cabinet, 23 March 1918.

37. AN, C7491, Foreign Affairs Commission, 25 March 1918.

38. Palmer, *Gardeners*, p. 178.

39. PRO, CAB 28/3/IC55a, procès-verbal, 3 April 1918.

40. AG, 16N3139, Clemenceau to Guillaumat, 7 April 1918.

41. PRO, CAB 25/26, Clemenceau to Guillaumat, 4 April 1918.

42. P.R.O., CAB 25/26/04A, Wilson to Milne, 12 April 1918; CAB 25/27/5FF, Wilson to Foch, 12 April 1918.

43. PRO, CAB 23/6/400, War Cabinet, 26 April 1918; Maurice, *Allied Cooperation*, p. 146.

44. AG, 6N256, Clemenceau to Guillaumat, 28 April 1918.

45. PRO, CAB 28/3/IC58, procès-verbal, 2 May 1918.

46. Palmer, *Gardeners*, p. 178.

47. PRO, CAB 23/6/421, War Cabinet, 30 May 1918.

48. PRO, CAB 23/6/430, War Cabinet, 12 June 1918

49. PRO, FO 371/3150, Granville to Balfour, 29 May and 15 June 1918. Milne noted on 8 June: '[Guillaumat] tells me he is off to France ... Don't know if he is pleased or not. Thinks he may replace Pétain or Foch.' G. Nicol, *Uncle George: Field-Marshal Lord Milne of Salonika and Rubislaw* (London, 1976), p. 166.

50. MAE, Série Z, Grèce Vol. 33, Graillet to Pichon, 20 June 1918; Falls, *Military Operations*, Vol. 2, p. 102; Palmer, *Gardeners*, p. 180; Maurice, *Allied Cooperation*, p. 151.

51. PRO, CAB 25/27/65A, Sackville-West to War Office, 22 June 1918.

52. AG, 16N3139, Clemenceau to d'Espérey, 22 June 1918.

53. PRO, CAB 25/26/6BA, joint note, 'Situation in the Balkans'.

54. LRO, 920 DER(17) 28/1/1, Derby diary, 3 July 1918.

55. Palmer, *Gardeners*, p. 189; Maurice, *Allied Cooperation*, p. 155; M. Hankey, *The Supreme Command, 1914–18*, Vol. 2 (London, 1961), p. 821; Watson, *Clemenceau*, p. 312.

56. PRO, CAB 28/4/IC70, procès-verbal, 3 July 1918; AG, 16N3140.
57. PRO, CAB 23/41/IWC23.
58. PRO, CAB 25/26/11A, resolutions of the Supreme War Council, 11 July 1918.
59. PRO, CAB 23/41/IWC25, Imperial War Cabinet, 18 July 1918.
60. PRO, CAB 25/26/19A, Milne to Wilson, 22 July 1918.
61. Palmer, *Gardeners*, p. 191.
62. Ibid., p. 192.
63. AG, 16N3140, note au sujet de l'offensive en Orient, 27 August 1918.
64. AG, 16N3140, Cambon to Clemenceau, 4 September 1918.
65. AG, 16N3140, Historique des opérations en Serbie, September 1918.
66. B. Hamard, 'Quand la Victoire s'est gagnée dans les Balkans: L'Assaut de l'Armée Alliée d'Orient de Septembre à Novembre 1918', *Guerres mondiales et conflits contemporains* 184 (1996), pp. 29–31.
67. G. Suarez, *Briand: Sa vie, son oeuvre*, Vol. 4 (Paris, 1940), p. 379.
68. LRO, 920 DER(17) 28/1/1, Derby diary, 24 September 1918.
69. R. Poincaré, *Au Service de la France*, Vol. 10 (Paris,1933), p. 357.
70. LRO, 920 DER(17) 28/1/1, Derby diary, 5 October 1918.
71. PRO, CAB 23/8/480.
72. Suarez, *Briand*, Vol. 4, p. 378.
73. PRO, CAB 23/14/482A; D. French, *The Strategy of the Lloyd George Coalition 1916–1918* (Oxford, 1995), p. 262.
74. PRO, FO 800/201, Balfour to Cecil, 7 October 1918.
75. Hankey, *Supreme Command*, Vol. 2, p. 842.
76. V. H. Rothwell, *British War Aims and Peace Diplomacy 1914–1918* (Oxford, 1971), p. 242.
77. House diary, 30 October 1918, cited in J. Nevakivi, *Britain, France and the Arab Middle East 1914–1920* (London, 1969), p. 70.
78. C. M. Andrew and A. S. Kanya-Forstner, *France Overseas: The Great War and the Climax of French Imperial Expansion* (London, 1981), p. 164.
79. Max of Baden, *Memoirs*, Vol. 2 (London, 1928), p. 19.
80. P. Ludendorff, *My War Memories, 1914–1918*, Vol. 2 (London, 1919), pp. 712ff.
81. J. Vincent (ed.), *The Crawford Papers* (Manchester, 1984), p. 395; J. Ramsden (ed.), *Real Old Tory Politics: The Political Diaries of Robert Sanders, Lord Bayford* (London, 1984), p. 110; J. Barnes and D. Nicholson (eds), *The Leo Amery Diaries*, Vol. 1 (London, 1980), p. 241.
82. T. Wilson, *The Myriad Faces of War* (Oxford, 1986), p. 620.
83. HLRO, Lloyd George MSS, F/47/7/35, Milne to Wilson, 27 July 1918.
84. MAE, Nouvelle Série Vol. 53, Pichon to Ministries of Finance and Commerce, 12 March 1918.
85. MAE, A-Guerre 310, Dussap to Pichon, 21 February 1918.
86. AG, 7N1342, A. Romanos to Pichon, 5 February 1918.
87. MAE, A-Guerre 310, de Billy to Pichon, 15 March 1918.
88. PRO, FO 371/3158, Granville to Balfour, 12 September 1918.

89. AG, 7N1344, note on propaganda, 31 March 1918.

90. MAE, Série Z, Grèce Vol. 98, Graillet to Pichon, 20 November 1918 and 13 December 1918.

91. MAE, A-Guerre 310, Jonnart to Pichon, 4 April 1918.

92. MAE, Nouvelle Série Vol. 19, Commission aux Transports Maritimes to MAE, 25 April 1918.

93. MAE, Série Z, Grèce Vol. 128, Bargeton to de Billy, 12 April 1918.

94. MAE, Série Z, Grèce Vol. 128, Guillaumat to Clemenceau, 5 May 1918.

95. MAE, Série Z, Grèce Vol. 128, Ministry of Blockade to Pichon, 12 July 1918.

96. MAE, Série Z, Grèce Vol. 128, Commission aux Transports Maritimes to Pichon, 30 July 1918.

97. MAE, Série Z, Grèce Vol. 128, Dussap to Pichon, 6 June 1918.

98. AG, 6N168, Situation Générale en Grèce, 28 February 1919.

99. E. Goldstein, 'Great Britain and Greater Greece 1917–1920', *Historical Journal* 32, 2 (1989), pp. 339–56.

100. AG, 16N3147, note by Guillaumat on the military situation in the Balkans, 2 October 1918.

101. PRO, CAB 23/8/484, War Cabinet, 11 October 1918.

102. AG, 16N3147, d'Espérey to Clemenceau, 9 October 1918.

103. AG, 14N23, note on the general situation in the East, for the office of Marshal Joffe, 15 December 1918.

104. AN, C7503, report on mission to the Armeé d'Orient, presented 22 May 1919.

105. AN, Painlevé MSS, 313AP110, *Commercial Bulletin* September–October 1918.

106. MAE, Série Z, Grèce vol 32, d'Espérey to Foch, 3 March 1919.

107. AG, 16N3194, rapport sur le rôle que doit jouer la France en Orient, 20 July 1919; see also 16N3061, note au sujet des effectifs et des possibilités d'action de l'Armée d'Orient, 19 February 1920, which stresses the importance of avoiding the dismemberment of the Ottoman Empire.

108. MAE, Série Z, Grèce Vol. 33, Pichon to Clemenceau, 21 December 1918.

109. AG, 20N168, report on the situation in Turkey by Lieutenant de Rollin, 26 September 1920.

110. C. M. Andrew and A. S. Kanya-Forstner, 'The French Colonial Party and French Colonial War Aims', *Historical Journal* 17 (1974), p. 105.

111. MAE, de Freycinet MSS, Vol. 1, d'Espérey to de Freycinet, 4 February 1919.

112. MAE, Série Z, Grèce Vol. 33, note pour le ministre, 21 April 1919.

113. MAE, A-Guerre 281, report by Pichery on his 'mission en Orient', March 1918.

114. MAE, A-Guerre 282, de Billy to Pichon, 29 May 1918.

115. AG, 7N1342, de Fontenay to Pichon, 28 July 1918.

116. AG, 7N1342, de Billy to Pichon, 4 December 1918.

117. AG, 7N1342, de Billy to Pichon, 2 December and 12 December 1918.

118. AG, 7N1344, undated note on British propaganda in Greece.

8. Conclusion

1. C. à C. Repington, *The First World War 1914–1918*, Vol. 1 (London, 1920), p. 254.

2. Ibid., Vol. 2, p. 14.

3. J. Lees-Milne, *The Enigmatic Edwardian: the Life of Reginald 2nd Viscount Esher* (London, 1986), p. 291.

4. G. H. Cassar, *Kitchener: Architect of Victory* (London, 1977), p. 398. As the journalist Leo Maxse put it: 'We appear to be quite unteachable. With the object lesson of the Dardanelles in front of us, in which a force of about 250,000 men has dwindled down to about 110,000 without having achieved anything material, it would be incredible that we should be prepared to repeat the disaster on a larger scale in the same part of the world.' University of Birmingham Library, Chamberlain MSS, AC13/3/61, Maxse to Austen Chamberlain, 13 October 1915.

5. HLRO, Lloyd George MSS, C/16/1/3, 'Suggestions as to the Military Position', 1 January 1915.

6. A. J. P. Taylor (ed.), *Lloyd George: A Diary by Frances Stevenson* (London, 1971), p. 66. In terms of cartography little seems to have been learnt during the course of the campaign. Four days before the armistice in November 1918, Henry Wilson found Lloyd George, Clemenceau and the Italian Prime Minister Orlando discussing Balkan strategy using a small hand-atlas of Europe, 'the whole page of Europe being about 8 inches by 6 inches!' Sir C. E. Callwell, *Field-Marshal Sir Henry Wilson: His Life and Diaries*, Vol. 2 (London, 1927), p. 132.

7. Howell to wife, 27 November 1915, cited in J. K. Tanenbaum, *General Maurice Sarrail 1856–1929: The French Army and Left-Wing Politics* (Chapel Hill, 1974), p. 75.

8. HLRO, Bonar Law MSS, 51/5/38, Wilson to Law, 20 November 1915.

9. HLRO, Lloyd George MSS, D/17/3/8, memorandum by Hankey, 8 December 1915.

10. Repington, *First World War*, Vol. 1, p. 414; see also P. G. Halpern (ed.), *The Keyes Papers: Selections from the Private and Official Correspondence of Admiral of the Fleet Baron Keyes of Zeebrugge*, Vol. 1 (London, 1972), p. 348.

11. G. Nicol, *Uncle George: Field-Marshal Lord Milne of Salonika and Rubislaw* (London, 1976), p. 128.

12. LHCMA, Robertson MSS, I/32/27, Robertson to Duff, 18 May 1916.

13. W. J. Philpott, *Anglo-French Relations and Strategy on the Western Front, 1914–18* (London, 1996), p. 13.

14. Liverpool Record Office, Derby MSS, 920 DER(17) 28/1/1, Derby diary, 13 July 1918.

15. LHCMA, Robertson MSS, I/32/77, Robertson to Allenby, 23 November 1917.

16. LHCMA, Robertson MSS, I/34/20, Robertson to Esher, 14 March 1917.

17. C. E. Callwell, *Stray Recollections*, Vol. 2 (London, 1923), pp. 283–4.

18. HLRO, Lloyd George MSS, F/50/3/40, Lloyd George to Clemenceau, 25 October 1918.

19. D. R. Woodward (ed.), *The Military Correspondence of Field-Marshal Sir William Robertson, Chief of General Staff, December 1915–February 1918* (London, 1989), p. 37.

20. PRO, CAB 42/9/3, 'The position of Great Britain with regard to her allies', 18 February 1916.

21. MAE, A-Guerre 256, P. Cambon to Briand, 21 October 1916.

22. D. French, *British Strategy and War Aims 1914–1916* (London, 1986), p. 62.

23. J. Barnes and D. Nicholson (eds), *The Leo Amery Diaries*, Vol. 1 (London, 1980), p. 129.

24. LRO, Derby MSS, 920 DER(17) 28/1/1, Derby diary, 2 June 1918.

25. M. and E. Brock (eds), *H. H. Asquith: Letters to Venetia Stanley* (Oxford, 1985), p. 422.

26. R. Blake (ed.), *The Private Papers of Douglas Haig 1914–1919* (London, 1952), p. 214.

27. LRO, Derby MSS, 920 DER(17) 28/2/1, Derby to Balfour, 6 June 1918.

28. W. K. Hancock and J. van der Poel (eds), *Selections from the Smuts Papers*, Vol. 3 (Cambridge, 1966), p. 488.

29. LHCMA, Robertson MSS, I/34/7, Robertson to Esher, 9 August 1916.

30. E. Grey, *Twenty-Five Years*, Vol. 2 (London, 1926), pp. 154, 160.

31. Repington, *First World War*, Vol. 1, p. 167.

32. 'I was afraid that the P. M. would find himself landed in considerable difficulties owing to the intrigues of Lloyd George with French politicians in opposition to our own military advisers': University of Birmingham Library, Chamberlain MSS, AC12/35, private note by Austen Chamberlain, 29 June 1916.

33. LHCMA, Robertson MSS, I/34/10, Robertson to Milne, 7 November 1916.

34. Repington, *First World War*, Vol. 1, p. 134.

35. LHCMA, Robertson MSS, I/33/73, Robertson to Repington, 31 October 1916.

36. Mathiez to Sarrail, 14 February 1916, cited in Tanenbaum, *Sarrail*, p. 142.

37. C. Petrie, *The Life and Letters of the Right Hon. Sir Austen Chamberlain*, Vol. 2 (London, 1940), p. 110.

Bibliography

Official Archives

Britain

Public Record Office

1. Cabinet Papers

CAB 23 (War Cabinet); CAB 24 (Cabinet Memoranda); CAB 25 (Supreme War Council); CAB 27 (Cabinet Committees); CAB 28 (Inter-allied Conferences); CAB 37 (Cabinet); CAB 42 (War Committee)

2. Foreign Office Papers

FO 371 (General Correspondence)

3. War Office Papers

WO 32 (War of 1914–1918); WO 106 (Military Operations and Intelligence); WO 158 (Military Headquarters); WO 159 (Kitchener Papers)

France

Ministère des Affaires Etrangères (MAE)

Série A-Guerre; Série A-Paix; Nouvelle Série; Série Z

Archives du Ministère de la Guerre, Château de Vincennes (AG)

5N (Cabinet du Ministre); 6N (Fonds Clemenceau); 7N (Attachés Militaires); 14N (Fonds Joffre); 16N (Grand Quartier Général); 20N (Armée d'Orient)

Archives Nationales (AN)

Archives of the Chamber of Deputies

Private Papers

Britain

Arthur Balfour MSS (PRO and British Library); Francis Bertie MSS (PRO); Robert Cecil MSS (PRO); Austen Chamberlain MSS (Birmingham University

Library); Lord Derby MSS (Liverpool Record Office/LRO); David Lloyd George MSS (House of Lords Record Office/HLRO); Edward Grey MSS (PRO); Howell Gwynne MSS (Bodleian Library); Douglas Haig MSS (Microfilm); Andrew Bonar Law MSS (House of Lords Record Office/HLRO); William Robertson MSS (Liddell Hart Centre for Military Archives/LHCMA)

France

Camille Barrère MSS (MAE); Philippe Berthelot MSS (MAE and in private possession); Edouard de Billy MSS (MAE); Léon Bourgeois MSS (MAE); Jules Cambon MSS (MAE); Paul Cambon MSS (MAE); Théophile Delcassé MSS (MAE); Charles de Freycinet MSS (MAE); Paul Painlevé MSS (AN); Maurice Pellé MSS (Institut de France); Stephen Pichon MSS (Institut de France)

Published Primary Sources

Barnes, J. and D. Nicholson (eds), *The Leo Amery Diaries*, Vol. 1 (London, 1980).

Blake, R. (ed.), *The Private Papers of Douglas Haig 1914–1919* (London, 1952).

Brock, M. and E. (eds), *H. H. Asquith: Letters to Venetia Stanley* (Oxford, 1985).

Cambon. H. (ed.), *Paul Cambon: Correspondance 1870–1924*, Vol. 3 (Paris, 1946).

David, E. (ed.), *Inside Asquith's Cabinet: From the Diaries of Charles Hobhouse* (London, 1977).

Esher, O. (ed.), *Journals and Letters of Reginald, Viscount Esher. Vol. 3: 1910–1915* (London, 1938).

Galliéni, G. (ed.), *Les Carnets de Galliéni* (Paris, 1932).

Halpern, P. G. (ed.), *The Keyes Papers: Selections from the Private and Official Correspondence of Admiral of the Fleet Baron Keyes of Zeebrugge*, Vol. 1 (London, 1972).

Hancock, W. K. and J. van der Poel (eds), *Selections from the Smuts Papers*, Vol. 3 (Cambridge, 1966).

Lennox, Lady A. G. (ed.), *The Diary of Lord Bertie of Thame 1914–1918*, 2 vols (London, 1924).

Marchand, R. (ed.), *Un Livre Noir: Diplomatie d'avant Guerre et de Guerre d'après les documents des Archives Russes 1910–1917*, Vol. 3, parts 2 and 4 (Paris, 1926–31).

Pimlott, B. (ed.), *The Second World War Diary of Hugh Dalton 1940–45* (London, 1986).

Ramsden, J. (ed.), *Real Old Tory Politics: The Political Diaries of Robert Sanders, Lord Bayford* (London, 1984).

Ribot, A. (ed.), *Journal d'Alexandre Ribot et Correspondances Inédites 1914–22* (Paris, 1936).

Taylor, A. J. P. (ed.), *Lloyd George: A Diary by Frances Stevenson* (London, 1971).

Vincent, J. (ed.), *The Crawford Papers* (Manchester, 1984).

Williamson, P. (ed.), *The Modernisation of Conservative Politics: The Diaries and Letters of William Bridgeman, 1904–1935* (London, 1988).

Woodward, D. R. (ed.), *The Military Correspondence of Field-Marshal Sir William Robertson, Chief Imperial General Staff, December 1915–February 1918* (London, 1989).

Published Memoirs etc

Asquith, H. H., *Memories and Reflections*, Vol. 2 (London, 1928).

Baden, Max of, *Memoirs*, Vol. 2 (London, 1928).

Chelwood, Viscount Cecil of, *All the Way* (London, 1949).

Churchill, W. S., *The World Crisis 1915* (London, 1923; 2 vol edn, 1938).

Clemenceau, G., *Grandeur and Misery of Victory* (London, 1930).

Fayolle, Maréchal, *Cahiers Secrets de la Grande Guerre* (Paris, 1964).

Ferry, A., *Les Carnets Secrets* (Paris, 1957).

Grey, E., *Twenty-Five Years*, Vols 1–2 (London, 1925–26).

Herbillon, E., *Souvenirs d'un officier de liaison pendant la guerre mondiale: du général en chef au gouvernement*, 2 vols (Paris, 1930).

Joffre, J., *The Memoirs of Marshal Joffre*, 2 vols (London, 1932).

Lloyd George, D., *War Memoirs*, 6 vols (London, 1933–36).

Loucheur, L., *Carnets Secrets 1908–1932* (Brussels, 1962).

Ludendorff, P., *My War Memories, 1914–1918*, Vol. 2 (London, 1919).

Mackenzie, C., *Greek Memories* (London, 1939).

— *Aegean Memories* (London, 1940).

Morand, P., *Journal d'un attaché d'ambassade, 1916–1917* (Paris, 1948).

Painlevé, P., *Comment j'ai nommé Foch et Pétain* (Paris, 1923).

Poincaré, R., *Au Service de la France*, Vols 4–10 (Paris, 1927–33).

Repington, C. à C., *The First World War 1914–1918*, 2 vols (London, 1920).

Ribot, A., *Letters to a Friend* (London, 1926).

Riddell, Lord, *War Diary 1914–1918* (London, 1933).

Robertson, W., *From Private to Field Marshal* (London, 1921).

— *Soldiers and Statesmen 1914–1918*, 2 vols (London, 1926).

Sarrail, M., *Mon Commandement en Orient 1916–1918* (Paris, 1920).

Other Published Books

Adamthwaite, A., *Grandeur and Misery: France's Bid for Power in Europe 1914–1940* (London, 1995).

Allard, P., *Les Dessous de la Guerre révélés par les Comités Secrets* (Paris, 1932).

Anderson, M. S., *The Eastern Question 1774–1923* (London, 1966).

Andrew, C. M. and A. S. Kanya-Forstner, *France Overseas: The Great War and the Climax of French Imperial Expansion* (London, 1981).

Azan, P., *Franchet d'Espérey* (Paris, 1949).

Barré, J.-L., *Le Seigneur Chat: Philippe Berthelot 1866–1934* (Paris, 1988).

238 · *The Politics of Diplomacy*

Bell, P. M. H., *France and Britain 1900–1940: Entente and Estrangement* (London, 1996).

Bernard, P., *La fin d'un monde 1914–1929* (Paris, 1975).

Bertin, C., *Marie Bonaparte: A Life* (New Haven, 1987).

Bond, B., (ed.), *Fallen Stars: Eleven Studies of Twentieth-Century Military Disasters* (London, 1991).

Bonnefous, G., *Histoire Politique de la Troisième République*, Vol. 2 (Paris, 1957).

Bourget, J. M., *Gouvernement et Commandement* (Paris, 1930).

Bourne, J. M., *Britain and the Great War 1914–1918* (London, 1989).

Bréal, A., *Philippe Berthelot* (Paris, 1937).

Brogan, D. W., *The Development of Modern France 1870–1939* (London, 1940).

Callwell, C. E., *Field Marshal Sir Henry Wilson: His Life and Diaries*, 2 vols (London, 1927).

Calvocoressi, P., et al., *Greece and Great Britain during World War One* (Thessaloniki, 1985).

Carroll, E. M., *French Public Opinion and Foreign Affairs 1870–1914* (New York, 1931).

Cassar, G. H., *The French and the Dardanelles* (London, 1971).

— *Kitchener: Architect of Victory* (London, 1977).

— *The Tragedy of Sir John French* (Newark, 1985).

— *Asquith as War Leader* (London, 1994).

Churchill, R. S., *Lord Derby: 'King of Lancashire'* (London, 1959).

Coblentz, P., *The Silence of Sarrail* (London, 1930).

Conte, A., *Joffre* (Paris, 1991).

Conwell-Evans, T. P., *Foreign Policy from a Back Bench 1904–1918: A Study Based on the Papers of Lord Noel-Buxton* (London, 1932).

Cosgrove, A. and J. I. McGuire (eds), *Parliament and Community* (Belfast, 1983).

David, R., *Le Drame Ignoré de l'Armée d'Orient* (Paris, 1927).

Delage, E., *The Tragedy of the Dardanelles* (London, 1932).

Dutton, D. (ed.), *Statecraft and Diplomacy in the Twentieth Century: Essays Presented to P. M. H. Bell* (Liverpool, 1995).

Eubank, W. K., *Paul Cambon, Master Diplomatist* (Oklahoma, 1960).

Falls, C. B., *Military Operations: Macedonia*, 2 vols (London, 1933–35).

Farrar, M. M., *Principled Pragmatist: The Political Career of Alexandre Millerand* (New York, 1991).

French, D., *British Economic and Strategic Planning 1905-1915* (London, 1982).

— *British Strategy and War Aims 1914–1916* (London, 1986).

— *The Strategy of the Lloyd George Coalition 1916–1918* (Oxford, 1995).

Fridenson, P., (ed.), *The French Home Front 1914–1918* (Oxford, 1992).

Fry, M. G., *Lloyd George and Foreign Policy Vol. 1: The Education of a Statesman 1890–1916* (Montreal, 1977).

Gheusi, P., *Guerre et Théâtre* (Paris, 1919).

Gilbert, B. B., *David Lloyd George: A Political Life. Organizer of Victory 1912–16* (London, 1992).

Gilbert, M., *Winston S. Churchill*, Vol. 3 (London, 1971).
Gooch, J., *The Plans of War: The General Staff and British Military Strategy c.1900–1916* (London, 1974).
Gorce, P. M. de la, *The French Army* (New York, 1963).
Gottlieb, W. W., *Studies in Secret Diplomacy during the First World War* (London, 1957).
Grigg, J., *Lloyd George: From Peace to War 1912–1916* (London, 1985).
Halle, K., *The Irrepressible Churchill: A Treasury of Winston Churchill's Wit* (Cleveland, 1966).
Halpern, P. G., *A Naval History of World War One* (Annapolis, 1994).
Hamilton, K., *Bertie of Thame: Edwardian Ambassador* (London, 1990).
Hankey, M., *The Supreme Command, 1914–1918*, 2 vols (London, 1961).
Hazlehurst, C., *Politicians at War, July 1914 to May 1915* (London, 1971).
Higgins, T., *Winston Churchill and the Dardanelles* (London, 1963).
Hinsley, F. H. (ed.), *British Foreign Policy under Sir Edward Grey* (Cambridge, 1977).
Horne, A., *The Price of Glory: Verdun 1916* (London, 1962).
— *The French Army and Politics 1870–1970* (New York, 1984).
Hunt, B. and A. Preston (eds), *War Aims and Strategic Policy in the Great War* (London, 1977).
Johnson, D., F. Bédarida and F. Crouzet (eds), *Britain and France: Ten Centuries* (Folkestone, 1980).
Keiger, J. F. V., *Raymond Poincaré* (Cambridge, 1997).
King, J. C., *Generals and Politicians: Conflict between France's High Command, Parliament and Government, 1914–1918* (Berkeley, 1951).
Leblond, M., *Galliéni Parle*, 2 vols (Paris, 1920).
Lees-Milne, J., *Harold Nicolson: A Biography*, Vol. 1 (London, 1980).
— *The Enigmatic Edwardian: the Life of Reginald 2nd Viscount Esher* (London, 1986).
Liddell Hart, B. H., *Reputations Ten Years After* (London, 1928).
Lowe, C. J. and M. L. Dockrill, *The Mirage of Power*, Vol. 2 (London, 1972).
Magnus, P., *Kitchener: Portrait of an Imperialist* (London, 1958).
Maurice, F., *Lessons of Allied Cooperation* (London, 1942).
Millett, A. R. and W. Murray (eds), *Military Effectiveness: The First World War*, Vol. 1 (Boston, 1988).
Ministère de la Guerre, Etat-Major de l'Armée, Service Historique, *Les Armées françaises dans la grande guerre*, Vol. 8 (Paris, 1924).
Mitrakos, A. S., *France in Greece during World War One: A Study in the Politics of Power* (Boulder, 1982).
Moorehead, A., *Gallipoli* (London, 1956).
Neilson, K., *Strategy and Supply: The Anglo-Russian Alliance, 1914–17* (London, 1984).
Neilson, K. and R. Prete (eds), *Coalition Warfare: An Uneasy Accord* (Waterloo, Ont., 1983).

Néré, J., The Foreign Policy of France from 1914 to 1945 (London, 1975).

Nevakivi, J., Britain, France and the Arab Middle East 1914–1920 (London, 1969).

Nicol, G., Uncle George: Field Marshal Lord Milne of Salonika and Rubislaw (London, 1976).

Nicolson, H., King George V: His Life and Reign (London, 1952).

Oudin, B., Aristide Briand: La Paix, une idée neuve en Europe (Paris, 1987).

Palmer, A., The Gardeners of Salonika: The Macedonian Campaign 1915–1918 (London, 1965).

Petrie, C., The Life and Letters of the Right Hon. Sir Austen Chamberlain, Vol. 2 (London, 1940).

Philpott, W. J., Anglo-French Relations and Strategy on the Western Front, 1914–18 (London, 1996).

Pingaud, A., Histoire Diplomatique de la France pendant la Grande Guerre, Vol. I (Paris, 1937).

Renouvin, P., The Forms of War Government in France (New Haven, 1927).

Rolo, P. J. V., Entente Cordiale: The Origins and Negotiation of the Anglo-French Agreements of 8 April 1904 (London, 1969).

Roskill, S., Hankey, Man of Secrets, Vol. 1 (London, 1970).

Rothwell, V. H., British War Aims and Peace Diplomacy 1914–1918 (Oxford, 1971).

Rowland, P., Lloyd George (London, 1975).

Schmidt, M. E., Alexandre Ribot: Odyssey of a Liberal in the Third Republic (The Hague, 1974).

Spears, E. L., Prelude to Victory (London, 1939).

Steiner, Z., The Foreign Office and Foreign Policy (Cambridge, 1969).

Stevenson, D., French War Aims against Germany 1914–1919 (Oxford, 1982).

— The First World War and International Politics (Oxford, 1988).

Suarez, G., Briand: Sa vie, son oeuvre, Vols 3–4 (Paris, 1939–40).

Tanenbaum, J. K., General Maurice Sarrail 1856–1929: The French Army and Left-Wing Politics (Chapel Hill, 1974).

Terrail, G., Joffre: La Première Crise du Commandement (Paris, 1919).

— Sarrail et les Armées d'Orient (Paris, 1920).

Turner, J., British Politics and the Great War: Coalition and Conflict 1915–1918 (New Haven, 1992).

— (ed.), Britain and the First World War (London, 1988).

Van der Kiste, J., Kings of the Hellenes: The Greek Kings 1863–1974 (Stroud, 1994).

Villari, L., The Macedonian Campaign (London, 1922).

Wallach, J. L., Uneasy Coalition: The Entente Experience in World War One (Westport, 1993).

Ward Price, G., The Story of the Salonika Army (London, 1918).

Watson, D. R., Georges Clemenceau: A Political Biography (London, 1974).

Watt, R. M., Dare Call it Treason (London, 1964).

Williamson, S. R., The Politics of Grand Strategy: Britain and France Prepare for War 1904–1914 (Cambridge, MA, 1969).

Wilson, K. (ed.), *Decisions for War, 1914* (London, 1995).
Wilson, T., *The Myriad Faces of War* (Oxford, 1986).
Winter, D., *Haig's Command* (London, 1991).
Woodward, D. R., *Lloyd George and the Generals* (Newark, 1983).

Articles

Andrew, C. M. and A. S. Kanya-Forstner, 'The French Colonial Party and French Colonial War Aims, 1914–18', *Historical Journal* 17 (1974).
Bliss, T. H., 'The Evolution of the Unified Command', *Foreign Affairs* 1, 2 (1922).
Dutton, D. J., 'The Fall of General Joffre: An Episode in the Politico-Military Struggle in Wartime France', *Journal of Strategic Studies* 1, 3 (1978).
— 'The Deposition of King Constantine of Greece, June 1917: An Episode in Anglo-French Diplomacy', *Canadian Journal of History* 12, 3 (1978).
— 'The Ministerial Career of Paul Painlevé and the end of the Sacred Union in Wartime France', *Journal of Strategic Studies* 4, 1 (1981).
Goldstein, E., 'Great Britain and Greater Greece 1917–1920', *Historical Journal* 32, 2 (1989)
Hamard, B., 'Quand la Victoire s'est gagnée dans les Balkans: L'Assaut de l'Armée Alliée d'Orient de Septembre à Novembre 1918', *Guerres mondiales et conflits contemporains* 184 (1996).
Helsey, E., 'Le Guet-apens d'Athènes (1er décembre 1916)', *Revue des deux mondes* (1955).
Lowe, C. J. , 'The Failure of British Diplomacy in the Balkans, 1914–1916', *Canadian Journal of History* 3 (1968).
Neilson, K., 'Kitchener: A Reputation Refurbished?', *Canadian Journal of History* 15, 2 (1980).
Philpott, W. J., 'Kitchener and the 29th Division: A Study in Anglo-French Strategic Relations, 1914–1915', *Journal of Strategic Studies* 16, 3 (1993).
Pingaud, A., 'Le second ministère Venizelos (24 août–5 octobre 1915) et les origines de l'expédition de Salonique', *Revue d'histoire de la guerre mondiale* 12 (1934).
— 'Les origines de l'expédition de Salonique', *Revue historique* 176 (1935).
Prete, R. A., 'French Military War Aims 1914–1916', *Historical Journal* 28, 4 (1985).
— 'French Strategic Planning and the Deployment of the BEF in France in 1914', *Canadian Journal of History* 26 (1989).
— 'Joffre and the Question of Allied Supreme Command, 1914–1916', *Proceedings of the Annual Meeting of the Western Society for French History* 16 (1989).
Renouvin, P., 'Les buts de guerre du gouvernement français, 1914–1918', *Revue historique* 225 (1966).

Robbins, K., 'British Diplomacy and Bulgaria, 1914–1915', *Slavonic and East European Review* 49 (1971).

Rousseau, G., 'Le Conseil des Ministres en 1916, d'après les notes d'Etienne Clémentel', *Guerres mondiales et conflits contemporains* 171 (1993).

Sarrail, M., 'La Grèce Venizeliste', *Revue de Paris*, 15 December 1919.

Smith Jr, C. J., 'Great Britain and the 1914–1915 Straits Agreement with Russia: The British Promise of November 1914', *American Historical Review* 70 (1965).

Soutou, G., 'La France et les marches de l'est, 1914–1919', *Revue historique* 528 (1978).

Torrey, G. E., 'The Rumanian Campaign of 1916: Its Impact on the Belligerents', *Slavic Review* 39 (1980).

Wilson, K., 'The Channel Tunnel Question at the Committee of Imperial Defence, 1906–1914', *Journal of Strategic Studies* 13, 2 (1990).

Wilson, T., 'Britain's Moral Commitment to France in August 1914', *History* 64 (1979).

Woodward, D. R., 'Britain in a Continental War: The Civil–Military Debate over the Strategical Direction of the Great War of 1914–1918', *Albion*, 12, 1 (1980).

Index

193; armistice with, 179; containment
of forces, 100; French economic
interest in, 184; loan agreement with
Germany, 27, 28; military collapse of,
180; proposed invasion of, 178
Buxton, Charles, 19
Buxton, Noel, 19

Cadorna, General Luigi, 137
Caillaux, Joseph, 35, 44, 54–5, 58–9, 60, 123,
137, 141, 190
Caillaux, Madame, 35
Calais, war conferences, 8, 43, 69, 70, 71,
72, 73, 74, 78, 81, 108, 121, 123
Callwell, General, 14, 54, 56, 65, 76
Calthorpe, Admiral, 180
Cambon, Jules, 70, 108
Cambon, Paul, 15, 36, 45, 46, 47, 67, 68, 69,
72, 73, 74, 92, 94, 95, 98, 99, 109, 127,
133, 139, 142, 154, 190
Caporetto, campaign disaster of, 172
Carol, King, of Romania, 19
Carson, Sir Edward, 51
de Castelnau, General, 104, 105
Cecil, Lord Robert, 12, 126, 127, 128, 129,
132, 144, 148, 178
Chamberlain, Austen, 56
Chantilly, war conference, 73, 74, 75, 78,
81, 86, 114
Chemin des Dames campaign, 171; disaster
of, 176
Churchill, Sir Winston, 13, 15, 19, 23, 25,
29, 51, 69
Cilicia, 165; French interest in, 154
Clark, George, 72
Clemenceau, Georges, 6, 14, 15, 53, 58, 60,
117, 137, 139, 141, 142, 155, 166, 167,
168, 169, 172, 174, 176, 179, 180, 181,
190; bitterness towards British, 189;
opposition to Balkans expedition, 177,
178; view of Salonika expedition, 169–
70
Clerk, George, 147, 148
Cochin, Denys, 44, 59, 64, 72, 107, 139
Combes, Emile, 59
Commercial Bureau for French
Importations, 181; *Bulletin*, 161, 162,
184; set up, 160
Compiègne war conference, 173
conscription, in Britain, 69, 116
Constantine, king of Greece, 28, 65, 108,
109, 110, 112, 146, 185; deposition of,
132, 133, 163, 167 (proposed, 107, 125,
126, 127, 129, 130, 131); German

sympathies of, 47, 67, 71; relations with
Venizelos, 110
Constantinople, 150, 152, 156; proposed
advance on, 179, 184; proposed Russian
attribution of, 153, 154, 155, 183;
proposed triumphal march into, 179,
180; Russians renounce interest in, 183
Crewe, Lord, 89
Curzon, Lord, 136

Dardanelles campaign, 15, 25, 28, 30, 38,
39, 40, 41, 44, 63, 153, 154, 155, 186
(need for troops, 42)
Dardanelles Committee, 50, 55, 56, 60, 61,
64, 143
Dartige du Fournet, Admiral, 108
Decrais, Commandant, 122, 140
Delcassée, Théophile, 1, 27, 28, 32, 43, 45,
48, 51, 52, 149, 153; resignation
proposed, 52, 53
Derby, Lord, 7, 129, 136, 171, 176, 189, 190,
191
Doullens, war conference, 172
Doumayrou, Captain, 68
Doumer, Paul, 40
Dreyfus affair, 34, 35
Dubail, General, 37, 38, 39

Eastern front, 69; British view of, 46;
proponents of, 20, 21, 51
Egypt, 2, 50, 71, 185; British forces in, 84,
92, 94, 100, 134; defence of, 165
Elliot, Sir Francis, 71, 127, 146, 147, 156
entente cordiale, 2, 53, 57, 63, 71, 135, 180
Esher, Lord, 12, 13, 30, 123, 190

Fashoda incident, 1
von Falkenhayn, Erich, 101
Fémau, General, 31
Ferry, Abel, 38, 85, 95
Fleurot, Paul, 96
Foch, General Ferdinand, 11, 35, 171, 172,
174, 175, 177, 194
de Fontenay, French minister, 156, 157
Forgeot, Pierre, 113
du Fournet, Admiral, 110
France: attitude to Salonika expedition,
145; British stereotypes of, 11, 12, 81;
casualties in early part of war, 79;
collapse of policy on Greece, 112;
confusion of decision-making
processes, 149; defence of Republican
ideal, 34, 35; economic dependence on
Britain, 7; economic dominance in

Plunkett, Lt-Col, 168
Poincaré, Raymond, 22, 31, 33, 34, 36, 39,
40, 41, 42, 43, 52, 53, 58, 105, 108, 131,
137, 138, 140, 149, 153, 154, 179
Porro, General, 74

Radical Socialist party (France), 34, 36, 41,
58, 77, 111, 112, 139
railway, at Salonika, 49, 61, 187
Reinach, Joseph, 113
Renaudel, Pierre, 53, 112
Repington, Charles à Court, 186, 188, 192
Ribot, Alexandre, 5, 27, 38, 53, 88, 122, 124,
125, 127, 129, 131, 132, 133, 135, 139,
140, 142, 149, 169; fall of government,
136
Roberts, Lord, 91
Robertson, Sir William, 12, 13, 27, 54, 79,
82, 83, 84, 87, 89, 90, 92, 93, 97, 98, 99,
100, 101, 102, 103, 105, 106, 113, 114,
115, 117, 120, 121, 123, 124, 125, 129,
131, 133, 134, 135, 136, 141, 143, 144,
188, 189, 190, 192; appointed CIGS, 8;
criticism of Salonika expedition, 193;
policy for war, 80; threat of resignation,
119; visit to Balkans, 81; waning
influence of, 138
Romania, 18, 20, 24, 25, 26, 28, 84, 87, 89,
102, 121, 134, 187; collapse of, 106;
defeat of, 113; French economic
interest in, 184; German offensive
against, 101; possible entry into war,
27, 46, 51, 62, 67, 83, 92, 100, 101, 151
Rome, war conference, 118
de Roquefeuil, Commandant, 109, 146
Roques, General, 97, 105
Rothwell, Dr, 79
Russia, 1, 3, 4, 5, 6, 13, 23, 24, 72, 73, 87,
99, 100, 121, 130, 133, 134, 153, 154,
156, 190; collapse of front, 136;
countering of, 150; renounces interest
in Constantinople, 183; withdrawal
from war, 5, 9, 116, 135, 143, 173 *see
also* Constantinople

Sacred Union, 31, 35, 52, 53, 59, 72, 73, 95,
117, 139, 191, 194; creation of, 30;
threat to, 41
Salonika: as base (defence of, 64, 65, 67, 75,
93, 114, 128, 173, 176, 184; not ideal
location, 187); as large-scale internment
camp, 15; British decision to maintain
troops, 71; economic potential of, 158;
fire in, 163; French educational
institutions in, 163; French interests in,

160, 161; port, allied control of, 62;
possible offensive at, 98, 176; possibility
of evacuation of, 66, 67, 68, 70, 71, 73,
75, 76, 77, 81, 82, 84, 97, 124, 128, 144,
173 (French opposition to, 70, 72);
possibility of reduction of troop levels,
65, 69, 88, 98, 123, 128, 134, 136, 143,
174, 175; problems of communications,
188; withdrawal to, 65, 66
Salonika expedition, 14, 16, 52, 58, 81, 86,
151, 155, 156, 157; agreed by French,
17; and 'easterner' position, 21; Anglo-
French war policy at its worst, 194; as
lever for French ambitions, 165; as price
of Anglo-French alliance, 188; at heart
of Briand's political troubles, 95; British
opposition to, 138; British sending of
troops, 25, 26, 27, 28, 51, 54, 55, 62, 63,
67, 68, 94, 104, 105, 115, 119 (proposed
increases in, 103); central to Anglo-
French relationship, 192; early
discussions of, 27, 30; end of campaign,
167–85; favoured by Sarrail, 42; French
attitude to, 145; French plan for, 22;
French sending of troops, 26, 27, 45, 47,
51, 67; French support for, 45, 51, 53,
57, 62, 140; governed by French
political situation, 143, 194; impossible
to abandon, 164; origins of, 17–48;
perceived inutility of, 16, 56, 87, 99;
possible evacuation of, 64; viewed as
major mistake, 186
Sarrail, General Maurice, 17, 40, 41, 42, 43,
44, 45, 47, 52, 53, 56, 57, 58, 63, 64, 68,
69, 70, 75, 82, 84, 90, 91, 92, 94, 96, 98,
100, 101, 104, 105, 108, 109, 111, 112,
118, 120, 121, 122, 128, 130, 131, 132,
133, 134, 136, 140, 143, 145, 146, 150,
158, 159, 162, 164, 166, 168, 169, 170,
181, 182, 193, 194; appointed to head
the Armée d'Orient, 41;
correspondence of, 96; criticism of, 37,
140; departure for Salonika, 48;
designated C-in-C of French army in
Serbia, 47; difficulties with Joffre, 36,
37; dismissal of, 175, 194; emergence of,
34, 35; military objectives of, 62, 157;
offensive launched, 124 (failure of, 129);
possible resignation of, 137; pressure to
replace, 131, 135; proposed as
commander of Salonika armies, 120;
proposed as head of Dardanelles
expedition, 40; recall of, 141, 167, 181;
replaced at head of Third Army, 38, 39;
signs circular letter, 159, 160; viewed as